# OVERSEAS AMERICANS

## The Essential Guide to Living and Working Abroad

### William Beaver

Paladin Press
Boulder, Colorado

To my fellow Americans here in Kuwait, especially those of the American Business Council . . .
and for the two expats who matter most—Jacob and Jasmin.

*Overseas Americans: The Essential Guide to Living and Working Abroad*
by William Beaver

Copyright © 2001 by William Beaver

ISBN 1-58160-259-6
Printed in the United States of America

Published by Paladin Press, a division of
Paladin Enterprises, Inc.
Gunbarrel Tech Center
7077 Winchester Circle
Boulder, Colorado 80301 USA
+1.303.443.7250

Direct inquiries and/or orders to the above address.

PALADIN, PALADIN PRESS, and the "horse head" design
are trademarks belonging to Paladin Enterprises and
registered in United States Patent and Trademark Office.

Visit our Web site at www.paladin-press.com

# TABLE OF CONTENTS

# ACKNOWLEDGMENTS

Many people have influenced my attitudes about living outside the United States. The first was a Pulitzer Prize–nominated writer named Mark Salzman, whose book *Iron and Silk* detailed his adventures teaching English in China. His prose showed the romantic adventure that can result from being an American in a foreign land. Years later, I was proud to ask him to be on my first cover of the martial arts magazine I edited.

While working on this book, I spent three weeks in Guildford, England. One wonderfully gray afternoon I found myself in a Waterstone's bookshop staring at a large cardboard display near the cash register. It featured the best-selling travel writer in England, Bill Bryson—*an American*. I bought all his books and marvelled at the humor of a man who thought that moving back to the United States after nearly 20 years abroad was like waking from a coma. His thoughts on being an expat influence me still.

Countless people have helped me with *Overseas Digest*, my monthly newsletter and Web site, and I thank you all. I want to especially praise Diane MacPherson of *Relocation Journal* and *Real Estate News*; Betsy Burlingame of Expat Exchange; Jane Bruno, my favorite tax expert; Michael Sedge, the definitive expat journalist; the helpful folks at American Citizens Abroad in Geneva; and Charles Wingate, the commercial attaché at the American Embassy in Kuwait.

Thanks also to Donna and Jon for making me look good. Yours is a thankless task.

# INTRODUCTION

This book is a collection of the most important government documents, pamphlets, and information related to Americans who live and work in foreign countries. These brave souls are known as *expatriates*, or *expats* for short.

I lived overseas for two years before I learned the meaning of the word *expatriate*. The official meaning is "to leave one's homeland." In this case, if you're an American citizen but live in a different country, then by definition you're an expat.

The Internal Revenue Service, however, has a completely different definition. To qualify for the tax breaks that go with being an expatriate, you must, in general, pass one or more of several different qualifying tests. One example of a qualifying condition is living outside the United States for at least 330 days in a row.

Romantic notions of the expatriate still survive, thanks in no small part to Turner Classic Movies. Picture Humphrey Bogart standing in the smoky black and white bar in Casablanca. Or maybe you've heard the stories of writer Ernest Hemingway tormenting himself in Havana. Then there was the famous group of artists and musicians who became known as the American expats in Paris in the period between the world wars. Maybe you've seen the 1951 movie *An American in Paris* starring Gene Kelly that memorializes the adventures of the American expat community in Paris during this time.

Today's reality is far less exciting. According to the U.S. State Department, more than three million Americans live in foreign countries. Some stay for just one year, others for 10, a few remain forever. Some are drawn abroad by promises of a tax-free lifestyle. Others seek the romance of a foreign land, the mixture of culture, the challenge of learning or using a foreign language, and the lure of travel. Many go overseas because they married a spouse from a different country.

## SHOULD YOU LIVE ABROAD?

Whatever reason drives you to consider a life abroad, there are several questions that you should be able to answer clearly before making such an important decision.

### Why Do You Want to Live Abroad?

Does the idea of a living in a foreign country appeal to you? If so, why? Is it the different culture or the need to learn a new language? Maybe you saw a movie that showed an American living abroad, and it looked like the good life: an American sitting in a sidewalk café, sipping espresso, and reading the *International Herald Tribune*. You can do that in New York, Los Angeles, or Wichita, so why live overseas? Try to be as honest as you can.

### Where Do You Want to Live?

Which country would you like to call your new home? Why? In my case, I've moved overseas twice. The first time, I spent three years in Germany simply because I was a soldier and Bavaria is where I was ordered. The second time I moved to Kuwait, where I've lived since 1992, mainly because it is my wife's country.

There are many reasons for choosing a particular place. You may have accepted a job somewhere, or perhaps you are considering a transfer with your company. Many people choose a country based on their travel experience or their high school and college language training. An article in the *International Herald Tribune* reported that most people who buy a home in one of the Caribbean islands leave within 5 to 10 years. The lifestyle change is too great for them to handle.

### What Will You Do When You Get There?

Most foreign countries require visas and work permits for foreigners to live as permanent residents. So what will you do when you get to your new country? How will you find a job before you go? Are you going to carry on with the career you have now, e.g., teaching or accounting? Do you want to start fresh? If so, why would someone in a foreign country hire you?

### How Will You Move Abroad?

Do you want to pack your house and move everything overseas? Do you plan to just go abroad with a couple of suitcases and buy what you need when you get there? Will your company or new job take care of these details for you?

### When Do You Want to Go Abroad?

If your plan is to move to a country and then try to settle in, buying what you need when you get there or even if you are taking everything with you, the time of year you relocate can be important to your mental health. Moving abroad is extremely stressful, so depending on where you are going, you don't want to add the additional stress of monsoons, snow storms, or other bad weather.

In the coming chapters, you'll find detailed discussions of all these questions. Much of the information is based on the rules and regulations of the U.S. government, so you will find the *actual documents* that describe such topics as marriages performed abroad, the citizenship status of children born in foreign countries, the tax maze an expatriate must wander through, and much more. By the end of this book you will have a fairly clear idea of what you might encounter if you choose to move overseas. But first, a few random thoughts about living abroad, just to set the stage.

## WHY EVERY AMERICAN ABROAD SHOULD BE GRANTED DIPLOMATIC IMMUNITY

I'm not running for president of the United States in the next election (actually, I'm undecided), but here's my solution for rapidly improving the United States. Every person whose parents and grandparents were born in the United States has to leave . . . at least for a little while. Grandparents who came through Ellis Island don't count. If you're a first- or second-generation immigrant, you can stay.

I know what you're thinking, so before you label me a fascist or worse, let me explain. Having spent nearly a quarter of my life abroad, I am totally convinced that truly enjoying life, especially American life, demands a perspective that only comes from leaving. If you've never left our national borders for any period longer than a summer vacation, odds are you could use a cultural coffee klatch.

For example, a favorite complaint of U.S. comedians is the eternal wait at the department of motor vehicles. I've been in countries where getting your driver's license before the next full moon was reason for celebration. In the United States, it may take a couple of hours, but at least you finish the same day.

If you think a speed trap is reason to abolish law enforcement, try living in parts of the world where police officers don't do their jobs at all. Can you imagine traffic anarchy? Trust me, you don't want it. That's the downside of anarchy. Just when you warm up to the idea of doing anything you want, the other guy reminds you that no rules for you means no rules for him. Say good-bye to your nerves and your brand-new car.

I wasn't going to mention the right to vote, especially when more than half of Americans who are eligible don't seem to care. But having lived in places still struggling and dying for basic human rights, including the right to vote, maybe I should say something.

Being patriotic isn't the point. What matters, especially for those of us who live outside the United States, is that like it or not, we all represent our country and that for which it stands.

Every U.S. expatriate has probably been told by someone somewhere that America sucks, and since we're Americans, so do we. On the other hand, most of us have probably been given a break or two simply because of our passport with the eagle on the cover.

And those of us who have lived in certain parts of the world have received the embassy telephone call warning us that we may have to leave in a hurry. Why? Not because we're black or white, but because we're Americans, and someone has decided he wants us dead. Again. Oh, and be sure to check your car for bombs before you rush to the airport.

We may not present our credentials to heads of state, but those of us living overseas do influence the day-to-day relationships between our country and others. We have a direct impact on the way other people think of Americans in general.

Maybe diplomatic immunity should be given to all of us. Imagine that: expatriate anarchy. I bet even with a choice, we'd fight for the right to stand in line.

## AMERICAN FOLLOWED ME ABROAD . . .

Spending a quarter of my life abroad has convinced me that there is something called "American" and it's spreading. It may not be the America we'd prefer, but I know it's there and it belongs to us. An example or two might make my case.

When I moved to the Middle East, I was informed that Thursday is Saturday, which is to say that this part of the world has a different week than the United States. The Islamic week begins on Saturday, which means that Thursday and Friday are the weekend.

When you don't work on Thursday and religious services are on Friday, you begin to realize that there is a real "feel" to a weekend. On Friday, for example, the roads don't seem as busy and the city doesn't seem as hectic. For three years, I couldn't stop calling that feeling "Saturday and Sunday."

Rupert Murdoch started beaming *Monday Night Football* into the Middle East, but Monday night is the middle of the week. Somehow it didn't have the same effect as starting off the week with a Packers and Patriots game. Then last year, when I returned to the United States for a short visit, I kept thinking Saturday was Thursday.

What does all this have to do with human nature? Human beings, especially Americans, crave a weekend, and it doesn't matter what you call it. After all, we spend the work week offering ourselves to the world, so we want to relax and have fun when the week's over. America's culture of leisure and fun is responsible for a great deal of how we are seen by others.

The first time I visited Kuwait in 1987, this small part of the world had a much different view of America than it does now. The walls in the local Hardees were covered with large movie poster blowups of *Dallas* (the TV show, not the city). I looked around at the people, happily devouring the new mushroom and Swiss sandwich, while Charlene Tilden smiled down her approval. I'd bet money that no one in the place could tell me who shot J.R. More important, none of them cared. But they did like *Dallas*. Why? Because it was American.

The Gulf War came and went. America came and stayed. Any American who has been abroad can tell you that at least 50 percent of anything found in his local K-Mart back home has magically reappeared within a 30-minute drive of his current location. I walk through local stores here in Kuwait, and the shelves are stuffed with Smucker's jams and Kellogg's Cornflakes, Craftsman tools and Chevrolet spare parts. Nearly anything I can think of from America, I can find abroad. And if I can't find it, I can order it from Amazon.com.

I left the United States in search of adventure the same week Bill Clinton began his as president. Bill's now out of office; I'm still abroad. And somehow America followed me.

## DOES LIVING OVERSEAS MAKE YOU MORE SOPHISTICATED?

When I was working on my master's degree in philosophy, the professors taught us that the "answer is in the question." Fair enough. Does living overseas make one more sophisticated? The word *sophisticated* itself gives us the first problem.

Consider the first definition of sophisticated: "worldly wise, not naive, or ingenuous." Some people claim that Americans living abroad, because of their exposure to other cultures, develop an understanding of the world that exceeds that of the typical American back home. We're dangerously close to making overseas Americans into some kind of social elite.

All social elites have problems of their own, and American expatriates, if we think of them this way, are no exception. In America, one problem is "latch-key kids," the children whose working parents leave them to more or less fend for themselves. The expatriate spin on the problem is called "third culture kids" (TCK). These are the "American" children who are sometimes born in a foreign country by American parents. They sometimes

can't figure out how to be an American without actually having lived there. How do they return "home" to a country they've never seen?

There are several groups that offer support and assistance for these "global nomads," as they like to call themselves. They even have their own magazine and alumni network. I like their name: Overseas Brats. Their literature claims that they are more attuned to international events and other cultures, which make them more worldly. This seems to fit the first definition of sophisticated.

The second definition of sophisticated is far less appealing: "characterized by a lack of simplicity or naturalness; refined to the point of being artificial." I haven't met many Americans overseas who are "refined to the point of being artificial," but I see the potential for such a thing as "refined to the point of being American."

An example: I recently took part in a practice evacuation of American expatriates from Kuwait. We ended up around the swimming pool at the embassy, watching a couple of fully clothed guys jump in the deep end to rescue a small girl who was drowning. When the applause for the two rescuers died down, we somehow got on the subject of the difference between British and American expats.

Probably under the influence of too many black-and-white British empire movies, someone commented that if we were British, we'd probably be standing around in a tuxedo and pith helmet, sipping Darjeeling tea, and ordering someone else into the pool.

Try as we might, we could only come up with one example of the worldly wise sophisticated (not refined to the point of being artificial) American expatriate: Humphrey Bogart in *Casablanca*. Actually, Ernest Hemingway was our second choice, but he liked to hang out in Havana. By the end of our mini-summit meeting on sophisticated expats, we agreed on three things:

1. American expatriates in white tuxedos don't exist anymore, especially here in the Middle East.
2. The world would probably be a better place if they did.
3. If they ever make a sequel to *Casablanca*, the producers will probably have Humphrey Bogart's character running an Internet cafe.

# CHAPTER 1
## Overseas Employment Scams

One reason you want to be an expatriate may be a strong desire to work abroad. But why? Perhaps the stories of easy money and romantic adventure drive you to leave the United States and find happiness in a foreign culture. These same stories give scam artists the fuel they need to bilk countless people out of millions of dollars.

Often it is not easy to spot a scam, especially about something you know little about, such as jobs supposedly available overseas. You will see advertisements in prestigious newspapers and magazine making legitimate-sounding claims of unparalleled excitement and salaries. The ads sound like the authentic ones you find in your local employment classifieds. But there are telltale signs that may indicate a scam.

1. The ad asks for money up front.
2. It uses a post office box instead of an office address.
3. It promises employment and guarantees a refund if you are not satisfied.
4. It charges a fee for giving you a job lead.

To see how these scam artists operate, consider the following three cases taken from the files of the U.S. Federal Trade Commission (FTC).

### CASE NUMBER ONE

The FTC accused a Las Vegas company and three individuals with deceptive practices in its overseas employment matching services. The company claimed to match consumers' qualifications and skills with companies that were hiring Americans in Australia and other countries. The firm typically sold its services for $290.

The FTC's complaint charged the company with falsely advertising the following:

- That clients were very likely to obtain overseas employment in Australia or other countries
- That the company had existing relationships with numerous firms that had overseas jobs available
- That the company derived most of its income from fees paid by hiring companies
- That the company had located specific employers interested in hiring particular clients

This company also implied that it would refund the fee to any client who was not satisfied with its services. However, according to the complaint, the company frequently refused to refund fees or made refunds only after clients filed complaints with government or consumer protection agencies.

In addition, the company sometimes had employees or associates contact potential clients and falsely represent that they were prospective employers interested in hiring the client, according to the complaint.

These misrepresentations "caused substantial financial injury to numerous individual consumers," the complaint alleged.

At the FTC's request, the U.S. District Court for the District of Nevada issued a temporary restraining order, froze the assets of the company and the individuals, and appointed a temporary receiver to run the company. The commission also asked the court to issue a permanent injunction against any misrepresentations in the sale of job placement, résumé preparation, or any other products or services, and to order the defendants to pay redress to consumers at the conclusion of the case.

The FTC's San Francisco Regional Office handled the investigation and litigation. The commission received substantial assistance in the investigation from the Nevada Labor Commission and the Better Business Bureau of Southern Nevada.

### CASE NUMBER TWO

The FTC charged Company B with conducting a fraudulent telemarketing scheme that promised to place consumers in overseas jobs but which had bilked approximately 70,000 consumers out of an estimated $25 million. According to the complaint, Company B and its two owners and officers allegedly offered overseas employment matching services. The company claimed to "match" job applicants with a computerized database of current job openings and to send customers'

résumés to companies that had job openings matching the customers' skills.

Company B sold its services for $395 to $550 and advertised in national and local magazines and newspapers, by telephone and by mailed promotional materials.

The FTC's complaint charged that owners falsely claimed the following:

- That customers were very likely to get overseas jobs through the company's placement services. In fact, the complaint alleged that many or most of the customers did not obtain jobs through Company B.
- That the company had information on 10,000 to 15,000 or more currently available overseas job openings. According to the complaint, the company actually had information on substantially fewer than 10,000 openings.
- That the company maintained "close working relationships" with hundreds of companies that had overseas jobs available and it they discussed individual customers' applications with those companies. The complaint charged that the firm had no such "close working relationships and that on few, if any, occasions had it discussed individual applications.
- That the company matched customers with at least three prospective employers within the time specified in the contract and made refunds to customers who were not provided matches. In fact, the complaint alleged, the firm did not match all customers with three prospective employers within the time limit and did not provide refunds.

Consumers had suffered "substantial injury" as a result of these actions, the complaint charged.

At the commission's request, the U.S. District Court for the Central District of California in Los Angeles issued a temporary restraining order, froze the assets of the company and the individuals, and appointed a receiver to run the company. The commission also asked the court to issue a permanent injunction against any misrepresentations in the sale of employment matching services and to order the defendants to pay redress to consumers at the conclusion of the case.

Company B was based in Los Angeles and maintained offices in Boise, Idaho; Newark, New Jersey; and Tampa, Florida. The commission had the cooperation of a number of state and federal officials in developing the case.

## CASE THREE

A federal district court has prohibited Company C of Coral Springs, Florida, from falsely promising that it had found jobs for individuals, was hiring workers on behalf of other firms, and that it would fully refund deposits that applicants had paid to hold purported jobs. The court order followed earlier FTC charges that the company had engaged in a deceptive scheme offering jobs in the Caribbean. The order also applied to company directors.

The court order stemmed from an FTC lawsuit alleging that Company C placed help-wanted ads in newspapers throughout the United States inviting job seekers to call an 800 telephone number for information about construction jobs featuring high pay—$70,000 to $85,000 a year—and good benefits. According to the FTC complaint detailing the charges, the defendants charged job seekers $289 each as a "refundable good faith" deposit for placement in a "guaranteed" position. In fact, the FTC charged, applicants received neither the promised jobs nor refunds of their deposits. Company C was not hiring for construction jobs with any firm in the Caribbean area, nor had the defendants reserved any construction jobs for the applications, the FTC charged.

At the time the FTC filed the complaint, the court granted the agency's request to freeze the defendants' assets to preserve any funds for consumer redress. After the defendants failed to respond to the complaint as required, the court entered defaults against them. The court order was a default final. In addition to the prohibitions on future conduct, the judgment required the defendants to pay $45,373 in redress, but the FTC said it was not certain how much of the judgment would be collected. The judgment also included various reporting requirements to assist the FTC in monitoring the defendants' compliance.

The FTC's San Francisco Regional Office handled the matter with substantial assistance from the Florida attorney general's office, which provided an assistant attorney general to help in prosecuting the case. The Coral Springs Police Department, the Broward County Sheriff's Department, and the U.S. Postal Service also provided assistance.

(Copies of all of the judgments, as well as the complaints and the news releases issued at the time of these cases, are available from the FTC's Public Reference Branch, Room 130, 6th Street and Pennsylvania Avenue, N.W., Washington, D.C. 20580.)

According to the Better Business Bureau and the FTC, you can protect yourself against overseas employment scams by using common sense and following a few basic rules:

1. Always ask for references.
2. Check out the company doing the advertising in the state it lists as an address.
3. Get everything in writing.
4. Forget about companies with no legitimate street address.
5. Be very skeptical of overseas employment opportunities that sound "too good to be true."
6. Never send cash in the mail, and be extremely cautious with firms that require a money order. This could indicate that the firm is attempting to avoid a traceable record of its transactions.
7. Do not be fooled by official-sounding

names. Many scam artists operate under names that sound like those of long-standing, reputable firms.

8. Avoid working with firms that require payment in advance.

9. Do not give your credit card or bank account number to these firms.

10. Read the contract very carefully. Have an attorney look over any documents you are asked to sign.

11. Beware of an agency that is unwilling to give you a written contract.

12. Do not hesitate to ask questions. You have a right to know what services to expect and the costs involved.

13. Do not make a hasty decision. Instead, take time to weigh all the pros and cons of the situation. Be wary of demands that "you must act now."

14. Keep a copy of all agreements you sign, as well as copies of checks you forward to the company.

# CHAPTER 2
## *Tips for Americans Residing Abroad*

(Department of State Publication 10391, Bureau of Consular Affairs, Revised Septmenber 1996)

*(Author's note: Most of the topics discussed in this chapter are examined in later chapters in more detail.)*

The Department of State's Bureau of Consular Affairs has prepared this publication for Americans considering residence abroad, as well as for the more than three million U.S. citizens who are currently residing in a foreign country. Our primary goal is to provide assistance to and protect the welfare of American citizens who live abroad.

Before taking up a foreign residence, there are many details that you will need to consider. This brochure will acquaint you with the wide range of services provided to American citizens by U.S. embassies and consulates worldwide. We are committed to providing prompt, courteous, and effective assistance.

Any additional guidance not specifically addressed in this publication may be obtained from the Bureau of Consular Affairs in the Department of State or from the nearest U.S. embassy or consulate if you are living overseas.

### BEFORE YOU GO: LEARN ABOUT THE HOST COUNTRY

Read as much as possible about the country where you plan to reside. Learning about a nation's culture, customs, people, and history will make your stay more meaningful. Libraries, bookstores, and tourist bureaus are good resources for this information. Keep abreast as well of the international news for the latest political developments in the country where you will live. Although English is spoken in many countries, learning the language of the nation in which you plan to reside will make the transition to your new environment easier.

One of the best ways to learn about living in a foreign country is to get advice from U.S. citizens already residing there. Countries with large numbers of U.S. expatriates often have a U.S. Chamber of Commerce, a bicultural organization, or clubs for Americans that could give you information on living in that country. In countries with fewer U.S.

residents, you may be able to meet fellow expatriates through a local international club. The Consular Section of the U.S. embassy or consulate may be able to assist you in finding these organizations.

### Background Notes

The Department of State publishes Background Notes on countries around the world. These are brief, factual pamphlets with information on each country's people, culture, geography, history, government, economy, and political conditions. They are available for about 170 countries worldwide and often include a reading list, travel notes, and maps. To purchase copies, contact the Superintendent of Documents, U.S. Government Printing Office, Washington, D.C. 20402 or call (202) 512-1800. Select issues are also available from the Bureau of Public Affairs, fax-on-demand by calling (202) 736-7720 from your fax machine or on the Department of States homepage on the Internet at http://www.state.gov.

### Consular Information Program

The U.S. Department of State issues fact sheets on every country in the world called Consular Information Sheets. The sheets contain information on crime and security conditions, areas of instability, and other details relevant to travel in a particular country.

The Department of State also issues Travel Warnings and Public Announcements. Travel Warnings are issued when the State Department recommends deferral of travel by Americans to a country because of civil unrest, dangerous conditions, terrorist activity, and/or because the U.S. has no diplomatic relations with the country and cannot assist an American in distress. Public Announcements are issued as a means to disseminate information quickly about terrorist threats and other relatively short-term and/or transnational conditions which would pose significant risks to American travelers.

### How to Access Consular Information Sheets, Travel Warnings, and Public Announcements

Consular Information Sheets, Travel Warnings, and Public Announcements may be heard any time by dialing the Office of Overseas Citizens Services at (202) 647-5225 from a Touch-Tone phone. The recording is updated as new information becomes available. They are also available at any of the 13 regional passport agencies and U.S. embassies and consulates abroad, or by sending a self-addressed, stamped envelope and indicating the desired country to the Office of Overseas Citizens Services, Bureau of Consular Affairs, Room 4811, U.S. Department of State, Washington, D.C. 20520-4818.

### By Fax

From your fax machine, dial (202) 647-3000, using the handset as you would a regular telephone. The system prompts you on how to proceed.

### By Internet

Information about travel and consular services is now available on the Internet's World Wide Web. The address is http://travel.state.gov. Visitors to the Web site will find Travel Warnings, Public Announcements, and Consular Information Sheets; passport and visa information; travel publications; background on international adoption and international child abduction services; international legal assistance; and the Consular Affairs mission statement. There is also a link to the State Department's main site on the Internet's World Wide Web that provides users with current foreign affairs information. The address is http://www.state.gov.

### Consular Affairs Bulletin Board (CABB)

If you have a personal computer, modem, and communication software, you can access the Consular Affairs Bulletin Board (CABB). This service is free of charge. To view or download the documents from a computer and modem, dial the CABB on (301) 946-4400. The login is travel; the password is travel.

### Tips for Travelers Series

The Department of State publishes a series of pamphlets on travel to specific regions of the world. The brochures cover topics such as currency and customs regulations, import and export controls, dual nationality, and photography restrictions. The following publications are available for $1 to $1.50 each from the Superintendent of Documents, U.S. Government Printing Office (GPO), Washington, D.C. 20402. (Availability and prices are subject to change without notice. Please check with the GPO before ordering at [202] 512-1800.)

* *Tips for Travelers to Sub-Saharan Africa*
* *Tips for Travelers to the Caribbean*
* *Tips for Travelers to Canada*
* *Tips for Travelers to Central and South America*
* *Tips for Travelers to the People's Republic of China*
* *Tips for Travelers to Mexico*
* *Tips for Travelers to the Middle East and North Africa*
* *Tips for Travelers to Russia and the Newly Independent States*
* *Tips for Travelers to South Asia*

## REQUIRED DOCUMENTS

### U.S. Passports

U.S. citizens should have a valid passport before taking up residence abroad. Once living overseas, Americans should continue to maintain a valid passport.

### *Applying in Person for a Passport*

In the United States, application for a U.S. passport may be presented in person at a passport agency or at one of the several thousand Federal or state courts or post offices which accept passport applications. If you are overseas, you may apply at the nearest U.S. embassy or consulate. U.S. citizens who cannot apply by mail (see requirements below) must appear in person and need to bring proof of U.S. citizenship such as a certified copy of their birth certificate, a Consular Report of Birth Abroad of a U.S. Citizen, a Certificate of Naturalization, or a previous U.S. passport. This should be accompanied by a completed DSP-11, Passport Application, two recent 2x2-inch identical photographs, proof of identity (a valid driver's license or other valid photo ID will suffice), and the appropriate application fee.

For more information on obtaining a U.S. passport, obtain a copy of the publication *Passports: Applying for Them the Easy Way*. This brochure provides basic information on applying for a U.S. passport and is available for 50 cents from the Consumer Information Center, Pueblo, CO 81009.

### *Passports by Mail*

You can apply for a passport by mail (without a personal appearance) if you meet the following requirements:

* you have had a passport issued within 12 years prior to the date of a new application;
* you are able to submit your most recent U.S. passport with your new application; and
* your previous passport was issued on or after your 16th birthday.

For further information and to obtain Form DSP-82, Application for Passport by Mail, contact the nearest U.S. passport agency or, if you are overseas, consult the nearest U.S. embassy or consulate. Not all embassies and consulates abroad are authorized to accept passport applications by mail or via a third party courier. Contact the U.S. embassy or consulate in your consular district to find out if it accepts passport applications by mail or via a third party courier.

Your previous passport, two identical photographs (2x2 inches), and the appropriate passport fee must accompany your application. Since it may take several weeks to prepare and mail your new passport to you, do not wait until it expires to apply for a new one.

### Visas

All governments require foreigners to have an appropriate visa to reside in their country. This endorsement or stamp placed in your passport by a foreign government permits you to enter that country for a specified purpose. If you are planning to reside in a country for an indefinite period of time, most countries will require you to seek residence status. See the section on Citizenship (page 19) to learn what effect this may have on your U.S. citizenship.

### *Applying for a Visa*

In most instances you must obtain the necessary visa before you leave the United States. Apply for your visa directly from the embassy or nearest consulate of the country in which you plan to reside. A listing of foreign embassies and consulates in the U.S. should be available at your local library or by ordering the publication *Foreign Consular Offices in the United States* from the U.S. Government Printing Office. You can write or call them at Superintendent of Documents, U.S. Government Printing Office, Washington, D.C. 20402; telephone (212) 512-1800 to check pricing and stock information.

### Work Permits

A work permit is usually required and is a separate document from your visa or residency permit. It is necessary if you plan on working in a foreign country. It may be obtained either before you leave the U.S. or after you arrive in the foreign country, depending on the laws of the particular country. It is usually applied for at the same time as the residency permit or visa. (Note: The Department of State cannot help you obtain visas or work permits.)

## HEALTH MATTERS

### Health Insurance

The Social Security Medicare Program does not cover hospital or medical services outside the United States. The Department of Veterans Affairs will only pay for hospital and medical service outside the United States if you are a veteran with a service-related disability.

When considering medical insurance, first find out how citizens of the country where you will reside pay their medical bills and if the same coverage is available to resident foreigners. Some countries have government-sponsored health insurance that may also provide coverage to foreign residents, while others have a dual system with national health supplemented by private insurance. In countries where many American expatriates reside, such as Mexico, you may find that local private international health insurance companies will offer coverage to U.S. citizen residents. Once you arrive, check with organized groups in the American community to learn about these companies.

Wherever possible, try to get the best medical insurance available. If good coverage is not available where you will live, you may have to rely on a U.S. medical insurance company. Before taking up residence abroad, learn which U.S. medical services or health insurance plans provide coverage for Americans living overseas. Check with the insurance company on whether the coverage offered abroad includes both routine and emergency medical treatment, hospitalization, and medical evacuation should it be necessary. Once you obtain health insurance, remember to carry your policy's identity card and to keep a supply of insurance claim forms handy. The U.S. government cannot pay for hospital or medical services for Americans overseas and cannot pay to evacuate you for treatment in the United States.

There are a number of emergency medical assistance companies operating internationally who offer urgent medical treatment for their member travelers. Although the service is designed primarily for tourists who encounter a medical or personal emergency while on vacation, some companies offer yearly memberships which may be available to Americans residing overseas. Contact a travel agent to learn more about these emergency assistance companies.

### Medication

For your protection, leave all medicines in their original, labeled containers. If you require medication containing habit-forming drugs or narcotics, carry a copy of the doctor's prescription attesting to that fact. These precautions will make customs processing easier and also will ensure you do not violate the laws of the country in which you live.

If you have allergies, reactions to certain medicines, or other unique medical problems, consider wearing a medical alert bracelet or carrying a similar warning at all times.

### Immunizations

Under the International Health Regulations adopted by the World Health Organization, some countries require International Certificates of Vaccination against yellow fever from international travelers. A few countries still require a certificate of cholera immunization as well. A helpful guide to immunizations and preventive measures for international travel is the booklet, *Health Information for International Travel*. It is available for $14 from the Superintendent of Documents, U.S. Government Printing Office, Washington, D.C. 20402. Specific information may also be obtained from local and state health departments, physicians, or travel clinics that advise international travelers. You may also reach the Centers for Disease Control & Prevention at (404) 332-4559 or via their Internet address at http://www.cdc.gov for immunization recommendations.

### AIDS /HIV Testing

Many countries require long-term foreign residents and students to submit proof that they are free of the HIV virus. Some of the countries that require this proof may accept certified test results from the United States. Consult the embassy of the country you will be residing in on whether an AIDS/HIV test is required and if test results from the United States are accepted. If not, check on the type of test to be performed and if it is permissible to supply your own disposable needle. If you are overseas, consult the nearest U.S. embassy or consulate for information and advice, keeping in mind that you are in a foreign country and are subject to its laws and requirements.

### Glazed Ceramic Purchases

Be careful when purchasing ceramic tableware and clay pottery while overseas. The U.S. Food and Drug Administration has determined that there are dangerous levels of lead found in the glazes of some ceramic dinnerware and pottery sold abroad. Because there is no way of knowing whether a particular item is safe, the Food and Drug Administration recommends that you use such wares for decorative purposes only.

## PRACTICAL MATTERS

### Federal Benefits

If you are receiving monthly benefits from a Federal or state agency (Social Security, Department of Veterans Affairs, Office of Personnel Management, etc.), contact the appropriate agency prior to your departure from the United States to advise them of your residence abroad and to inquire about the procedures for having your benefits checks sent overseas.

### Driver's License

Many countries do not recognize a U.S. driver's license. Some, however, will accept an international driver's permit, but it would be a good idea to qualify for an in-country driver's license as soon as possible. International driver's permits are not always valid in every country for the length of your stay. It is usually only a matter of courtesy that the holder of the permit is allowed to drive with it for any length of time.

International driver's licenses are usually only valid if presented in conjunction with a valid U.S. or local license. To renew a license contact the Department of Motor Vehicles in your home state. It is illegal to drive without a valid license and insurance in many countries. You should check with the embassy of the country where you plan to reside to find out more about driver's license requirements.

### Customs Hints

The pamphlet *Know Before You Go* contains information about U.S. Customs regulations and procedures. Single copies are available from any U.S. Customs office abroad or by writing to U.S. Customs, P.O. Box 7407, Washington, D.C. 20044.

### Taking a Pet Overseas

If you decide to bring your pet with you overseas, check specific requirements with the country's embassy. Many countries have strict health, quarantine, agriculture, wildlife, and customs requirements and prohibitions. (Note: There are U.S. government regulations forbidding evacuation or emergency assistance to pets during a crisis abroad.)

## LIVING OVERSEAS

### Help from the U.S. Government

#### *Assistance from American Consuls*

U.S. consular officers are located in over 260 foreign service posts abroad. They are available to advise and help you, especially if you are in any kind of serious trouble. In addition, consular agents in approximately 46 foreign cities without U.S. embassies or consulates provide a limited range of emergency and other consular services.

Consular officers are responsive to the needs of Americans traveling or residing abroad. However, the majority of their time is devoted to assisting Americans who are in serious legal, medical, or financial difficulties. They can provide the names of local doctors, dentists, medical specialists, and attorneys, and give you information about any dangerous or unusual situations. Consular officers also perform nonemergency services, including information on absentee voting, selective service registration, and acquisition and loss of U.S. citizenship. They can arrange for the transfer of Social Security and other U.S. government benefits to beneficiaries residing abroad, provide U.S. tax forms, and notarize documents. They may also provide information on how to obtain foreign public documents.

Because of the limited number of consular officers and the growing number of U.S. tourists and residents abroad, consuls cannot provide tourism or commercial services. For example, consuls cannot perform the work of travel agencies, lawyers, information bureaus, banks, or the police. They cannot find you jobs, get residence or driving permits, act as interpreters, search for missing luggage, or settle commercial disputes.

### Registration at U.S. Embassies or Consulates

As soon as you arrive at your permanent residence abroad, you should register in person or by telephone with the nearest U.S. embassy or consulate. Registration will make your presence and whereabouts known in case it is necessary to contact you in an emergency. In accordance with the Privacy Act, information on your welfare or whereabouts may not be released to inquirers without your expressed written authorization. If you register in person, you should bring your U.S. passport with you. Your passport data will be recorded at the embassy or consulate, thereby making it easier for you to apply for a replacement passport should it be lost or stolen.

### Missing Persons

When a U.S. citizen abroad loses contact with friends or relatives in the United States, the U.S. consul is often requested to give information about that individual's welfare and whereabouts. Similar requests often come from American private and official welfare organizations attempting, for example, to track down an errant parent who failed to make child support payments. The U.S. consul tries to comply with such requests after determining carefully the reasons for the inquiry. If the consul has the address of the U.S. citizen about whom the inquiry is being made, the consul will inform the American of the inquirer's interest in getting in touch with them and pass on any urgent messages. Consistent with the Privacy Act, the consul then reports back to the inquirer the results of their search efforts. Except in emergency situations, the consul will not release any details about a U.S. citizen's welfare and whereabouts without the citizen's expressed consent.

### Helpful Information for Americans Arrested Abroad

When living abroad, you are subject to local—i.e., foreign—laws. If you experience difficulties with the local authorities, remember American officials are limited by foreign laws, U.S. regulations, and geography as to what they can do to assist you. The U.S. government cannot fund your legal fees or other related expenses.

Should you find yourself in a dispute that may lead to police or legal action, consult the nearest U.S. consular officer. Although consular officers cannot get you out of jail, serve as your attorneys, or give legal advice, they can provide lists of local attorneys and help you find legal representation. However, neither the Department of State nor U.S. embassies or consulates can assume any responsibility for the caliber, competence, or professional integrity of these attorneys.

If you are arrested, immediately ask to speak to the consular officer at the nearest U.S. embassy or consulate. Under international agreements and practice, you have a right to get in touch with the U.S. consul. If you are turned down, keep asking—politely, but persistently.

Consular officers will do whatever they can to protect your legitimate interests and ensure that you are not discriminated against under local law. Upon learning of your arrest, a U.S. consular officer will visit you, provide a list of local attorneys and, if requested, contact family and friends. In cases of arrest, consuls can help transfer money, food, and clothing from your family and friends to you. They also try to get relief if you are held under inhumane or unhealthy conditions or treated less equitably than others in the same situation.

### Drug Arrests

Despite repeated warnings, drug arrests and convictions of American citizens are still a problem. If you are caught with any type of narcotics overseas, you are subject to local—not U.S.—laws. Penalties for possession or trafficking are often the same. If you are arrested, you will find the following:

- Few countries provide a jury trial.
- Most countries do not accept bail.
- Pre-trial detention, often in solitary confinement, may last many months.
- Prisons may lack even minimal comforts—bed, toilet, washbasin.
- Diets are often inadequate and require supplements from relatives and friends.
- Officials may not speak English.
- Physical abuse, confiscation of personal property, degrading or inhumane treatment, and extortion are possible.

If you are convicted, you may face one of the following sentences:

- Two to ten years in most countries.
- A minimum of six years' hard labor and a stiff fine.

- The death sentence in some countries.

Learn what the local laws are and obey them.

### Marriage Abroad

Consular officers abroad cannot perform a marriage for you. Marriages abroad are generally performed by local civil or religious officials. Once your marriage is performed overseas, U.S. consular officers can advise you on how your foreign marriage document can be authenticated. A marriage which is valid under the laws of the country where the marriage was performed is generally recognized by most states in the United States. If you are married abroad and need confirmation that your marriage will be recognized in the United States, consult the Attorney General of your state of residence in the United States.

Marriages abroad are subject to the residency requirements of the country where the marriage is performed. There is almost always a lengthy waiting period. Some countries require that the civil documents which are presented to the marriage registrar abroad be translated and authenticated by a foreign consular official in the United States.

This process can be time consuming and expensive. Unlike in the United States, civil law countries require proof of legal capacity to enter into a marriage contract. If it is necessary to obtain this proof overseas, you can execute an affidavit of eligibility to marry at a U.S. embassy or consulate for a small fee (currently $10). There are also individual requirements which vary from country to country, i.e., parental consent and blood tests. Before going abroad, check with the embassy or tourist information bureau of the country where you plan to marry to learn of any specific requirements. In addition, the Office of Overseas Citizens Services, Room 4811, Department of State, Washington, D.C. 20520, has some general information on marriage in a number of countries overseas. If you are already abroad, consult with the nearest U.S. embassy or consulate.

### Divorce Abroad

The validity of divorces obtained overseas will vary according to the requirements of an individual's state of residence. Consult the authorities of your state of residence in the United States for these requirements.

### Birth Abroad of a U.S. Citizen

Most children born abroad to a U.S. citizen parent or parents acquire U.S. citizenship at birth. As soon as possible after the birth, the U.S. citizen parent should contact the nearest American embassy or consulate. When it is determined that the child has acquired U.S. citizenship, a consular officer prepares a Consular Report of Birth Abroad of a Citizen of the United States of America (Form FS-240). This document is recognized by U.S. law as proof of acquisition of U.S. citizenship and is acceptable evidence of citizenship for obtaining a passport, entering school, and most other purposes.

### Death of a U.S. Citizen Abroad

When a U.S. citizen dies abroad, the nearest U.S. embassy or consulate should be notified as soon as possible. Upon notification, the consular officer, in accordance with local laws, may do the following:

- Require proof of the decedent's citizenship (for example, U.S. passport, birth certificate, or naturalization certificate).
- Report the death to the next of kin or legal representative.
- Obtain instructions and funds from the family to make arrangements for local burial or return of the body to the United States.
- Obtain the local death certificate and prepare a "Report of Death of an American Citizen Abroad" (Form OF-180) to forward to the next of kin or legal representative. (This document may be used in U.S. courts to settle estate matters.)

- Serve as provisional conservator of a deceased American's estate and arrange for disposition of those effects.

Because the costs for local burial or transporting a deceased body back to the United States can be quite expensive, you may wish to obtain insurance to cover this cost. Otherwise, your relative or next of kin must bear these expenses. The U.S. Government cannot pay to have your body buried overseas or returned to the United States.

### Federal Benefits Services Abroad

Federal agency monthly benefits checks are generally sent from the Department of the Treasury to the U.S. embassies or consulates in the countries where the beneficiaries are residing. When you move overseas, report your change of residence to the nearest U.S. embassy or consulate. The usual procedure is for the embassy or consulate to then forward the check through the local mail system to you. It may be possible to make arrangements to have your check deposited directly into a bank account located in the United States or in the country where you reside. Check with the benefits paying agency or the nearest U.S. embassy or consulate for further information.

If your check does not arrive or you have other questions about your benefits, contact a consular officer at the nearest U.S. embassy or consulate. If the consular officer cannot answer your inquiry, he or she will contact the appropriate paying agency, such as the Social Security Administration, and make inquiries on your behalf. If you move, notify the nearest U.S. embassy or consulate at least 60 days before the move. This will enable the Federal agency to update its records so your checks are sent to the correct address.

### Assistance in Voting in U.S. Elections

Americans who reside abroad are usually eligible to vote by absentee ballot in all Federal elections and may also be eligible to vote in many state and local U.S. elections.

Eligibility depends upon the laws and regulations of your state of residence in the United States. To vote absentee, you must meet state voter registration requirements and apply for the ballot as early as possible from the state of your last domicile. Should your state ballot not arrive in sufficient time, you may be eligible to use a Federal write-in ballot known as a F.W.A.B. You should consult the nearest U.S. embassy or consulate for additional information.

### Selective Service Registration

Section I-202 of the Presidential Proclamation of July 2, 1980, reinstituting registration under the Military Selective Service Act, states:

Citizens of the United States who are to be registered and who are not in the United States on any of the days set aside for their registration shall present themselves at a U.S. embassy or consulate for registration before a diplomatic or consular officer of the United States or before a registrar duly appointed by a diplomatic or consular officer of the United States.

Check with the nearest U.S. embassy or consulate if you need to comply.

## FAMILY MATTERS

### Adopting a Child Overseas

If you plan to adopt a child overseas, you should be aware that the U.S. Government considers foreign adoptions to be a private legal matter within the judicial sovereignty of the nation where the child is residing. U.S. authorities have no right to intervene on behalf of American citizens in the courts in the country where the adoption takes place. However, there are a number of ways that U.S. embassies and consulates can assist prospective parents.

The U.S. embassy or consulate can provide you with information on the adoption process in the country where you reside. Consular officers can make inquiries on your behalf regarding the status of your case in the foreign court and will assist in clarifying documentary requirements if necessary. Embassies and consulates will also ensure that as an American you are not being discriminated against by foreign courts and will provide you with information on the visa application process for your adopted child.

Because children in foreign adoptions are considered to be nationals of the country of origin, prospective parents must comply with local laws. One way to achieve this is by dealing only with a reputable international adoption agency experienced in handling adoptions in the country where you are living. In the case of a private adoption, you should hire a local attorney with expertise in adoptions. Because of the potential for fraud in international adoptions, you need to be aware of the pitfalls. The U.S. embassy or consulate can offer you advice on what problems you might encounter.

Foreign children adopted overseas by U.S. citizens can gain U.S. citizenship if the adoptive parents apply for the child's naturalization after they return to the United States. In most cases, the adoptive parents would merely apply for a "Certificate of Citizenship from the Immigration and Naturalization Service" (INS) after the adoption. However, until they return to the United States, the adopted child remains a national of their country of origin. Before returning to the United States with your adopted child, you will need to petition the INS for your child's immigrant visa. For further information on adoption procedures, obtain INS Form M-249 entitled, "The Immigration of Adopted and Prospective Adoptive Children." You can also contact the Department of State, Overseas Citizens Services Office of Children's Issues, Room 4818, Washington, D.C. 20520, telephone (202) 736-7000 to learn more about foreign adoption procedures and to order the booklet *International Adoptions*. This booklet is also available on the Internet at http://travel.state.gov and contains useful information for U.S. citizens who plan to adopt a foreign child.

Author's note: In 2000 the U.S. Congress passed the Child Citizenship Act, which took effect February 22, 2001. This act granted automatic citizenship to most foreign-born adoptees who are under 18 and have at least one parent or legal guardian who is a U.S. citizen.

### International Child Custody Disputes

For parents involved in a child custody dispute, there are limits on the assistance that U.S. authorities can provide. In cases where an American child is abducted overseas by a parent, the U.S. Government's role is confined to helping the remaining parent locate the child, monitoring the child's welfare, and providing general information about child custody laws and procedures in the country where the abduction took place. Consular officers overseas can issue a U.S. passport to a child involved in a custody dispute if the child appears in person at the U.S. embassy or consulate and there is no court order issued by the foreign court of that country which bars the child's departure from the country.

U.S. consuls cannot take custody of a child, force the child's return to the United States, or attempt to influence child custody proceedings in foreign courts. If the parents cannot work out an amicable settlement of a child custody dispute, the only recourse is usually court action in the country where the child is residing. A custody decree originating in the United States is not automatically recognized overseas. On the contrary, foreign courts will decide custody in accordance with the laws of that country. If you are involved in a custody dispute, you will need to obtain a foreign attorney to represent you in court. You can obtain a list of such attorneys from the U.S. embassy or consulate in the country where your child has been taken.

Parents who are involved in a custody battle overseas should find out whether the country you are in is a party to the Hague Convention on the Civil Aspects of International Child Abduction. Under the Hague Convention, a child who has been wrongfully removed may be returned to his or her place of habitual residence. For further information on the Hague Convention contact the Office of Children's Issues in Overseas Citizens Services. That office also has copies of the booklet *International Parental Child Abduction,* which contains helpful information on what U.S. citizen parents can do to prevent their child from becoming a victim of parental child abduction. If you are overseas and would like information on this subject, contact the nearest U.S. embassy or consulate for guidance.

## PRECAUTIONS

### Safeguarding Your Passport

Your passport is a valuable document which should be carefully safeguarded. When living overseas, the Department of State recommends that you keep your passport at home in a safe, secure place. Although a passport kept at an available storage facility outside the home might offer maximum security, keep in mind that an emergency requiring immediate travel may make it difficult or impossible to obtain your passport before departure. In such a case, it may not be possible to obtain a replacement or temporary passport in time to make the intended travel.

### Loss or Theft of a U.S. Passport

If your passport is lost or stolen abroad, report the loss immediately to the nearest foreign service post and to local police authorities. If you can provide the consular officer with the information in the old passport, it will facilitate issuance of a new passport. Therefore, you should photocopy the data page of your passport and keep it in a separate place for easy retrieval.

### Passport Fraud

Multiple and fraudulent U.S. passports are used in many types of criminal activity, including illegal entry into the United States. In processing lost passport cases, the Department of State must take special precautions that may delay the issuance of a new passport. If you suspect a U.S. passport is being used fraudulently, do not hesitate to contact the nearest passport agency in the United States or American embassy or consulate overseas.

## CITIZENSHIP AND NATIONALITY

### U.S. Citizenship and Residence Abroad

U.S. citizens who take up residence abroad or who are contemplating doing so frequently ask whether this will have any effect on their citizenship. Residence abroad, in and of itself, has no effect on U.S. citizenship, and there is no requirement of U.S. law that a person who is a naturalized U.S. citizen must return to the United States periodically to preserve his or her U.S. citizenship. Contact the nearest U.S. embassy or consulate if you have any questions about nationality.

### Acquisition and Loss of Citizenship

U.S. citizenship may be acquired by birth in the United States or by birth abroad to a U.S. citizen parent or parents. However, there are certain residency or physical presence requirements that U.S. citizens may need to fulfill before the child's birth in order to transmit citizenship to their child born overseas. A child born abroad in wedlock to one citizen parent and one alien parent acquires U.S. citizenship only if the citizen parent was physically present in the United States for 5 years prior to the child's birth, at least 2 years of which were after the age of 14. Living abroad in military service or U.S. Government employment, or as an unmarried dependent in the household of someone so employed, can be considered as presence in the United States. A child born out of wedlock to a U.S. citizen mother acquires U.S. citizenship if the mother was physically present in the United States for 1 continuous year prior to the child's birth. A child born out of wedlock to a U.S. citizen father must establish a legal relationship to the father before age 18 or be legitimated before reaching age 21, depending on the date of birth, if he/she is to acquire U.S. citizenship through the father. For further information on these legal requirements, consult the nearest U.S. embassy or consulate. Citizenship may also be acquired subsequent to birth through the process of naturalization. (For more information, contact the Immigration and Naturalization Service at 1-800-755-0777.)

Loss of citizenship can occur only as the result of a citizen voluntarily performing an act of expatriation as set forth in the Immigration and Nationality Act with the intent to relinquish citizenship. Such acts most frequently performed include the following:

- Naturalization in a foreign state;
- Taking an oath or making an affirmation of allegiance to a foreign state;
- Service in the armed forces of a foreign state;
- Employment with a foreign government; or
- Taking a formal oath of renunciation of allegiance before a U.S. consular or diplomatic officer.

If you have any question about any aspect of loss of nationality, contact the nearest U.S. embassy or consulate or the Office of Overseas Citizens Services, Bureau of Consular Affairs, Room 4811, Department of State, Washington, D.C. 20520.

### Dual Nationality

A foreign country might claim you as a citizen of that country if:

- You were born there.
- Your parent or parents are or were citizens of that country.

- You are a naturalized U.S. citizen but are still considered a citizen under that country's laws.

If you fall into any of the above categories, consult the embassy of the country where you are planning to reside or are presently living. While recognizing the existence of dual nationality, the U.S. Government does not encourage it as a matter of policy because of the problems it may cause. Claims of other countries upon dual-national U.S. citizens often place them in situations where their obligations to one country are in conflict with U.S. law. Dual nationality may hamper efforts by the U.S. Government to provide diplomatic and consular protection to individuals overseas. When a U.S. citizen is in the other country of their dual nationality, that country has a predominant claim on the person. If you have any question about dual nationality, contact the nearest U.S. embassy or consulate or the Office of Overseas Citizens Services at the address in the previous section.

### FINANCIAL AND BUSINESS MATTERS

#### U.S. Taxes

U.S. citizens must report their worldwide income on their Federal income tax returns. Living or earning income outside the United States does not relieve a U.S. citizen of responsibility for filing tax returns. However, U.S. citizens living and/or working abroad may be entitled to various deductions, exclusions, and credits under U.S. tax laws, as well as under international tax treaties and conventions between the United States and a number of foreign countries. Consult the Internal Revenue Service (IRS) for further information.

For information on taxes and locations of IRS offices overseas, contact any office of the IRS or write to the Forms Distribution Center, Post Office Box 25866, Richmond, Virginia 23289. That office also has copies of Publication 54, *Tax Guide for U.S. Citizens and*

*Resident Aliens Abroad;* Publication 901, *U.S. Tax Treaties;* Publication 514, *Foreign Tax Credit for Individuals,* and Publication 520, *Scholarships and Fellowships.* The IRS has also put together a package of forms and instructions (Publication 776) for U.S. citizens living abroad. The package is also available through the Forms Distribution Center. During the filing period, you can usually obtain the necessary Federal income tax forms from the nearest U.S. embassy or consulate.

If you have access to a personal computer and a modem, you can get forms and publications electronically from the IRS. The forms and publications are available through IRIS, the Internal Revenue Information Services on FedWorld, a government bulletin board. On the Internet, you can telnet to fedworld.gov. or for file transfer protocol services, connect to ftp.fedworld.gov. If you are using the Internet's World Wide Web, connect to http://www.ustreas.gov.

### Foreign Country Taxes

If you earn any income while you are overseas, you may be required to pay tax on that income. You should check the rules and regulations with that country's embassy or consulate before you leave the United States or consult the nearest U.S. embassy or consulate abroad.

### Bank Accounts

Some countries will permit you to maintain a local bank account denominated in dollars or in another foreign currency of your choice. This may be a good idea if the U.S. dollar is strong and the local currency in the country you reside in is weak. If that country does not permit you to maintain U.S. dollar bank accounts, another idea would be to keep your dollars in a bank in the United States. That way you could convert them to the local currency as you need them rather than all at once. This would protect you in the event that the country you are living in devalues its currency.

### Wills

To avoid the risk of running afoul of foreign laws, if you own property or other assets both in the United States and overseas, consider the idea of having two wills drawn up. One should be prepared according to the legal system of your adopted country and the other according to the legal system of the U.S. Each will should mention the other.

Having two wills should ensure that your foreign property is disposed of in accordance with your wishes in the event of your death.

### Property Investment

A major decision that you will have to face when you live abroad is whether or not to purchase a home or property. Because prices in many foreign countries may seem like a bargain compared to the United States, there may be some merit to investing in real estate. However, you will need to keep several things in mind. First, check to see whether the country where you plan to invest permits foreigners to own property. Many foreign countries do not permit foreigners without immigrant status to buy real estate. Also, there may be restrictions on areas in which you may buy property and on the total number of foreigners who may purchase property in any one year.

One way for a foreigner to purchase real estate overseas may be to set up a bank trust and then lease the property. For your protection, you should first consult with a local real estate agent and then hire a reputable attorney. Check with the U.S. embassy or consulate in the country where you plan to purchase property to obtain a list of lawyers. A good lawyer will provide you with information about having your real estate contract notarized, registered, and, if necessary, translated. Your attorney should also be able to advise you on protection against unscrupulous land deals.

Before you make a real estate purchase, learn the customs and laws of the foreign government with regard to real estate. In the event of a dispute, you will have to abide by local and not U.S. laws. A good rule to follow is that before you invest in any real estate take the same precautions which you normally would take before you make a sizable investment in the United States.

## RETURNING TO THE U.S.

### U.S. Immigration and Customs

If you leave the U.S. for purposes of traveling, working, or studying abroad, and return to resume U.S. residence, you are considered a returning U.S. resident by the U.S. Customs Service.

When you go through immigration and customs at the port of entry, have your passport ready. Where possible, pack separately the articles you have acquired abroad to make inspection easy. Have your receipts handy in case you need to support your customs declaration. If you took other documents with you, such as an International Certification of Vaccination, a medical certificate, or a customs certificate of registration for foreign-made personal articles, have them ready also. If you are returning to the U.S. by car from either Mexico or Canada, a certificate of vehicle registration should be available.

Articles acquired abroad and brought back with you are subject to duty and internal revenue tax. As a returning U.S. resident, you are allowed to bring back $400 ($600, if you are returning directly from a Caribbean Basin Economy Recovery Act country) worth of merchandise duty free. However, you must have been outside the United States for at least 48 hours, and you must not have used this exemption within the preceding 30-day period. The next $1,000 worth of items you bring back with you for personal use or gifts are dutiable at a flat 10% rate. (Your duty free exemption may include 100 cigars, 200 cigarettes, and 1 liter of wine, beer, or liquor.)

### Restrictions on Products Entering the U.S.

Fresh fruit, meat, vegetables, plants in soil, and many other agricultural products are prohibited from entering the United States because they may carry foreign insects and diseases that could damage U.S. crops, forests, gardens, and livestock. Other items may also be restricted, so be sure to obtain details of regulations before departing for your trip back to the U.S. These restrictions also apply to mailed products. Prohibited items confiscated and destroyed at U.S. international postal facilities have almost doubled in recent years. For more information and to request the pamphlet *Travelers Tips on Prohibited Agricultural Products,* contact the agricultural affairs office at the nearest U.S. embassy or consulate, or write to the Animal and Plant Health Inspection Service, U.S. Department of Agriculture, 4700 River Road, Unit 51, Riverdale, MD 20737.

### Importing a Car

If you plan to bring a car back with you, before purchasing it make sure it conforms to U.S. emission standards established by the Environmental Protection Agency. If your vehicle does not conform to standards, it may be banned from entering the country. For further information, obtain the pamphlet *Buying a Car Overseas? Beware!* from the U.S. Environmental Protection Agency, Public Information Center, Mail Code 3406, 401 M Street, S.W., Washington, D.C. 20460.

### Wildlife and Wildlife Products

While you were overseas, if you purchased any articles made from endangered animals and plants or any live wild animals to bring back as pets, you need to be aware that U.S. laws and international treaties make it a crime to bring many wildlife souvenirs into the United States. Some prohibited items include those made from sea turtle shell, most reptile skins, crocodile leather, ivory, furs from endangered cat species, and those from coral reefs. Do not buy wildlife souvenirs if you are unsure of being able to bring them legally into the United States. The penalties you risk are severe, and your purchases could be confiscated. To learn more about endangered wildlife and guidelines governing restrictions on imports into the United States, you can obtain the pamphlet *Buyer Beware!* For a free copy, contact the Publications Unit, U.S. Fish and Wildlife Service, Department of the Interior, Washington, D.C. 20240. Additional information on the import of wildlife and wildlife products can be obtained through TRAFFIC (U.S.A.), World Wildlife Fund—U.S., 1250 24th Street, N.W., Washington, D.C. 20037.

## OTHER IMPORTANT PUBLICATIONS

### U.S. Embassies and Consulates

*Key Officers of Foreign Service Posts: Guide for Business Representatives* has names of key officers and addresses for U.S. embassies, consulates, and missions abroad. Updated two times a year; a 1-year subscription is $5. Order from the Superintendent of Documents, U.S. Government Printing Office (GPO), Washington, D.C. 20402, telephone: (202) 512-1800 or fax: (202) 512-2250.

*Your Trip Abroad* contains helpful tips on obtaining a passport, things to consider in preparing for your overseas trip, other resources for travel and customs information. To obtain a copy, contact the GPO for price and availability.

*Travel Tips for Older Americans* provides general information on passports, visas, health, currency, and other travel tidbits for elderly U.S. citizens planning to travel overseas. Copies are available from the Internet at http://travel.state.gov or Consular Affairs automated fax at (202) 647-3000.

*A Safe Trip Abroad* contains helpful precautions to minimize the chance of becoming a victim of terrorism and also provides other safety tips for Americans traveling overseas. To obtain a copy, contact the GPO for price and availability.

*Crisis Abroad—What the State Department Does* summarizes the work by the State Department during a crisis and its efforts to obtain reliable information from local authorities abroad for concerned relatives and friends of Americans located in the disaster area. Copies are free by sending a stamped, self-addressed business-size envelope (SASE) to CA/P, Room 6831, Department of State, Washington, D.C. 20520-4818.

*Office of Overseas Citizens Services* contains information about the assistance that the office provides in four major categories: deaths, arrests, welfare/whereabouts inquiries, and financial-medical emergencies. The booklet is free by sending a SASE to CA/P at the address above.

# CHAPTER 3
## *Know Before You Go*
(U.S. Customs Service Pamphlet, Revised January 1997)

On behalf of U.S. Customs, let me wish you a wonderful trip. We know you will be anxious to reach your destination upon your return, so we want to do everything we can to facilitate your entry into the United States. You are our customers, and we hope to serve you well by making your Customs clearance as pleasant and unobtrusive as possible.

I hope this booklet will help you understand our mission to protect your interests. Please read it carefully and don't hesitate to contact us if there is anything you would like clarified.

With your help, we can protect our borders and the interests of all citizens of this great nation. The Customs Service has an effect on nearly every aspect of American life. We protect industry, trademarks, and products; interdict illicit drugs; support the American farmer and the environment by guarding against contaminated products and foodstuffs; and for every dollar provided to this agency, we return approximately $20 directly to the U.S. Treasury.

I am proud of this agency's heritage and its continued commitment to serving and protecting you. If you have any suggestions, questions, or problems with the Customs Service, do not hesitate to contact us. We have over 300 ports around the country, and they are committed to helping you. You can find our phone number in the federal government section of your phone book, listed under the U.S. Department of the Treasury.

Thank you for your support.

Commissioner
U.S. Customs Service

## WARNING!

If you understate the value of an article you declare, or if you otherwise misrepresent an article in your declaration, you may have to pay a penalty in addition to payment of duty. Under certain circumstances, the article could be seized and retained by Customs if the penalty is not paid.

It is well known that some merchants abroad offer travelers invoices or bills of sale showing false or understated values. This practice not only delays your Customs examination, but can result in civil and/or criminal penalties.

If you fail to declare an article acquired abroad, not only is the article subject to seizure and/or retention, but you will be liable for a personal penalty in an amount equal to the value of the article in the United States. In addition, you may also be liable for criminal prosecution.

Don't rely on advice given by persons outside the Customs Service. It may be misleading. You could violate Customs laws and incur costly penalties. Any questions should be directed to the nearest Customs Office before you leave or upon entry into the United States.

If in doubt about whether an article should be declared, always declare it first and then direct your question to the Customs inspector. If in doubt about the value of an article, declare the article at the actual price paid (transaction value).

Customs inspectors routinely handle tourist items and become acquainted with the foreign prices. Moreover, current commercial prices of foreign items are available at all times and on-the-spot comparisons of these values can be made.

Be wary of an individual who asks you to carry an item back to the United States.

You are responsible for everything in your possession when you clear Customs. Packages from other individuals have been known to contain contraband and/or currency. You would be responsible for any penalties that may be assessed on these packages.

Play it safe—declare it all!

## YOUR DECLARATION

You must declare all articles acquired during your trip and in your possession at the time of your return. This includes:

- Articles that you purchased.
- Articles presented to you while abroad, such as wedding and birthday presents or inherited items.
- Articles purchased in duty-free shops or on board a carrier.
- Repairs or alterations made to any articles taken abroad and returned, whether or not repairs or alterations were free of charge.
- Items you have been requested to bring home for another person.
- All articles you intend to sell or use in your business. Promotional items and samples for Customs purposes are only those items that are valued at $1 or less.

In addition, you must declare any articles acquired in the U.S. Virgin Islands, American Samoa, Guam, or a country of the Caribbean Basin Economic Recovery Act and not accompanying you at the time of your return.

The price actually paid for each article must be stated on your declaration in U.S. currency or its equivalent in the country of acquisition. The stated price must include any "value added tax" (VAT) if it was not refunded prior to arrival. If the article was not purchased, obtain an estimate of its fair retail value in the country in which it was acquired.

Note: The wearing or use of any article acquired abroad does not exempt it from duty. It must be declared at the price you paid for it.

### Oral Declaration

Customs declaration forms are distributed on vessels and planes and should be prepared in advance of arrival for presentation to

Immigration and Customs inspectors. You may declare orally to the Customs inspector the articles you acquired abroad if the articles are accompanying you and have not exceeded the duty-free exemption allowed. A Customs officer may, however, ask you to prepare a written list of the articles.

### Written Declaration

A written declaration will be necessary when:

- The total fair retail value of articles acquired abroad exceeds your personal exemption. More than one liter (33.8 fl. oz.) of alcoholic beverages, 200 cigarettes (one carton), and 100 cigars are included.
- Some of the items are not intended for your personal or household use, such as commercial samples, items for sale or use in your business, or articles you are bringing home for another person.
- Articles acquired in the U.S. Virgin Islands, American Samoa, Guam, or a Caribbean Basin Economic Recovery Act country are being sent to the United States.
- A Customs duty or Internal Revenue Tax is collectible on any article in your possession.
- A Customs officer requests a written list of articles acquired.
- You have used your exemption in the last 30 days.

### Family Declaration

The head of a family may make a joint declaration for all members residing in the same household and returning together to the United States. Family members making a joint declaration may combine their personal exemptions. For example, Mrs. Smith purchased an item for $600, but Mr. Smith only purchased $200 worth of merchandise. Mr. and Mrs. Smith may combine their $400 exemptions and will not have to pay duty on the items they acquired.

Infants and children returning to the United States are entitled to the same exemptions as adults (except for alcoholic beverages). Children born abroad, who have never resided in the United States, are entitled to the Customs exemptions granted nonresidents.

Visitors to the United States should obtain the leaflet *Visiting the U.S., Customs Requirements for Non-Residents.*

Military and civilian personnel of the U.S. Government should obtain the leaflet *Customs Highlights for Government Personnel* for information about their Customs exemptions when returning from an extended duty assignment abroad.

### YOUR EXEMPTIONS

In clearing U.S. Customs, a traveler is considered either a "returning resident of the United States" or a "nonresident."

Generally speaking, if you leave the United States for purposes of traveling, working, or studying abroad and return to resume residency in the United States, you are considered a returning resident by Customs.

However, U.S. residents living abroad temporarily are entitled to be classified as nonresidents, and thus receive more liberal Customs exemptions, on short visits to the United States, provided they export any foreign-acquired items at the completion of their visit.

Residents of American Samoa, Guam, or the U.S. Virgin Islands, who are American citizens, are also considered as returning U.S. residents.

Articles acquired abroad and brought into the United States are subject to applicable duty and Internal Revenue Tax, but as a returning resident you are allowed certain exemptions from the payment of duty on items obtained while abroad.

### Exemptions

Articles totaling $400, $600, or $1,200, depending on your trip, may be entered free of duty, subject to the limitations on liquors, cigarettes, and cigars, if:

- Articles were acquired during your trip for your personal or household use.
- You bring the articles with you at the time of your return to the United States and they are properly declared to Customs. Articles purchased and left for alterations or other reasons cannot be applied to your $400 exemption when shipped to follow at a later date. The flat rate of duty does not apply to mailed articles. Duty is assessed when received.
- You are returning from a stay abroad of at least 48 hours. Example: A resident who leaves United States territory at 1:30 P.M. on June 1st would complete the required 48-hour period at 1:30 P.M. on June 3rd. This time limitation does not apply if you are returning from Mexico or the Virgin Islands of the U.S.
- You have not used either the $400, $600, or $1,200 exemption, or any part of it, within the preceding 30-day period. Also, your exemption is not cumulative. If you use a portion of your exemption on entering the United States, then you must wait 30 days before you are entitled to another exemption, other than a $200 exemption.
- Articles are not prohibited or restricted.

### $400 Exemption

Residents of the U.S. who meet the above conditions are entitled to a $400 dollar exemption from paying duty on goods that would otherwise be dutiable. This means that articles acquired abroad with a total value of up to $400 will be admitted duty-free, as long as they accompany you. (Purchases you mail home have a different exemption, see the sections on "Gifts" and "Customs Pointers" for more information.)

Additional acquisitions may qualify for duty-free treatment under other exemption authorities, such as the Generalized System of Preferences, which awards duty-free treatment to many goods from developing countries. Fine art (not handicrafts) and antiques over 100 years old are commonly acquired items that also do not require the payment of duty.

This means that a resident could spend more than $400 and still not be charged duty on any purchases when reentering the U.S. For instance, a traveler buys a $300 gold bracelet, a $40 hat, and a $60 purse. Duty would not be charged on these items, because they qualify for the $400 exemption. In addition, this same traveler buys a $200 unframed painting. Because fine art is not subject to duty, the traveler will be able to bring in $600 worth of goods without paying any duty. (Be aware, if the painting is framed, duty may be charged on the value of the frame.)

### $1,200 Exemptions

If you return directly or indirectly from a U.S. insular possession—American Samoa, Guam, or the U.S. Virgin Islands—you may receive a Customs exemption of $1,200.

You may also bring in 1,000 cigarettes, but only 200 of them may have been acquired elsewhere.

### $600 Exemption

If you are returning directly from any of the following 24 beneficiary countries, yourcustoms exemption is $600:

Antigua and Barbuda
El Salvador
Netherlands, Antilles
Aruba
Grenada
Nicaragua
Bahamas
Guatemala
Panama
Barbados
Guyana
Saint Kitts and Nevis
Belize
Haiti
Saint Lucia
Costa Rica
Honduras

Saint Vincent and the Grenadines
Dominica
Jamaica
Trinidad and Tobago
Dominican Republic
Montserrat
Virgin Islands, British

In the case of the $1200 exemption, up to $600 worth of the merchandise may havebeen obtained in any of the beneficiary countries listed above, or up to $400 in anyother country. For example, if you traveled to the U.S. Virgin Islands and Jamaica and then returned home, you would be entitled to bring in $1,200 worth of merchandise duty-free. Of this amount, $600 worth may have been acquired in Jamaica.

In the case of the $600 exemption for the Caribbean Basin Economic Recovery Act countries, up to $400 worth of merchandise may have been acquired in other foreign countries. For instance, if you travel to England and the Bahamas, and then return home, your exemption is $600, $400 of which may have been acquired in England.

### $200 Exemption

If you cannot claim the $400, $600, or $1,200 exemption because of the 30-day or 48-hour minimum limitations, you may bring in free of duty and tax articles acquired abroad for your personal or household use if the total fair retail value does not exceed $200. This is an individual exemption and may not be grouped with other members of a family on one Customs declaration.

You may include any of the following: 50 cigarettes, 10 cigars, 150 milliliters (4 fl. oz.) of alcoholic beverages, or 150 milliliters (4 fl. oz.) of perfume containing alcohol.

If any article brought with you is subject to duty or tax, or if the total value of all dutiable articles exceeds $200, no article may be exempted from duty or tax.

*Cigars and Cigarettes:* Not more than 100 cigars and 200 cigarettes (one carton) may be included in your $400 exemption. (See other exemption levels for exceptions.)

Products of Cuban origin may be included if purchased in Cuba. This exemption is available to each person. Your cigarettes, however, may be subject to a tax imposed by state and local authorities.

*Liquor:* One liter (33.8 fl. oz.) of alcoholic beverages may be included in the $400 exemption if:

- You are 21 years of age or older.
- It is for your own use or for use as a gift.
- It is not in violation of the laws of the state in which you arrive.

(See other exemption levels for exceptions.)

Note: Most states restrict the quantity of alcoholic beverages you may import. If the state in which you arrive permits less liquor than you have legally brought into the United States, that state's laws prevail. Information about state restrictions and taxes should be obtained from the state government as laws vary from state to state.

Alcoholic beverages in excess of the one-liter limitation are subject to duty and Internal Revenue Tax.

Shipping alcoholic beverages by mail is prohibited by United States postal laws. Alcoholic beverages include wine and beer as well as distilled spirits.

### Gifts

Gifts accompanying you are considered to be for your personal use and may be included in your exemption. This includes gifts given to you by others while abroad and those you intend to give to others after you return. Gifts intended for business, promotional, or other commercial purposes may not be included.

Bona fide gifts of not more than $100 in fair retail value may be shipped and received by friends and relatives in the United States free of duty and tax, if the same person does not receive more than $100 in gift shipments in one day. The "day" in reference is the day in which the parcel(s) are received for Customs processing.

This amount is increased to $200 if shipped from the U.S. Virgin Islands, American Samoa, or Guam. You do not declare these gifts upon your return to the United States.

Perfume containing alcohol and valued at more than $5 retail, tobacco products, and alcoholic beverages are excluded from the gift provision.

Gifts intended for more than one person may be shipped in the same package provided they are individually wrapped and labeled with the name of the recipient.

Be sure the outer wrapping of the package is marked: 1) unsolicited gift, 2) nature of the gift, and 3) its fair retail value. In addition, a consolidated gift parcel should be marked as such on the outside with the names of the recipients listed and the value of each gift. This will facilitate Customs clearance of your package.

If any article imported in the gift parcel is subject to duty and tax, or should any single gift within a consolidated package exceed the bona fide gift allowance, then that gift will be dutiable.

You, as a traveler, cannot send a "gift" parcel to yourself, nor can persons traveling together send "gifts" to each other. Gifts ordered by mail from the United States do not qualify under this duty-free gift provision and are subject to duty.

If a parcel is subject to duty, the United States Postal Service will collect the duty plus handling charges. Duty cannot be prepaid.

### Duty on Articles Not Covered by Your Exemption

Duty preferences are granted to certain developing countries under the Generalized System of Preferences (GSP). Some products from these countries have been exempted from duty which would otherwise be collected if imported from any other country. For details, obtain the leaflet *GSP & The Traveler*

from your nearest Customs office. Many products of certain Caribbean and Andean countries are also exempt from duty under the Caribbean Basin Initiative and Andean Trade Preference Act.

Most products of Israel may enter the United States either free of duty or at a reduced duty rate. Check with Customs.

The North American Free Trade Agreement (NAFTA) was implemented on January 1, 1994. U.S. residents returning directly or indirectly from Canada or Mexico are eligible for free or reduced duty rates as applicable, on goods originating in Canada or Mexico as defined in the Agreement.

Personal belongings of United States origin are entitled entry free of duty. Personal belongings taken abroad, such as worn clothing, etc., may be sent home by mail before you return and receive free entry provided they have not been altered or repaired while abroad. These packages should be marked "American Goods Returned."

When a claim of United States origin is made, marking on the article to so indicate facilitates Customs processing.

Foreign-made personal articles taken abroad are dutiable each time they are brought into our country unless you have acceptable proof of prior possession.

Documents which fully describe the article, such as a bill of sale, insurance policy, jeweler's appraisal, or receipt for purchase, may be considered reasonable proof of prior possession.

Items such as watches, cameras, tape recorders, or other articles which may be readily identified by serial number or permanently affixed markings, may be taken to the Customs office nearest you and registered before your departure. The "Certificate of Registration" (CF 4457) provided will expedite free entry of these items when you return. Keep the certificate as it is valid for any future trips as long as the information on it remains legible.

Registration cannot be accomplished by telephone nor can blank registration forms be given or mailed to you to be filled out at a later time.

Vehicles, boats, planes, or other vehicles taken abroad for noncommercial use may be returned duty free by proving to the Customs officer that you took them out of the United States. This proof may be the state registration card for an automobile, the Federal Aviation Administration certificate for an aircraft, a yacht license or motorboat identification certificate for a pleasure boat, or a Customs certificate of registration obtained before departure.

Dutiable repairs or accessories acquired abroad for articles taken out of the United States must be declared on your return.

*Warning:* Catalytic-equipped vehicles (1976 or later model years) driven outside the United States, Canada, or Mexico will not, in most cases, meet EPA standards when brought back to the United States. As unleaded fuel generally is not available in other countries, the catalytic converter will become inoperative and must be replaced. Contact Environmental Protection Agency, Washington, D.C. 20460, for details and exceptions.

Your local Customs office has the following leaflets which will be of interest—*Importing a Car* and *Pleasure Boats.* You may purchase *Customs Guide for Private Flyers* from your local Government Printing Office bookstore. Consult your local telephone book under "U.S. Government."

Household effects and tools of trade or occupation which you take out of the United States are duty free at the time you return if properly declared and entered.

All furniture, carpets, paintings, tableware, linens, and similar household furnishings acquired abroad may be imported free of duty, if:

- They are not imported for another person or for sale.
- They have been used abroad by you for at least one year or were available for use in a household in which you were a resident member for one year. This privilege does not include articles placed in storage outside the home. The year of use need not be continuous, nor does it need to be the year immediately preceding the date of importation. Shipping time may not be included when you compute the "one year of use."

Items such as wearing apparel, jewelry, photograph equipment, tape recorders, stereo components, and vehicles are considered personal articles and cannot be passed free of duty as household effects, although the duty rate on them will be assessed on devalued basis according to age of the item.

Articles imported in excess of your Customs exemption will be subject to duty unless the items are entitled to free entry or prohibited.

The inspector will place the items having the highest rate of duty under your exemption, and duty will be assessed on the lower-rated items.

After deducting your exemptions and the value of any articles duty free, a flat 10 percent rate of duty will be applied to the next $1,000 worth (fair retail value) of merchandise. Any dollar amount of an article or articles over $1,000 will be dutiable at the various rates of duty applicable to the articles.

Articles to which the flat rate of duty is applied must be for your personal use or for use as gifts. You cannot receive this flat-rate provision more than once every 30 days, excluding the day of your last arrival.

There are special flat rates of duty for articles made in and acquired in either Canada or Mexico.

The flat rate of duty is 5% for articles purchased in the U.S. Virgin Islands, American Samoa, or Guam, whether the articles accompany you or are shipped.

Example: You acquire goods valued at $2,500 from:

**U.S. insular possessions:**

| | |
|---|---|
| Total Declared Value: | $2,500 |
| Personal exemption up to: | $1,200 |

| Flat duty rate at 5%: | next $1,000 |
| Various rates of duty: | remaining $300 |

**Caribbean Basin Economic Recovery Act:**

| Total Declared Value: | $2,500 |
| Personal exemption (free of duty) up to: | $600 |
| Flat duty rate at 10%: | next $1,000 |
| Various rates of duty: | remaining $900 |

**Other countries or locations:**

| Total Declared Value: | $2,500 |
| Personal exemption (free of duty) up to: | $400 |
| Flat duty rate at 10%: | next $1,000 |
| Various rates of duty: | remaining $1,100 |

The flat rate of duty will apply to any articles which are dutiable and cannot be included in your personal exemption, even if you have not exceeded the dollar amount of your exemption. Example: you are returning from Europe with $200 worth of articles which includes 2 liters of liquor. One liter will be free of duty under your exemption, the other dutiable at 10%, plus any Internal Revenue Tax.

Members of a family residing in one household traveling together on their return to the U.S. will group articles for application of the flat duty rate, no matter which family member may be the owner of the articles.

Rates of duty on imported goods are provided for in the Harmonized Tariff Schedule of the United States. There are two duty rates for each item, known as "column 1" and "column 2." Column 1 rates vary from free (prism binoculars, books, antiques) to 34.6% (man-made fiber wearing apparel) and are applicable to most favored nations.

Column 2 rates are higher and apply to products from the following countries:

Afghanistan
North Korea
Cuba
Laos

Note: The tariff duty status accorded these countries is subject to change. Please check with Customs for updated information.

Products of the above-listed column 2 countries are dutiable at the column 2 rates of duty, even if purchased in or sent from another country. Example: A crystal vase made in Laos and purchased in Switzerland would be dutiable at the column 2 rate. If the article accompanies you, however, it may be entered under your duty-free personal exemption or the flat rate of duty allowance.

Payment of duty, required at the time of your arrival on articles accompanying you, may be made by any of the following ways:

- U.S. currency (foreign currency is not acceptable).
- Personal check in the exact amount of duty, drawn on a national or state bank or trust company of the United States, made payable to the "U.S. Customs Service."
- Government check, money orders, or traveler's checks are acceptable if they do not exceed the duty amount by more than $50. [Second endorsements are not acceptable. Identification must be presented; e.g. traveler's passport or driver's license.]
- In some locations you may pay duty with credit cards from Mastercard or VISA.

Goods covered by an ATA Carnet: Residents returning to the U.S. with goods covered by an ATA Carnet are reminded to report to a Customs inspector upon their arrival. The inspector will examine the covered goods against the carnet and certify the appropriate reimportation counterfoil and voucher. The carnet will serve as the Customs control registration document, and no entry or payment of duty will be necessary as long as the goods qualify as U.S. goods returned and are being brought back into the United States within the validity period of the carnet. (See Customs pamphlet *ATA Carnet*).

## Prohibited and Restricted Articles

Because Customs inspectors are stationed at ports of entry and along our land and sea borders, they are often called upon to enforce laws and requirements of other Government agencies. This is done to protect community health, preserve domestic plant and animal life, and for other reasons.

Certain articles considered injurious or detrimental to the general welfare of the United States are prohibited entry by law. Among these are: lottery tickets, narcotics and dangerous drugs, obscene articles and publications, seditious and treasonable materials, hazardous articles (e.g., fireworks, dangerous toys, toxic or poisonous substances), and switchblade knives (however, a one-armed person may import a switchblade knife for personal use, if the blade is 3 inches in length or less.)

Other items must meet special requirements before they can be released. You will be given a receipt for any articles retained by Customs.

## Artifacts/Cultural Property (Objects/Artifacts)

U.S. law prohibits the importation of pre-Columbian monumental and architectural sculpture and murals from certain countries in Central and South America without proper export permits. These importations are restricted no matter where the artifacts are shipped from, be it the country of origin or elsewhere.

Federal law and international treaties prohibit the importation of any articles of stolen cultural property from museums, religious, or secular public monuments. Would-be buyers of such property should be aware that, unlike purchases of customary tourist merchandise, purchases of cultural objects do not confer ownership should such an object be found to be stolen. Imports of certain archeological and ethnographic material (e.g., masks or textiles) from Bolivia, El Salvador, Guatemala, Peru, and Mali are restricted and require export certificates from the country of origin. Purveyors of such merchandise have been known to offer phony export certificates, and again, prospective buyers should be aware that Customs inspectors are expert at spotting fraudulent export certificates that accompany cultural property. Additional restrictions are expected to be imposed on material from countries in Europe, Asia, Africa, and Central America. These restrictions are aimed at providing international access to cultural objects to all members of the public for legitimate scientific, cultural, and educational purposes. For more information, contact the United States Information Agency, Washington, D.C., (202) 619-6612.

## Automobiles

Automobiles imported into the United States must conform to Environmental Protection Agency (EPA) emission requirements and Department of Transportation (DOT) safety, bumper and theft prevention standards. See Customs pamphlet *Importing a Car* and *Pleasure Boats*.

Almost all automobiles purchased overseas do not comply with U.S. standards and will require modification. Vehicles imported conditionally for modification to U.S. specifications, and not modified, or are not modified acceptably, must either be exported or destroyed under Customs supervision.

Also, vehicles that were originally manufactured to meet EPA emission requirements may, depending upon what countries the car was driven in, be subject to additional EPA requirements or require a bond upon entry. You are advised to call the EPA for further assistance.

Information on importing vehicles may be obtained from the Environmental Protection Agency, Attn: 6405J, Washington, D.C. 20460, telephone (202) 233-9660, and the Department of Transportation, Office of Vehicle Safety Compliance (NEF 32), Washington, D.C. 20590. Copies of the Customs pamphlet *Importing a Car* and EPA's *Automotive Imports*

*Fact Manual* may be obtained by writing, respectively, the U.S. Customs Service, P.O. Box 7407, Washington, D.C. 20044, or the Environmental Protection Agency, Washington, D.C. 20460.

### Biological Materials

Biological materials of public health or veterinary importance (disease organisms and vectors for research and educational purposes) require import permits. Write to the Foreign Quarantine Program, U.S. Public Health Service, Center for Disease Control, Atlanta, GA 30333.

### Books, Video Tapes, Computer Programs and Cassettes

Pirated copies of copyrighted articles— unlawfully made articles produced without the authorization of the copyright owner—are prohibited from importation into the United States. Pirated copies may be seized and destroyed.

### Trademarked Articles

Foreign-made trademarked articles may be limited as to the quantity which may be brought into the United States if the registered trademark has been recorded with Customs by an American trademark owner.

The types of articles usually of interest to tourists are 1) lenses, cameras, binoculars, optical goods; 2) tape recorders, musical instruments; 3) jewelry, precious metal-ware; 4) perfumes; 5) watches, clocks.

Persons arriving in the United States with a trademarked article are allowed an exemption, usually one article of a type bearing a protected trademark. An exempted trademark article must accompany you, and you can claim this exemption for the same type of article only once each 30 days. The article must be for your personal use and not for sale. If an exempted article is sold within one year following importation, the article or its value is subject to forfeiture.

If the trademark owner allows a quantity in excess of the aforementioned exemption for its particular trademarked article, the total of those trademarked articles authorized may be entered. Articles bearing counterfeit trademarks, if the amount of such articles exceeds the traveler's personal exemption, are subject to seizure and forfeiture.

### Ceramic Tableware

Some ceramic tableware sold abroad contains dangerous levels of lead in the glaze that can leach into certain foods and beverages served in them.

The Food and Drug Administration recommends that ceramic tableware, especially when purchased in Mexico, China, Hong Kong, or India, be tested for lead release on your return or be used for decorative purposes only.

### Drug Paraphernalia

The importation, exportation, manufacture, sale, and transportation of drug paraphernalia are prohibited. Persons convicted of these offenses are subject to fines and imprisonment. As importations contrary to law, drug paraphernalia may be seized by U.S. Customs.

### Firearms and Ammunition

Firearms and ammunition are subject to restrictions and import permits approved by the Bureau of Alcohol, Tobacco and Firearms (ATF). Applications to import may be made only by or through a licensed importer, dealer, or manufacturer. Weapons, ammunition, or other devices prohibited by the National Firearms Act will not be admitted into the United States unless specifically authorized by ATF.

No import permit is required when it is proven that the firearms or ammunition were previously taken out of the United States by the person who is returning with such firearms or ammunition. To facilitate reentry, persons may have them registered before departing from the United States at any Customs office or ATF field office.

Exports are subject to the export licensing requirements of the Office of Defense Trade Controls, Department of State, Washington, D.C. 20520, (703) 875-6644.

For further information on imports, contact the Bureau of Alcohol, Tobacco and Firearms, Department of the Treasury, Washington, D.C. 20226, (202) 927-8320.

Residents of the United States carrying firearms or ammunition with them to other countries should consult in advance the Customs officials or the respective embassies of those countries as to their regulations.

### Fish and Wildlife

Fish and wildlife are subject to certain import and export restrictions, prohibitions, permits or certificates, and quarantine requirements. This includes:

- Wild birds, mammals including marine mammals, reptiles, crustaceans, fish, and mollusks and invertebrates.
- Any part or product, such as skins, feathers, eggs.
- Products and articles manufactured from wildlife and fish.

Endangered species of wildlife and products made from them are generally prohibited from being imported or exported. All ivory and ivory products made from elephant or marine mammal ivory are also generally prohibited from being imported. Antiques containing wildlife parts may be imported if accompanied by documentation proving that they are at least 100 years old. (Certain other requirements for antiques may apply.) If you contemplate purchasing articles made from wildlife, such as tortoise shell jewelry, leather goods, or other articles made from whalebone, ivory, skins, or fur, please contact—before you go—the U.S. Fish and Wildlife Service, Division of Law Enforcement, P.O. Box 3247, Arlington, VA 22203-3247. Information on the limit for migratory game birds for import and export can also be obtained from this office.

Ask for their pamphlet *Facts About Federal Wildlife Laws.*

If you plan to import fish or wildlife, or any product, article, or part, check with Customs or the Fish and Wildlife Service first, as only certain ports are designated to handle these entries. Additional information is contained in our leaflet *Pets and Wildlife*, U.S. Customs.

Federal regulations do not authorize the importation of any wildlife or fish into any state of the United States if the state's laws or regulations are more restrictive than any applicable Federal treatment. Wild animals taken, killed, sold, possessed, or exported to the United States in violation of any foreign laws are not allowed entry into the United States.

### *Hunting Trophies*

If you plan to import a hunting trophy or game, check with the Fish and Wildlife Service first. Such items generally require a Fish and Wildlife license and only certain ports are designated to handle these entries. Trophies may also be subject to an inspection by APHIS for sanitary purposes. General guidelines for importing trophies may be found in their publication: *Traveler's Tips.*

*Warning:* There are many different regulations governing the importation of animals and animal parts. Failure to comply could result in extensive and expensive delays in clearing your trophy through Customs.

In addition, federal regulations do not authorize the importation of any wildlife or fish into any state of the United States if the state's laws or regulations are more restrictive than any applicable Federal treatment. Wild animals taken, killed, sold, possessed, or exported to the United States in violation of any foreign laws are not allowed entry into the United States.

### Food Products

Bakery items and all cured cheeses are admissible. The USDA Animal and Plant Health Inspection Service leaflet, *Traveler's Tips*, provides detailed information on bringing food, plant, and animal products into the United States. Imported foods are also subject to requirements of the Food and Drug Administration.

### Fruits and Vegetables

Most fruits and vegetables are either prohibited from entering the country or require an import permit. Every fruit or vegetable must be declared to the Customs officer and must be presented for inspection, no matter how free of pests it appears to be.

Most canned or processed items are admissible.

Applications for import permits or requests for information should be addressed to Quarantines, USDA-APHIS-PPQ, Federal Bldg., Hyattsville, MD 20782, or call (301) 734-8645.

### Meats, Livestock, Poultry

Meats, livestock, poultry, and their by-products (such as ham, frankfurters, sausage, paté) are either prohibited or restricted from entering the United States, depending on the animal disease condition in country of origin. Fresh meat is generally prohibited from most countries. Canned meat is permitted if the inspector can determine that it is commercially canned, cooked in the container, hermetically sealed, and can be kept without refrigeration. Other canned, cured, or dried meat is severely restricted from most countries.

You should contact USDA-APHIS-VS, Federal Building, 6506 Belcrest Road, Hyattsville, MD 20782, for detailed requirements or call (301) 734-7830.

### Plants

Plants, cuttings, seeds, unprocessed plant products and certain endangered species either require an import permit or are prohibited from entering the United States.

Endangered or threatened species of plants and plant products, if importation is not prohibited, will require an export permit from the country of origin. Every single plant or plant product must be declared to the Customs officer and must be presented for inspection,

no matter how free of pests it appears to be. Applications for import permits or requests for information should be addressed to: Quarantines, USDA-APHIS-PPQ, Federal Building, Room 632, 6505 Belcrest Road, Hyattsville, MD 20782, (301) 734-8645.

### Gold

Gold coins, medals, and bullion, formerly prohibited, may be brought into the United States. However, under regulations administered by the Office of Foreign Assets Control, such items originating in or brought from Cuba, Iran, Iraq, Libya, and North Korea are prohibited entry. Copies of gold coins are prohibited if not properly marked by country of issuance.

### Medicine/Narcotics

Narcotics and dangerous drugs, including anabolic steroids, are prohibited entry and there are severe penalties if imported. A traveler requiring medicines containing habit-forming drugs or narcotics (e.g., cough medicines, diuretics, heart drugs, tranquilizers, sleeping pills, antidepressants, stimulants, etc.) should:

- Have all drugs, medicinals, and similar products properly identified;
- Carry only such quantity as might normally be carried by an individual having some sort of health problem;
- Have either a prescription or written statement from your personal physician that the medicinals are being used under a doctor's direction and are necessary for your physical well-being while traveling.

### Warning

The Food and Drug Administration prohibits the importation, by mail or in person, of fraudulent prescription and non-prescription drugs and medical devices. These may include unorthodox "cures" for medical conditions including cancer, AIDS, and multiple sclerosis. While these drugs and devices may be completely legal elsewhere, they may not have been approved for use in the United States, even under a prescription issued by a foreign physician. They may not legally enter the United States and may be confiscated.

For additional information, contact your nearest FDA office or write:

Food and Drug Administration
Division of Import Operations and Policy
Room 12-8 (HFC-170)
5600 Fishers Lane
Rockville, MD 20857

### Merchandise from Embargoed Countries

The importation of goods from the following countries is generally prohibited under regulations administered by the Office of Foreign Assets Control: Cuba, North Korea, Libya, Iraq, and Iran.

These restrictions do not apply to informational materials such as pamphlets, books, tapes, films, or recordings.

Specific licenses from the Office of Foreign Assets Control are required to bring prohibited merchandise into the United States, but they are rarely granted. Foreign visitors to the United States may be permitted to bring in small articles for personal use as accompanied baggage, depending upon the goods' country of origin.

Travelers should be aware of certain travel restrictions that may apply to these countries. Because of the strict enforcement of these prohibitions, those anticipating foreign travel to any of the countries listed above would do well to write in advance to the Office of Foreign Assets Control, Department of the Treasury, Washington, D.C. 20220, U.S.A.

### Money and Other Monetary Instruments

There is no limit on the total amount of monetary instruments which may be brought into or taken out of the United States, nor is it illegal to do so. However, if you transport or cause to be transported (including by mail or other means) more than $10,000 in monetary instruments on any occasion into or out of the United States, or if you receive more than that amount, you must file a report (Customs Form 4790) with U.S. Customs (Currency & Foreign Transactions Reporting Act, 31 U.S.C. 1101, et seq.). Failure to comply can result in civil, criminal, and/or forfeiture penalties.

Monetary instruments include U.S. or foreign coin in current circulation, currency, traveler's checks in any form, money orders, and negotiable instruments or investment securities in bearer form.

### Pets

There are controls, restrictions, and prohibitions on entry of animals, birds, turtles, wildlife, and endangered species.

Cats must be free of evidence of diseases communicable to man when examined at the port of entry. If the animal is not in apparent good health, further examination by a licensed veterinarian may be required at the expense of the owner.

Dogs must be free of evidence of diseases communicable to man. Dogs, except those less than 3 months of age, must be vaccinated against rabies not less than 30 days prior to arrival. A valid rabies vaccination certificate must accompany the animal. This certificate should identify the animal, specify the date of vaccination, date of expiration, and bear the signature of a licensed veterinarian. If no date of expiration is specified, the certificate is acceptable if the date of vaccination is no more than 12 months before the date of arrival. Vaccination against rabies is not required for dogs arriving from rabies-free countries.

Personally-owned pet birds may be entered (limit of two if of the psittacine family), but APHIS and Public Health Service requirements must be met, including quarantine at any APHIS facility at specified locations, at the owner's expense. Advance reservations are required.

Non-human primates such as monkeys, apes, and similar animals may not be imported.

If you plan to take your pet abroad or

import one on your return, obtain a copy of our leaflet, *Pets and Wildlife*, U.S. Customs.

You should check with state, county, and municipal authorities about any restrictions and prohibitions they may have before importing a pet.

### Textiles

Textile and apparel items which accompany you and which you have acquired abroad for personal use or as gifts are generally not subject to quantitative restrictions.

However, unaccompanied textile and apparel items may be subject to certain quantitative restrictions (quotas) which require a document called a "visa" or "export license" or exempt certificate as appropriate from the country of production. Check with Customs before you depart on your trip.

## CUSTOMS POINTERS

### Traveling Back and Forth Across Border

After you have crossed the United States boundary at one point and you swing back into the United States to travel to another point in the foreign country, you run the risk of losing your Customs exemption unless you meet certain requirements. If you make a "swing back," don't risk your exemptions—ask the nearest Customs officer about these requirements.

### "Duty-Free" Shops

Articles bought in "duty-free" shops in foreign countries are subject to U.S. Customs duty and restrictions but may be included in your personal exemption.

Articles purchased in U.S. "duty-free" shops are subject to U.S. Customs duty if reentered into the United States. Example: Liquor bought in a "duty-free" shop before entering Canada and brought back into the United States may be subject to duty and Internal Revenue Tax.

Note: Many travelers are confused by the term "duty-free" as it relates to shops. Articles

sold in duty-free shops are free of duty and taxes only for the country in which that shop is located. Articles sold in duty-free shops are intended for export and are not to be returned to the country of purchase. So if your purchases exceed your personal exemption, that item may be subject to duty. Articles acquired in a U.S. duty-free shop before you left the United States, may be included in your exemption.

### Keep Your Sales Slips

You will find your sales slips, invoices, or other evidence of purchase not only helpful when making out your declaration, but necessary if you have unaccompanied articles being sent from the U.S. Virgin Islands, American Samoa, Guam, or any of the Caribbean Basin Countries.

### Packing Your Baggage

Pack your baggage in a manner that will make inspection easy. Do your best to pack separately the articles you have acquired abroad. When the Customs officer asks you to open your luggage or the trunk of your car, please do so without hesitation.

### Photographic Film

All imported photographic film that accompanies a traveler, if not for commercial purposes, may be released without examination by Customs unless there is reason to believe it contains objectionable matter.

Films prohibited from entry are those that contain obscene matter, advocate treason or insurrection against the United States, advocate forcible resistance to any law of the United States, or films that threaten the life of or infliction of bodily harm upon any person in the United States.

Developed or undeveloped U.S. film exposed abroad (except motion-picture film to be used for commercial purposes) may enter free of duty and need not be included in your Customs exemption.

Foreign film purchased abroad and prints made abroad are dutiable but may be included in your Customs exemption.

## Procedures for Shipping Goods to the U.S.

Merchandise acquired abroad may be sent home by you or by the store where purchased. As these items do not accompany you on your return, they cannot be included in your Customs exemption and are subject to duty when received in the United States. Duty cannot be prepaid. There are, however, special procedures to follow for merchandise acquired in and sent from the U.S. Virgin Islands, American Samoa, Guam, or Caribbean Basin countries.

All incoming shipments must be cleared through U.S. Customs. Customs employees cannot, by law, perform entry tasks for the importing public, but they will advise and give information to importers about Customs requirements.

Customs collects duty (if any) as provided for in the tariff schedule, certain Internal Revenue taxes and sometimes, a user fee. Any other charges paid on import shipments are for handling by freight forwarders, commercial brokers, or for other delivery services. Some carriers may add other clearance charges that have nothing to do with Customs duties.

Note: Customs brokers are not U.S. Customs employees. Brokers' fees are based on the amount of work done, not on the value of the personal effects or tourist purchases you shipped. The fee may seem excessive to you in relation to the value of the shipment. The most cost-effective thing to do is to take your purchases with you if at all possible.

Mail shipments (including parcel post) are generally cost-efficient. Parcels must meet the mail requirements of the exporting country as to weight, size, or measurement.

The U.S. Postal Service sends all incoming foreign mail shipments to Customs for examination. Packages free of Customs duty are returned to the Postal Service for delivery to you by your home post office without additional postage, handling costs, or other fees.

For packages containing dutiable articles, the Customs officer will attach a mail entry showing the amount of duty to be paid and return the parcel to the Postal Service.

The duty and a $5 processing fee on dutiable packages will be assessed. In addition, the U.S. Postal Service changes a handling fee on the package when delivered.

Formal entry may be required for some shipments (certain textiles, wearing apparel, and small leather goods) regardless of value. Customs employees cannot prepare this type of entry for you. Only you or a licensed Customs broker may prepare a formal entry.

If you pay the duty on a package but feel that the duty was not correct, you may file a protest. This protest can be acted on only by the Customs office that issued the mail entry receipt—Customs Form 3419A—attached to your package. Send a copy of this form with your protest letter to the Customs office at the location and address shown on the left side of the form. That office will review the duty assessment based on the information furnished in your letter and, if appropriate, authorize a refund.

Another procedure would be to not accept the parcel. You would then have to provide, within five days, a written statement of your objections to the Postmaster where the parcel is being held. Your letter will be forwarded to the issuing Customs office. The shipment will be detained at the post office until a reply from Customs is received.

Express shipments may be sent to the United States from anywhere in the world.

The express company usually provides or arranges for Customs clearance of the merchandise for you. A fee is charged for this service.

Freight shipments, whether or not they are free of duty at the time of importation, must clear Customs at the first port of arrival into the United States, or, if you choose, the merchandise may be forwarded in Customs custody (in bond) from the port of arrival to another Customs port of entry for Customs clearance.

All arrangements for Customs clearance and forwarding in bond must be made by you or someone you designate to act for you. Frequently, a freight forwarder in a foreign country will handle all the necessary arrangements, including the clearance through Customs in the United States by a Customs broker. A fee is charged for this service.

This fee is not a Customs charge. If a foreign seller consigns a shipment to a broker or agent in the United States, the freight charge is usually paid only to the first port of arrival in the United States. This means there will be additional inland transportation or freight forwarding charges, brokers' fees, insurance, and other items.

An individual may also effect the Customs clearance of a single, noncommercial shipment not requiring formal entry for you, if it is not possible for you to personally secure the release of the goods. You must authorize and empower the individual in writing to execute the Customs declaration and the entry for you as your unpaid agent. The written authority provided to the individual should be addressed to the "Officer in Charge of Customs" at the port of entry.

Unaccompanied tourist purchases acquired in and sent directly from the U.S. Virgin Islands, American Samoa, Guam, or a Caribbean Basin country, may be entered, if properly declared and processed, as follows:

- Up to $1,200 free of duty under your personal exemption if from an insular possession; $600 if from a Caribbean Basin country. Remember that if up to $400 of this amount was acquired elsewhere than these countries, those articles must accompany you at the time of your return in order to claim duty-free entry under your personal exemption.
- An additional $1,000 worth of articles, dutiable at a flat five percent rate if from an insular possession, or various percentage rates found in the Harmonized Tariff Schedules of the United States (based on the fair retail value in the country where purchased) if the merchandise is from a Caribbean Basin country. Any amount over the above, dutiable at various rates of duty.

The procedure outlined below must be followed:

*Step 1.* You will: a) list all articles acquired abroad on your Customs declaration (Customs Form 6059B) except those sent under the $100 or the $200 bona fide gift provision to friends, relatives, and business associates, etc., in the U.S.; b) indicate which articles are unaccompanied; c) fill out a Declaration of Unaccompanied Articles (Customs Form 255) for each package or container to be sent. This form may be obtained when you clear Customs if it was not available where you made your purchase.

*Step 2.* At the time of your return, Customs will: a) collect duty and tax if owed on goods accompanying you; b) verify your unaccompanied articles against sales slips, invoices, etc.; c) validate Form 255 as to whether goods are free of duty under your personal exemption or subject to a flat rate of duty. Two copies of the three-part form will be returned to you.

*Step 3.* You will return the yellow copy of the form to the shopkeeper (or vendor) holding your purchase and keep the other copy for your records. You are responsible for advising the shopkeeper at the time you make your purchase that your package is not to be sent until this form is received.

*Step 4.* The shopkeeper will place the form in an envelope and attach the envelope securely to the outside of the package or container, which must be clearly marked "Unaccompanied Tourist Purchase." Please note that a form must be placed on each box or container. This is the most important step to be followed in order for you to receive the benefits allowed under this procedure.

*Step 5.* The Postal Service will deliver the package, if sent by mail, to you after Customs clearance. Any duty owed will be collected by the Postal Service plus a postal handling fee; or you will be notified by the carrier as to the arrival of your shipment, at which time you will go to the Customs office that has processed your shipment and make entry. Any duty or tax owed will be paid at that time. You may employ a Customs broker to do this for you. A fee will be charged by the broker.

### Storage Charges

Freight and express packages delivered before you return (without prior arrangements for acceptance) will be placed in storage by Customs after five days, at the expense and risk of the owner. If not claimed within six months, the items will be sold.

Mail parcels not claimed within 30 days will be returned to the sender unless a duty assessment is being protested.

### State "Use Tax"

Merchandise purchased abroad and brought back may be subject to a "use tax" in a number of states. The use tax on these purchases is assessed by states using information from Customs declarations completed by returning travelers at ports of entry. The use-tax rate is usually the same as the sales-tax rate in the traveler's county of residence.

## FOR FURTHER INFORMATION

Every effort has been made to indicate essential requirements; however, all regulations of Customs and other agencies cannot be covered in full.

Customs offices will be glad to advise you of any changes in regulations which may have occurred since publication of this leaflet. Please consult your local telephone directory under "U.S. Government, Department of the Treasury, U.S. Customs Service," for a telephone number of the nearest Customs office.

### Complaints

Should your contact with Customs be less than favorable, the Customs Service is interested in hearing about it. Complaints of rude treatment may be reported to a Customs supervisor at your port of entry, a Passenger Service Representative (PSR), if available, or the appropriate Customs Port Director from the above list. Allegations of criminal or serious misconduct may be reported to the Office of Internal Affairs hotline at 1-800-232-5378.

### Passenger Service Representative Program.

Passenger Service Representatives (PSRs) are located at most major international airports. The program is another example of Customs' commitment to quality service by providing personalized service to the airlines, travel agents, and the traveling public. They:

- Answer questions and distribute information regarding Customs regulations and procedures;
- Address passenger's concerns or complaints;
- Provide speakers to groups related to the travel industry and to members of service organizations; and,
- Represent Customs at travel fairs.

Frequently, we are asked questions which are not Customs matters. If you want to know about . . .

*Immigration*—The Immigration and Naturalization Service (INS) is responsible for the movement of people in and out of the United States. Please contact the Department of Justice, INS, for questions concerning resident alien and non-resident visa and passport information.

*Passports*—Contact the Passport Agency nearest you at the following Zip Codes:

Boston 02222-0123

Chicago 60604-1564
Honolulu 96850
Houston 77002-4874
Los Angeles 90024-3614
Miami 33130-1680
New Orleans 70113-1931
New York 10111-0031
Philadelphia 19106-1684
San Francisco 94105-2773
Seattle 98174-1091
Stamford, CT 06901-2767
Washington, D.C. 20524-0002.

Some Clerks of Court and Postal Clerks also accept passport applications.

*Baggage Allowance*—Ask the airline or steamship line you are traveling on about this.
*Currency of Other Nations*—Your local bank can be of assistance.
*Foreign Countries*—For information about the country you will visit or about what articles may be taken into that country, contact the appropriate Embassy, consular office, or tourist information office.

# CHAPTER 4
## *U.S. Consuls Help Americans Abroad*
### (Department of State Publication 10176, June 1994)

### PART I:
### BUREAU OF CONSULAR AFFAIRS

There are U.S. embassies in more than 160 capital cities of the world. Each embassy has a consular section. Consular officers in consular sections of embassies do two things:

- They issue visas to foreigners;
- They help U.S. citizens abroad.

There are also consular officers at about 60 U.S. consulates general and 20 U.S. consulates around the world. (Consulates general and consulates are regional offices of embassies.)

U.S. consuls usually are assisted by local employees who are citizens of the host country. Because of the growing number of Americans traveling abroad, and the relatively small number of consuls, the expertise of local employees is invaluable.

In this pamphlet, we highlight ways in which consular officers can assist you while you are traveling or residing abroad.

To help us help you while you are abroad, register with the nearest U.S. embassy or consular. This makes it easier for consular officers to reach you in an emergency or to replace a lost passport.

Consular officers provide a range of services—some emergency, some non-emergency.

### EMERGENCY SERVICES

#### Replace a Passport
If you lose your passport, a consul can issue you a replacement, often within 24 hours. If you believe your passport has been stolen, first report the theft to the local police and get a police declaration.

#### Help Find Medical Assistance
If you get sick, you can contact a consular officer for a list of local doctors, dentists, and medical specialists, along with other medical information. If you are injured or become seriously ill, a consul will help you find

medical assistance and, at your request, inform your family or friends. (Consider getting private medical insurance before you travel to cover the high cost of getting you back to the U.S. for hospital care in the event of a medical emergency.)

### Help Get Funds

Should you lose all your money and other financial resources, consular officers can help you contact your family, bank, or employer to arrange for them to send you funds. In some cases, these funds can be wired to you through the Department of State.

### Help in an Emergency

Your family may need to reach you because of an emergency at home or because they are worried about your welfare. They should call the State Department's Overseas Citizens Services at (202) 647-5225. The State Department will relay the message to the consular officers in the country in which you are traveling. Consular officers will attempt to locate you, pass on urgent messages, and, consistent with the Privacy Act, report back to your family.

### Visit in Jail

If you are arrested, you should ask the authorities to notify a U.S. consul. Consuls cannot get you out of jail (when you are in a foreign country you are subject to its laws). However, they can work to protect your legitimate interests and ensure you are not discriminated against. They can provide a list of local attorneys, visit you, inform you generally about local laws, and contact your family and friends. Consular officers can transfer money, food, and clothing to the prison authorities from your family or friends. They can try to get relief if you are held under inhumane or unhealthful conditions.

### Make Arrangements after the Death of an American

When an American dies abroad, a consular officer notifies the American's family and informs them about options and costs for disposition of remains. Costs for preparing and returning a body to the U.S. may be high and must be paid by the family. Often, local laws and procedures make returning a body to the U.S. for burial a lengthy process. A consul prepares a "Report of Death" based on the local death certificate; this is forwarded to the next of kin for use in estate and insurance matters.

### Help in a Disaster/Evacuation

If you are caught up in a natural disaster or civil disturbance, you should let your relatives know as soon as possible that you are safe, or contact a U.S. consul who will pass that message to your family through the State Department. Be resourceful. U.S. officials will do everything they can to contact you and advise you. However, they must give priority to helping Americans who have been hurt or are in immediate danger. In a disaster, consuls face the same constraints you do—lack of electricity or fuel, interrupted phone lines, closed airports.

### NONEMERGENCY SERVICES

### Issue a Consular Report of Birth

A child born abroad to U.S. citizen parents usually acquires U.S. citizenship at birth. The parents should contact the nearest U.S. embassy or consulate to have a "Report of Birth Abroad of a U.S. Citizen" prepared. This is proof of citizenship for all purposes.

### Issue a Passport

Consuls issue approximately 200,000 passports abroad each year. Many of these are issued to persons whose current passports have expired.

### Distribute Federal Benefits Payments

Over a half-million people living overseas receive monthly federal benefit payments. In many countries, the checks are mailed to the U.S. embassy or consulate and distributed through the local postal service.

### Assist in Child Custody Disputes

In an international custody dispute, a consul can try to locate the child abroad, monitor the child's welfare, and provide general information to the American parent about laws and procedures which may be used to effect the child's return to the United States. Consuls may not take custody of a child, or help a parent regain custody of a child illegally or by force or deception.

### Help in Other Ways

Consuls handle personal estates of deceased U.S. citizens, assist with absentee voting and Selective Service registration, notarize documents, advise on property claims, and provide U.S. tax forms. They also perform such functions as adjudicating U.S. citizenship claims and assisting U.S. courts in legal matters.

### WHAT CONSULAR OFFICERS CANNOT DO

In addition to the qualifications noted above, consular officers cannot act as travel agents, banks, lawyers, investigators, or law enforcement officers. Please do not expect them to find you employment, get you residence or driving permits, act as interpreters, search for missing luggage, or settle disputes with hotel managers. They can, however, tell you how to get help on these and other matters.

If you need to pick up mail or messages while traveling, some banks and international credit card companies handle mail for customers at their overseas branches. General Delivery (Poste Restante) services at post offices in most countries will hold mail for you.

### PRIVACY ACT

The provisions of the Privacy Act are designed to protect the privacy rights of Americans. Occasionally they complicate a consul's efforts to assist Americans. As a general rule, consular officers may not reveal information regarding an individual American's location, welfare, intentions, or problems to anyone, including the family members and Congressional representatives, without the expressed consent of that individual. Although sympathetic to the distress this can cause concerned families, consular officers must comply with the provisions of the Privacy Act.

For more information, contact: Overseas Citizens Services, Department of State, Room 4811, Washington, D.C. 20520.

• • •

### PART II:
### U.S. DEPARTMENT OF STATE
### BUREAU OF CONSULAR AFFAIRS
### THE OFFICE OF OVERSEAS CITIZENS SERVICES
(Department of State Publication 10252)

Overseas Citizens Services (OCS) in the State Department's Bureau of Consular Affairs is responsible for the welfare and whereabouts of U.S. citizens traveling and residing abroad. OCS has three offices: American Citizens Services (ACS) and Crisis Management, the Office of Children's Issues (CI), and the Office of Policy Review and Interagency Liaison (PRI).

### AMERICAN CITIZENS SERVICES
### AND CRISIS MANAGEMENT

American Citizens Services and Crisis Management corresponds organizationally to American Citizens Services offices set up at U.S. embassies and consulates throughout the world. ACS has six geographical divisions with case officers who assist in all matters involving protective services for Americans abroad, including arrests, death cases, financial or medical emergencies, and welfare and whereabouts inquiries. The office also issues Travel Warnings and Consular Information Sheets and provides guidance on nationality and citizenship determination, document issuance, judicial and notarial services, estates and property claims, third-country representation, and disaster assistance.

### Arrests

Over 2,500 Americans are arrested abroad annually. More than 30% of these arrests are drug related. Over 70% of drug related arrests involve marijuana or cocaine.

The rights an American enjoys in this country do not travel abroad. Each country is sovereign and its laws apply to everyone who enters regardless of nationality. The U.S. government cannot get Americans released from foreign jails. However, a U.S. consul will insist on prompt access to an arrested American, provide a list of attorneys, and provide information on the host country's legal system, offer to contact the arrested American's family or friends, visit on a regular basis, protest mistreatment, monitor jail conditions, provide dietary supplements, if needed, and keep the State Department informed.

ACS is the point of contact in the U.S. for family members and others who are concerned about a U.S. citizen arrested abroad.

### Deaths

Approximately 6,000 Americans die outside of the U.S. each year. The majority of these are long-term residents of a foreign country. ACS assists with the return of remains for approximately 2,000 Americans annually.

When an American dies abroad, a consular officer notifies the next of kin about options and costs for disposition of remains. Costs for preparing and returning a body to the U.S. are high and are the responsibility of the family. Often local laws and procedures make returning a body to the U.S. for burial a lengthy process.

### Financial Assistance

If destitute, Americans can turn to a U.S. consular officer abroad for help. ACS will help by contacting the destitute person's family, friends, or business associates to raise private funds. It will help transmit these funds to destitute Americans.

ACS transfers approximately 3 million dollars a year in private emergency funds. It can approve small government loans to destitute Americans abroad until private funds arrive.

ACS also approves repatriation loans to pay for destitute Americans' direct return to the U.S. Each year over $500,000 are loaned to destitute Americans.

### Medical Assistance

ACS works with U.S. consuls abroad to assist Americans who become physically or mentally ill while traveling. ACS locates family members, guardians, and friends in the U.S., assists in transmitting private funds, and, when necessary, assists in arranging the return of ill or injured Americans to the U.S. by commercial carrier.

### Welfare and Whereabouts of U.S. Citizens

ACS receives approximately 12,000 inquiries a year concerning the welfare or whereabouts of an American abroad. Many inquiries are from worried relatives who have not heard from the traveler. Others are attempts to notify the traveler about a family crisis at home.

Most welfare/whereabouts inquiries are successfully resolved. However, occasionally, a person is truly missing. It is the responsibility of local authorities to investigate and U.S. consuls abroad will work to ensure their continued interest in cases involving Americans. Unfortunately, as in the U.S., sometimes missing persons are never found.

### Consular Information Program

ACS issues fact sheets on every country in the world called Consular Information Sheets (CIS). The CIS contains information on entry requirements, crime and security conditions, areas of instability, and other details relevant to travel in a particular country.

The Office also issues Travel Warnings. Travel Warnings are issued when the State Department recommends deferral of travel by Americans to a country because of civil unrest, dangerous conditions, terrorist activity, and/or because the U.S. has no diplomatic relations with the country and cannot assist an American in distress.

Consular Information Sheets and Travel Warnings may be heard anytime, by dialing the Office of Overseas Citizens Services travelers' hotline at (202) 647-5225 from a touchtone phone. They are also available via Consular Affairs' automated fax system at (202) 647-3000, or at any of the 13 regional passport agencies, at U.S. embassies and consulates abroad, and through the airline computer reservation systems, or, by sending a self-addressed, stamped business size envelope to the Office of Overseas Citizens Services, Bureau of Consular Affairs, Room 4811, U.S. Department of State, Washington, D.C. 20520-4818.

If you have a personal computer, modem, and communications software, you can access them and other consular handouts and publications through the Consular Affairs Bulletin Board (CABB). This service is free of charge. To access CABB, dial the modem number—(301) 946-4400. The login is travel; the password is info.

### Disaster Assistance

ACS coordinates the Bureau's activities and efforts relating to international crises or emergency situations involving the welfare and safety of large numbers of Americans residing or traveling in a crisis area. Such crises can include plane crashes, hijackings, natural disasters, civil disorders, and political unrest.

## CHILDREN'S ISSUES

The Office of Children's Issues formulates, develops, and coordinates policies and programs, and provides direction to foreign service posts on international parental child abduction and international adoptions. It also fulfills U.S. treaty obligations relating to the abduction of children.

### International Adoptions

CI coordinates policy and provides information on international adoption to the potential parents. In 1994, over 8,000 foreign born children were adopted by U.S. citizens. The Department of State cannot intervene on behalf of an individual in foreign courts because adoption is a private legal matter within the judicial sovereignty of the country where the child resides. This office can, however, offer general information and assistance regarding the adoption process in over 60 countries.

### International Parental Child Abductions

In recent years, the Bureau of Consular Affairs has taken action in thousands of cases of international parental child abduction. The Bureau also provides information in response to thousands of additional inquiries pertaining to international child abduction, enforcement of visitation rights, and abduction prevention techniques. CI works closely with parents, attorneys, other government agencies, and private organizations in the U.S. to prevent international abductions.

The Hague Convention provides for the return of a child to his or her habitual place of residence if the child has been wrongfully removed or retained. CI has been designated by Congress as the Central Authority to administer the Hague Convention in the United States.

## POLICY REVIEW AND INTERAGENCY LIAISON

The Office of Policy Review and Interagency Liaison provides guidance concerning the administration and enforcement of laws on U.S. citizenship and on the documentation of Americans traveling and residing abroad. The Office also provides advice on matters involving treaties and agreements, legislative matters, including implementation of new laws; conducts reconsiderations of acquisition and loss of U.S. citizenship in complex cases abroad; and administers the overseas federal benefits program.

### Consular Conventions and Treaties

PRI works closely with other offices in the State Department in the negotiation of consular conventions and treaties, including prisoner transfer treaties.

As a result of these prisoner transfer treaties, many U.S. citizens convicted of crimes and incarcerated abroad have returned to the U.S. to complete their sentences.

### Federal Benefits

Over a half-million people receive monthly federal benefits payments outside the U.S. In many countries, the monthly benefits checks are mailed or pouched to the consular post and then distributed through the local postal service. In other countries, the checks are mailed directly into the beneficiaries' foreign bank accounts. Consular officers assist in the processing of individual benefits claims and problems; investigate claims on behalf of the agency concerned; and perform other tasks requested by the agencies or needed by the beneficiaries or survivors.

### Legislation

PRI is involved with legislation affecting U.S. citizens abroad. The Office participates in hearings and provides testimony to Congress on proposed legislation, particularly legislation relating to the citizenship and welfare of U.S. citizens. They also interpret laws and regulations pertaining to citizens consular services, including the administration of the Immigration and Nationality Act.

### Privacy Act

PRI responds to inquires under the Privacy Act. The provisions of the Privacy Act are designed to protect the privacy and rights of Americans but occasionally complicate efforts to assist U.S. citizens abroad. As a general rule, consular officers may not reveal information regarding an individual American's location, welfare, intentions, or problems to anyone, including family members and Congressional representatives, without the expressed consent of that individual. In all potential cases, consular officers explain Privacy Act restrictions and requirements so that all individuals involved in a case understand the Privacy Act's constraints.

### Hours of Operation

Monday–Friday: 8:15 A.M.–10:00 P.M.
Saturday: 9:00 A.M.–3:00 P.M.
Telephone: (202) 647-5225*

For after-hours emergencies, Sundays, and Holidays:
Telephone: (202) 647-4000
Request the OCS duty officer.

* Overseas Citizens Services has a 24-hours a day hotline at (202) 647-5225 for American Citizens Services (including travel and citizenship information). Policy Review and Interagency Liaison can also be reached at this number.

The Office of Children's Issues can be reached by calling (202) 736-7000.

Bureau of Consular Affairs
Office of Public Affairs
U.S. Department of State

# CHAPTER 5
# U.S. Department of State's Judicial Assistance

## PART I:
### MARRIAGE OF UNITED STATES CITIZENS ABROAD

### WHO MAY PERFORM MARRIAGES ABROAD

American diplomatic and consular officers are NOT permitted to perform marriages (Title 22, Code of Federal Regulations 52.1). Marriages abroad are almost always performed by local (foreign) civil or religious officials.

As a rule, marriages are not performed on the premises of an American embassy or consulate. The validity of marriages abroad is not dependent upon the presence of an American diplomatic or consular officer, but upon adherence to the laws of the country where the marriage is performed. Consular officers may authenticate foreign marriage documents. The fee for authentication of a document is $32.00.

### VALIDITY OF MARRIAGES ABROAD

In general, marriages which are legally performed and valid abroad are also legally valid in the United States. Inquiries regarding the validity of a marriage abroad should be directed to the attorney general of the state in the United States where the parties to the marriage live.

### Foreign Laws and Procedures

The embassy or tourist information bureau of the country in which the marriage is to be performed is the best source of information about marriage in that country. Some general information on marriage in a limited number of countries can be obtained from Overseas Citizens Services, Room 4811, Department of State, Washington, D.C. 20520. In addition, American embassies and consulates abroad frequently have information about marriage in the country in which they are located.

### Residence Requirements

Marriages abroad are subject to the residency requirements of the country in which the marriage is to be performed. There is almost always a lengthy waiting period.

### Documentation and Authentication

Most countries require that a valid U.S. passport be presented. In addition, birth certificates, divorce decrees, and death certificates are frequently required. Some countries require that the documents presented to the marriage registrar first be authenticated in the United States by a consular official of that country. This process can be time consuming and expensive.

### Parental Consent

The age of majority for marriage varies from one country to another. Persons under the age of 18 must, as a general rule, present a written statement of consent executed by their parents before a notary public. Some countries require the parental consent statement to be authenticated by a consular official of that foreign country in the United States.

### Affidavit of Eligibility to Marry

All civil law countries require proof of legal capacity to enter into a marriage contract in the form of certification by competent authority that no impediment exists to the marriage. No such document exists in the United States. Unless the foreign authorities will allow such a statement to be executed before one of their consular officials in the United States, it will be necessary for the parties to a prospective marriage abroad to execute an affidavit at the American embassy or consulate in the country in which the marriage will occur, stating that they are free to marry. This is called an affidavit of eligibility to marry and the fee for the American consular officer's certification of the affidavit is $55.00, subject to change. Some countries also require witnesses who will execute affidavits to the effect that the parties are free to marry.

### Additional Requirements

Many countries, like the United States, require blood tests.

Some countries require that documents presented to the marriage registrar be translated into the native language of that country.

## LOSS OF U.S. NATIONALITY

In some countries, marriage to a national of that country will automatically make the spouse either a citizen of that country or eligible to become naturalized in that country expeditiously. The automatic acquisition of a second nationality will not affect U.S. citizenship. However, naturalization in a foreign country on one's own application or the application of a duly authorized agent may cause the loss of American citizenship. Persons planning to apply for a foreign nationality should contact an American embassy or consulate for further information.

## MARRIAGE TO AN ALIEN

Information on obtaining a visa for a foreign spouse may be obtained from any office of the Immigration and Naturalization Service, U.S. embassies and consulates abroad, or the Department of State Visa Office, Washington, D.C. 20520-0113. General information regarding visas may be obtained by calling the Visa Office at 202-663-1225.

## PART II:
### ACQUISITION OF U.S. CITIZENSHIP BY A CHILD BORN ABROAD

### BIRTH ABROAD TO TWO U.S. CITIZEN PARENTS IN WEDLOCK

A child born abroad to two U.S. citizen parents acquires U.S. citizenship at birth under section 301(c) of the Immigration and Nationality Act (INA). One of the parents MUST have resided in the U.S. prior to the child's birth. No specific period of time for such prior residence is required.

### BIRTH ABROAD TO ONE CITIZEN AND ONE ALIEN PARENT IN WEDLOCK

A child born abroad to one U.S. citizen parent and one alien parent acquires U.S.

citizenship at birth under Section 301(g) INA provided the citizen parent was physically present in the U.S. for the time period required by the law applicable at the time of the child's birth. (For birth on or after November 14, 1986, a period of five years' physical presence, two after the age of fourteen is required. For birth between December 24, 1952, and November 13, 1986, a period of ten years, five after the age of fourteen are required for physical presence in the U.S. to transmit U.S. citizenship to the child.)

## BIRTH ABROAD OUT-OF-WEDLOCK TO A U.S. CITIZEN FATHER

A child born abroad out-of-wedlock to a U.S. citizen father may acquire U.S. citizenship under Section 301(g) INA, as made applicable by Section 309(a) INA provided:

1) a blood relationship between the applicant and the father is established by clear and convincing evidence;
2) the father had the nationality of the United States at the time of the applicant's birth;
3) the father (unless deceased) had agreed in writing to provide financial support for the person until the applicant reaches the age of 18 years, and
4) while the person is under the age of 18 years—
   A) applicant is legitimated under the law of their residence or
   B) father acknowledges paternity of the person in writing under oath, or
   C) the paternity of the applicant is established by adjudication court.

## BIRTH ABROAD OUT-OF-WEDLOCK TO A U.S. CITIZEN MOTHER

A child born abroad out-of-wedlock to a U.S. citizen mother may acquire U.S. citizenship under Section 301(g) INA, as made applicable by Section 309(c) INA if the mother was a U.S. citizen at the time of the child's

birth, and if the mother had previously been physically present in the United States or one of its outlying possessions for a continuous period of one year.

## PART III: CONSULAR REPORT OF DEATH OF A U.S. CITIZEN ABROAD

## FOREIGN DEATH CERTIFICATE

Foreign death certificates are issued by the local registrar of deaths or similar local authority. The certificates are written in the language of the foreign country and prepared in accordance with the laws of the foreign country.

Although authenticated copies of the foreign death certificate can be obtained, since the documents are written in the language of the foreign country they are sometimes unacceptable in the United States for insurance and estate purposes. In the United States, a "Report of Death of an American Citizen Abroad" issued by the U.S. consular officer is generally used in lieu of a foreign death certificate as proof of death.

## REPORT OF DEATH OF A U.S. CITIZEN ABROAD

The consular "Report of Death of an American Citizen Abroad" is a report that provides the essential facts concerning the death of a U.S. citizen, disposition of remains, and custody of the personal effects of a deceased citizen. This form is generally used in legal proceedings in the United States in lieu of the foreign death certificate. The Report of Death is based on the foreign death certificate, and cannot be completed until the foreign death certificate has been issued.

This can sometimes take from four to six weeks or longer after the date of the death, depending on how long it takes local authorities to complete the local form. U.S. Embassies and Consulates work with local authorities to see that this time is as short as possible.

## Copies of the Report of Death

The U.S. consular officer will send the family up to 20 certified copies of the "Report of Death" at the time the initial report is issued. Additional copies can be obtained subsequently by contacting the Department of State, Passport Services, Correspondence Branch, 1111 19th Street, N.W., Suite 510, Washington, D.C. 20522-1705, tel (202) 955-0307.

Submit a signed, written request including all pertinent facts along with requester's return address and telephone number. There is a $20.00 fee for the first copy and a $10.00 fee for each additional copy, payable to the Department of State. See also the Department of State, Consular Affairs home page on the Internet at http://travel.state.gov/ under "Passport Services" for further information about obtaining copies of "Reports of Death."

## LEGAL AUTHORITY

U.S. insurance companies and other agencies sometimes inquire regarding the authority for issuance of "Reports of Death." See 22 U.S. Code 4196; 22 Code of Federal Regulations 72.1.

## ADDITIONAL INFORMATION

For additional information concerning "Reports of Death," contact the appropriate geographic division of the Office of American Citizens Services and Crisis Management, Department of State, 2201 C Street N.W., Room 4817 N.S., Washington, D.C. 20520, tel: (202) 647-5225 or (202) 647-5226.

## PART IV:
### ESTATES OF DECEASED U.S. CITIZENS

The authority and responsibilities of a U.S. consular officer concerning the personal estate of a citizen who dies abroad or who resided abroad at the time of death are based on U.S. laws, treaties, and international practice, subject to local (foreign) law. (22 C.F.R. 72.16-72.55; 22 U.S.C. 4195-4197).

## NOTIFICATION OF NEXT OF KIN

When a U.S. citizen dies abroad, and no legal representative is present in the country at the time of death, the consular officer usually notifies the decedent's next of kin by official telegram relayed through the Department of State in Washington, D.C. On the basis of instructions received from the legal representative or other qualified party, the consular officer arranges for the disposition of the remains.

## PROVISIONAL CONSERVATOR OF THE ESTATE

The consular officer also acts as provisional conservator of the decedent's personal effects, after receiving them from police officials, hospital authorities, tour managers, or other persons who have had temporary custody of the effects.

The consular officer usually takes physical possession of convertible assets, luggage, wearing apparel, jewelry, articles of sentimental value, non-negotiable instruments, personal documents, and other miscellaneous effects. The consular officer has no authority to withdraw funds from bank accounts in foreign countries or to obtain the face value of traveler's checks.

If the personal effects are not located within a reasonable distance from the Foreign Service post, the consular officer will request the temporary custodian of the effects to send them to the post at the expense of the estate or of the legal representative. The U.S. Government has no independent authority to pay for any expenses incurred relating to the effects of a deceased private citizen.

Large, bulky articles found in residences are seldom taken into actual possession by the consular officer. However, reasonable steps are taken to ensure that the effects are adequately safeguarded until arrangements for disposition can be made by the legal representative.

The responsibilities of a consular officer as provisional conservator include taking possession of, inventorying, and appraising personal effects; paying local debts such as hospital and hotel bills from funds available in the estate or from funds received from the legal representative; and delivering effects to the person entitled to receive them.

A legal representative, as relates to the personal estate of a deceased person, may be:

(1) An executor appointed in testate proceedings;
(2) An administrator appointed in intestate proceedings;
(3) An agent of the executor or administrator, qualifying by power of attorney;
(4) A surviving spouse;
(5) A child of legal age;
(6) A parent;
(7) A sibling; or
(8) Next of kin.

## ENTITLEMENT TO RECEIVE PERSONAL ESTATE

The consular officer does not establish the ownership of nor entitlement to the personal estate of the person(s) who will receive it in the absence of presentation of proof of entitlement by the potential legal claimant.

Depending on the value of the estate and whether there is a disagreement among claimants, the consular officer may require that a document issued under the seal and signature of a court official be submitted to establish a claimant's proof of entitlement to receive the effects. Satisfactory proof may take the form of "Letters Testamentary," which are generally issued by a U.S. court when a person has left a valid will, or "Letters of Administration", which are issued by a U.S. court when a person dies without a will or leaves no valid will. In most cases, when the monetary value of the personal estate is small, an affidavit of surviving spouse or next of kin is sufficient to effect the release of the personal estate.

## SHIPMENT OF PERSONAL EFFECTS

After the personal effects have been inventoried and documentary proof of entitlement has been furnished, the consular officer requests instructions from the claimant regarding shipment of the effects. Because of the high costs of shipment, many persons instruct the consular officer to ship only items of commercial and sentimental value and to donate the remaining effects to a local charity or to dispose of them in another manner. In some instances a forwarding company in the foreign country must be selected by a legal claimant to ship the effects to a designated address. It is the responsibility of the forwarding company to obtain the necessary customs clearance from the country of departure. Additional customs clearance required by the United States at the port of entry is the responsibility of the person receiving the effects.

Questions: For additional information, you may contact the Office of American Citizens Services at (202) 647-5225 or 5226; fax: 202-647-2835.

## PART V:
## RETURN OF REMAINS OF DECEASED AMERICANS

### SUMMARY

One of the most essential tasks of the Department of State and of U.S. embassies and consulates abroad is to provide assistance to families of U.S. citizens who die abroad. The U.S. consular officer in the foreign country will assist the family in making arrangements with local authorities for preparation and disposition of the remains, following the family's instructions in accordance with local law. The authority and responsibilities of a U.S. consular officer concerning return of remains of a deceased U.S. citizen abroad are based on U.S. laws (22 U.S.C. 4196; 22 CFR 72.1), treaties, and international practice. Options available to a family depend upon local law and practice in the foreign country. Certain documents are required by U.S. and foreign law before remains can be sent from one country to another. These requirements may vary depending on the circumstances of the death.

## CONSULAR MORTUARY CERTIFICATE

A U.S. consular mortuary certificate is required to ensure orderly shipment of remains and to facilitate U.S. Customs clearance. The certificate is in English and confirms essential information concerning the cause of death. The U.S. consular officer will prepare the certificate and ensure that the foreign death certificate (if available), affidavit of the foreign funeral director, and transit permit, together with the consular mortuary certificate accompany the remains to the United States.

## AFFIDAVIT OF FOREIGN FUNERAL DIRECTOR AND TRANSIT PERMIT

The U.S. consular officer will ensure that the required affidavit is executed by the local (foreign) funeral director. This affidavit attests to the fact that the casket contains only the remains of the deceased and the necessary clothing and packing materials. The affidavit may also state that the remains have been embalmed or otherwise prepared. In addition, the U.S. consular officer ensures that a transit permit accompanies the remains. The transit permit is issued by local health authorities at the port of embarkation.

## U.S. ENTRY REQUIREMENTS FOR QUARANTINE AND CUSTOMS

In general, if remains have been embalmed, the documentation which accompanies the consular mortuary certificate will satisfy U.S. public health requirements. If the foreign death certificate is not available at the time the remains are returned, the consular mortuary certificate will include reference to the fact that the deceased did not die from a quarantineable disease and that the remains have been embalmed. The affidavit of the funeral director which is attached to the consular mortuary certificate complies with the U.S. Customs requirement that the casket and the packing container for the casket contain only the remains. If the remains are not accompanied by a passenger, a bill of lading must be issued by the airline carrier company to cover the transport. The customs house permit for entry to the United States is obtained by the airline carrier at the point of departure.

## SHIPMENT OF UNEMBALMED REMAINS

If the remains are not embalmed, the U.S. consular officer should alert U.S. Customs and the U.S. Public Health Service at point of entry in advance, faxing copies of the consular mortuary certificate, local death certificate (if available), affidavit of foreign funeral director, and a formal statement from competent foreign authorities stating that the individual did not die from a communicable disease. This statement generally is required even if the exact cause of death is unknown in order for unembalmed remains to enter the United States.

## ADDITIONAL INFORMATION

For additional information concerning return of remains of a diseased U.S. citizen, contact the appropriate geographic division of the Office of American Citizens Services, Department of State, Room 4817 N.S., 2201 C. Street, N.W., Washington, D.C. 20520, tel: (202) 647-5225 or (202) 647-5226 or the consular officer in the American Citizens Services Section of the U.S. embassy or consulate in the foreign country where the death occurred.

# CHAPTER 6
## *Staying Out of Legal Trouble*

DISCLAIMER: THE FOLLOWING IS A SUMMARY OF SERVICES PROVIDED TO U.S. CITIZENS ARRESTED ABROAD BY U.S. CONSULAR OFFICERS. SINCE CONDITIONS VARY FROM COUNTRY TO COUNTRY, THE PRECISE NATURE OF SERVICES MAY VARY LIKEWISE, DEPENDING ON INDIVIDUAL CIRCUMSTANCES IN A PARTICULAR CASE.

### SUMMARY

One of the most essential tasks of the Department of State and of U.S. embassies and consulates abroad is to provide assistance to U.S. citizens incarcerated abroad. The State Department is committed to ensuring fair and humane treatment for American citizens imprisoned overseas. We stand ready to assist incarcerated citizens and their families within the limits of our authority, in accordance with international law. We can and do monitor conditions in foreign prisons and immediately protest allegations of abuse against American prisoners. We work with prison officials to ensure treatment consistent with internationally recognized standards of human rights and to ensure that Americans are afforded due process under local laws.

### BACKGROUND

While in a foreign country, a U.S. citizen is subject to that country's laws and regulations, which sometimes differ significantly from those in the United States and may not afford the protections available to the individual under U.S. law. As our Consular Information Sheets explain, penalties for breaking the law can be more severe than in the United States for similar offenses.

Persons violating the law, even unknowingly, may be expelled, fined, arrested, or imprisoned. Penalties for possession, use, or trafficking in illegal drugs are strict, and convicted offenders can expect jail sentences and fines. If arrested abroad, a citizen must go through the foreign legal process for being charged or indicted, prosecuted, possibly convicted and sentenced, and for any appeals process. Within this framework, U.S. consular

officers provide a wide variety of services to
U.S. citizens arrested abroad and their families.

## CONSULAR ACCESS TO PRISONERS

Article 36(a) of the Vienna Convention on
Consular Relations of 1963, 21 UST 77, TIAS
6820, 596 UNST 261—a multilateral treaty to
which many, but not all, countries are party—
provides that consular officers shall be free to
communicate with their nationals and to have
access to them. However, Article 36(b)
provides that the foreign authorities shall
inform the consular officer or the arrest of a
national "without delay" (no time frame
specified), if the national requests such
notification. Bilateral Consular Conventions
between the United States and individual
countries are more specific, requiring
notification, regardless of whether the arrested
person requests it, and generally specifying
the time period in which such notification is to
be made. When there is no treaty in force,
notification and access are based on comity
and largely dependent on whether the two
countries have diplomatic relations.

## CONSULAR SERVICES

Consular officers abroad provide a wide
variety of services to U.S. citizens incarcerated
abroad. Specific services vary depending on
local laws and regulations, the level of local
services available in the country in question,
and the circumstances of the individual
prisoner. The frequency of U.S. consular visits
to citizens arrested abroad may likewise vary,
depending upon circumstances.
Consular services include:

- Upon initial notification of arrest:
  —visiting the prisoner as soon as possible
  after notification of the arrest;
  —providing a list of local attorneys to assist
  the prisoner obtain legal representation;
  —providing information about judicial
  procedures in the foreign country;

  —notifying family and/or friends, if
  authorized by the prisoner;
  —obtaining a Privacy Act Consent;
  —relaying requests to family and friends
  for money or other aid;

- On-going support to incarcerated
  Americans:
  —providing regular consular visits to the
  prisoner and reporting on those visits to
  the Department of State;
  —providing loans to qualified destitute
  prisoners through the Emergency
  Medical/Dietary Assistance (EMDA)
  program;
  —arranging dietary supplements
  (vitamins/minerals) to qualified prisoners;
  —arranging for medical and dental care if
  not provided by prison, to be paid for from
  prisoner's funds, funds provided by family,
  or funds loaned to the prisoner by the U.S.
  Government under the EMDA program for
  destitute Americans incarcerated abroad
  under the conditions specified at 22 CFR
  71.10.;
  —arranging for examinations by an
  independent physician if needed;
  —arranging special family visits, subject to
  local law;
  —protesting mistreatment or abuse to the
  appropriate authorities;
  —attending the trial, if the
  embassy/consulate believes that
  discrimination on the basis of U.S.
  nationality might occur or if specifically
  requested by the prisoner or family, if
  possible.
  —providing information about procedures
  to applications for pardons or prisoner
  transfer treaties, if applicable.

- Discretionary support provided as needed:
  —providing reading materials subject to
  local laws and regulations;
  —arranging with American community to
  provide holiday meals;
  —providing personal amenities such as

stamps, toiletries, and stationery, if permitted by prison authorities, from prisoner's or family's private funds;
—assisting in finding ways to expedite prisoners' mail;
—inquiring about the possibility of prison employment;
—assisting in arranging correspondence courses.
—arranging for American community volunteer visits to prisoners;

- A consular officer cannot:
  —demand the immediate release of a U.S. citizen arrested abroad or otherwise cause the citizen to be released.
  —represent a U.S. citizen at trial, give legal advice or pay legal fees and/or fines with U.S. Government funds.

### ADDITIONAL INFORMATION

Lists of foreign attorneys and country-specific information sheets regarding arrests abroad from the Department of State, Office of American Citizens Services, or directly from U.S. embassies and consulates abroad. General information about retaining a foreign attorney and prisoner transfer treaties is also available via our automated fax service which can be accessed by dialing (202) 647-3000 using the phone on your fax machine and following the prompts and via our home page on the Internet. See our home page at http://travel.state.gov which is linked to the home pages of our embassies and consulates abroad.

### QUESTIONS

Additional questions regarding services to Americans incarcerated abroad and prisoner transfer treaties may be addressed to the appropriate geographic division of the Office of American Citizens Services, Department of State, Room 4817 N.S., 2201 C Street N.W., Washington, D.C. 20520, tel: (202) 647-5225; 647-5226.

## PART II:
### TRAVEL WARNING ON DRUGS ABROAD

### THINGS YOU SHOULD KNOW BEFORE YOU GO ABROAD

#### Hard Facts

- Each year, 2,500 Americans are arrested overseas. One-third of the arrests are on drug-related charges. Many of those arrested assumed as U.S. citizens that they could not be arrested. From Asia to Africa, Europe to South America, U.S. citizens are finding out the hard way that drug possession or trafficking equals jail in foreign countries.
- There is very little that anyone can do to help you if you are caught with drugs.
- It is your responsibility to know what the drug laws are in a foreign country before you go, because "I didn't know it was illegal" will not get you out of jail.
- In recent years, there has been an increase in the number of women arrested abroad. The rise is a result of women who serve as drug couriers or "mules" in the belief they can make quick money and have a vacation without getting caught. Instead of a short vacation, they get a lengthy stay or life sentence in a foreign jail.
- A number of the Americans arrested abroad on drug charges in 1994 possessed marijuana. Many of these possessed one ounce or less of the substance. The risk of being put in jail for just one marijuana cigarette is not worth it.
- If you are purchasing prescription medications in quantities larger than that considered necessary for personal use, you could be arrested on suspicion of drug trafficking.
- Once you're arrested, the American consular officer CANNOT get you out!

You may say, "It couldn't happen to me," but the fact is that it could happen to you if you find yourself saying one of the following:

- "I'm an American citizen, and no foreign government can put me in their jail."
- "If I only buy or carry a small amount, it won't be a problem."

If you are arrested on a drug charge it is important that you know what your government CAN and CANNOT do for you.

The U.S. Consular Officer CAN:

- visit you in jail after being notified of your arrest;
- give you a list of local attorneys (the U.S. Government cannot assume responsibility for the professional ability or integrity of these individuals);
- notify your family and/or friends and relay requests for money or other aid—but only with your authorization;
- intercede with local authorities to make sure that your rights under local law are fully observed and that you are treated humanely, according to internationally accepted standards;
- protest mistreatment or abuse to the appropriate authorities.

The U.S. Consular Officer CANNOT:

- demand your immediate release or get you out of jail or the country!
- represent you at trial or give legal counsel;
- pay legal fees and/or fines with U.S. Government funds.

If you are caught buying, selling, carrying, or using drugs—from hashish to heroin, marijuana to mescaline, cocaine to quaaludes, to designer drugs like ecstasy, IT COULD MEAN:

- Interrogation and Delays Before Trial—including mistreatment and solitary confinement for up to one year under very primitive conditions;
- Lengthy Trials—conducted in a foreign language, with delays and postponements;

- Weeks, Months, or Life in Prison—some places include hard labor, heavy fines, and/or lashings, if found guilty;
- The Death Penalty—in a growing number of countries (e.g., Malaysia, Pakistan, and Turkey).

Although drug laws vary from country to country, it is important to realize before you make the mistake of getting involved with drugs that foreign countries do not react lightly to drug offenders. In some countries, anyone who is caught with even a very small quantity for personal use may be tried and receive the same sentence as the large-scale trafficker.
DON'T LET YOUR TRIP ABROAD BECOME A NIGHTMARE!
This information has been provided to inform you before it is too late.
SO THINK FIRST!

- A number of countries, including the Bahamas, the Dominican Republic, Jamaica, Mexico, and the Philippines, have enacted more stringent drug laws which impose mandatory jail sentences for individuals convicted of possessing even small amounts of marijuana or cocaine for personal use.
- Once you leave the United States, you are not covered by U.S. laws and constitutional rights.
- Bail is not granted in many countries when drugs are involved.
- The burden of proof in many countries is on the accused to prove his/her innocence.
- In some countries, evidence obtained illegally by local authorities may be admissible in court.
- Few countries offer drug offenders jury trials or even require the prisoner's presence at his/her trial.
- Many countries have mandatory prison sentences of seven years or life, without the possibility of parole for drug violations.

REMEMBER!

- If someone offers you a free trip and some quick and easy money just for bringing back a suitcase . . . SAY NO!
- Don't carry a package for anyone, no matter how small it might seem.
- The police and customs officials have a right to search your luggage for drugs. If they find drugs in your suitcase, you will suffer the consequences.
- You could go to jail for years and years with no possibility of parole, early release, or transfer back to the U.S.
- Don't make a jail sentence part of your trip abroad.

The Department of State's Bureau of Consular Affairs' Office of Overseas Citizens Services provides emergency services pertaining to the protection of Americans arrested or detained abroad, the search for U.S. citizens overseas, the transmission of emergency messages to those citizens or their next of kin in the United States, and other emergency and non-emergency services. Contact the Office of Overseas Citizens Services from Monday through Friday, 8:15 A.M. to 10:00 P.M. at (202) 647-5225. For an emergency after hours or on weekends and holidays, ask for the Overseas Citizens Services' duty officer at (202) 647-4000. Internet home page: http://travel.state.gov

# CHAPTER 7
*Internal Revenue Service, Publication 54:*
*Tax Guide for U.S. Citizens and Resident Aliens Abroad,*
# Part One

## INTRODUCTION

This publication discusses the special tax rules for U.S. citizens and resident aliens who work abroad or who have income earned in foreign countries. As a U.S. citizen or resident alien, your worldwide income generally is subject to U.S. income tax, regardless of where you are living. Also, you are subject to the same income tax filing requirements that apply to U.S. citizens or residents living in the United States.

### Filing information

The publication begins with general filing information such as:

- Whether you must file a U.S. tax return,
- When and where to file your return,
- How to report your income if it is paid in foreign currency,
- How to determine your filing status if your spouse is a nonresident alien, and
- Whether you must pay estimated tax.

If you own stock in a foreign corporation or have an interest in a foreign partnership, you may have to file information returns. See the instructions under Information Returns and Reports in Chapter 1.

### Withholding Tax

Chapter 7 discusses the withholding of income taxes and social security and Medicare taxes from the pay of U.S. citizens, resident aliens, and nonresident aliens. It will help you determine if the correct amounts of taxes are being withheld and how to adjust your withholding if too much or too little is being withheld.

### Self-Employment Tax

If you are self-employed, you generally are required to pay self-employment tax. Chapter 8 discusses who must pay self-employment tax and who may be exempt from self-employment tax.

### Foreign Earned Income Exclusion and Housing Exclusion and Deduction

There are income tax benefits that might apply if you meet certain requirements while living abroad. You may qualify to treat up to $72,000 of your income as not taxable by the United States. You may also be able to either deduct part of your housing expenses from your taxable income or treat a limited amount of income used for housing expenses as not taxable by the United States. These benefits are called the foreign earned income exclusion and the foreign housing deduction and exclusion.

To qualify for either of the exclusions or

the deduction, you must have a tax home in a foreign country and earn income in a foreign country. These rules are explained in Chapter 9. If you are going to exclude or deduct your income as discussed above, you must file Form 2555 or Form 2555-EZ. You will find an example with filled-in Forms 2555 and 2555-EZ in this publication.

### Exemptions, Deductions, and Credits

If you are a U.S. citizen or resident alien living outside the United States, you are generally allowed the same exemptions, deductions, and credits as those living in the United States. However, if you choose to exclude foreign earned income or housing amounts, you cannot deduct or exclude any item or take credit for any item that is related to the amounts you exclude. Among the topics discussed in Chapter 10 are:

- Exemptions you can claim,
- Contributions you can deduct,
- Moving expenses you can deduct, and
- Foreign taxes you can either deduct or take a credit for.

### Tax Treaty Benefits

Chapter 11 discusses some benefits that are common to most tax treaties and explains how to get help if you think you are not getting a benefit to which you are entitled. It also explains how to get copies of tax treaties.

### How to Get More Information

Chapter 11 is an explanation of how to get information (including forms and publications) and assistance from the IRS.

### FILING REQUIREMENTS

If you are a U.S. citizen or resident alien living or traveling outside the United States, you generally are required to file income tax returns, estate tax returns, and gift tax returns and pay estimated tax in the same way as those residing in the United States.

Your income, filing status, and age generally determine whether you must file a return. Generally, you must file a return if your gross income is at least the amount shown for your filing status in the following table:

| FILING STATUS | AMOUNT |
| --- | --- |
| Single | $7,050 |
| 65 or older | $8,100 |
| Head of household | $9,100 |
| 65 or older | $10,150 |
| Qualifying widow(er) | $9,950 |
| 65 or older | $10,800 |
| Married filing jointly | $12,700 |
| Not living with spouse at end of year | $2,750 |
| One spouse 65 or older | $13,550 |
| Both spouses 65 or older | $14,400 |
| Married filing separately | $2,750 |

If you are the dependent of another taxpayer, see the instructions for Form 1040 for more information on whether you must file a return.

### Gross Income

This includes all income you receive in the form of money, goods, property, and services that is not exempt from tax.

In determining whether you must file a return, you must consider as gross income any income that you exclude as foreign earned income or as a foreign housing amount. If you must file a return and you exclude all or part of your income under these rules, you must prepare Form 2555, discussed later. You may be able to file Form 2555-EZ if you are claiming only the foreign earned income exclusion.

### Self-Employed Individuals

If you are self-employed, your gross income includes the amount on line 7 of Schedule C (Form 1040), "Profit or Loss from Business," or line 1 of Schedule C-EZ (Form 1040), "Net Profit from Business."

If your net self-employment income is $400 or more, you must file a return even if your gross income is below the amount for filing purposes listed above.

### 65 or Older

You are 65 on the day before your 65th birthday. If your 65th birthday is on January 1, you would be 65 on December 31 of the previous year.

### When to File and Pay

If you file on the calendar year basis, the due date for filing your return is April 15 of the following year. (If April 15 falls on Saturday, the due date for your return will be April 17; if it falls on Sunday, it will be April 16.) If you file on a fiscal year basis (a year ending on the last day of any month except December), the due date is 3 months and 15 days after the close of your fiscal year. In general, the tax shown on your return should be paid by the due date of the return, without regard to any extension of time for filing the return.

A tax return delivered by the U.S. mail or a designated delivery service that is postmarked or dated by the delivery service on or before the due date is considered to have been filed on or before that date. This rule does not apply if a return is filed late. A return postmarked or date marked after the due date is not considered filed until it is received by Internal Revenue Service (IRS).

You can use certain private delivery services designated by the IRS to meet the "timely mailing as timely filing/paying" rule for tax returns and payments. The IRS publishes a list of the designated private delivery services in September of each year.

### Extensions

You can be granted an extension of time to file your return. In some circumstances, you can also be granted an extension of time to file and pay any tax due.

However, if you pay the tax due after the regular due date, interest will be charged from the regular due date until the date the tax is paid.

#### Automatic 2-Month Extension

You may be allowed an automatic 2-month extension to file your return and pay any federal income tax that is due. You will be allowed the extension if you are a U.S. citizen or resident and on the regular due date of your return:

1. You are living outside of the United States and Puerto Rico and your main place of business or post of duty is outside the United States and Puerto Rico, or
2. You are in military or naval service on duty outside the United States and Puerto Rico.

If you use a calendar year, the regular due date of your return is April 15.

#### Service in a Combat Zone

If you served in a combat zone or qualified hazardous duty area, see "Extension of Deadline" in Publication 3: Armed Forces' Tax Guide found at http://www.irs.ustreas.gov/plain/forms_pubs/pubs/p3toc.htm.

#### Married Taxpayers

If you file a joint return, either you or your spouse can qualify for the automatic extension. If you and your spouse file separate returns, this automatic extension applies only to the spouse who qualifies.

#### How to Get the Extension

To use this automatic 2-month extension, you must attach a statement to your return explaining which of the two situations listed earlier qualified you for the extension.

#### Extensions Beyond 2 Months

If you are unable to file your return within the automatic 2-month extension period, you may be able to get an additional 2-month extension of time to file your return, for a total of 4 months.

This additional 2-month extension of time to file is not an extension of time to pay. See "Time to Pay Not Extended" below.

#### 4-Month Extension

If you are not able to file your return by

the due date, you may be able to get an automatic 4-month extension of time to file. To get this automatic extension, you must file Form 4868 or pay the tax due by credit card (see the form instructions).

### You May Not Be Eligible

You cannot use the automatic 4-month extension of time to file if:

- You want the IRS to figure your tax, or
- You are under a court order to file by the regular due date.

### When to File

Generally, you must request the 4-month extension by the regular due date for your return.

### 2-Month Extension

If you qualify for the 2-month extension discussed above because your tax home and abode are outside the United States and Puerto Rico, that extension and the 4-month extension start at the same time.

You do not have to request the 4-month extension until the new due date allowed by the first extension, but the total combined extension will still only be 4 months from the regular due date.

### Time to Pay Not Extended

A 4-month extension of time to file is not an extension of time to pay. You must make an accurate estimate of your tax and send any necessary payment with your Form 4868 or pay the tax due by credit card. If you find you cannot pay the full amount due with Form 4868, you can still get the extension. You will owe interest on the unpaid amount.

You also may be charged a penalty for paying the tax late unless you have reasonable cause for not paying your tax when due. Interest and penalties are assessed (charged) from the original due date of your return.

### Extension Beyond the 4 Months

If you qualify for the 4-month extension and you later find that you are not able to file within the 4-month extension period, you may be able to get 2 more months to file, for a total of 6 months.

You can apply for an extension beyond the 4-month extension either by sending a letter to the IRS or by filing Form 2688. You should request the extension early so that, if refused, you still will be able to file on time. Except in cases of undue hardship, Form 2688 or a request by letter will not be accepted until you have first used the 4-month extension. Form 2688 or your letter will not be considered if you send it after the extended due date.

To get an extension beyond the automatic 4-month extension, you must give all the following information.

- The reason for requesting the extension.
- The tax year to which the extension applies.
- The length of time needed for the extension.
- Whether another extension for time to file has already been requested for this tax year.

You can sign the request for this extension, or it can be signed by your attorney, CPA, enrolled agent, or a person with a power of attorney. If you are unable to sign the request because of illness or for another good reason, a person in close personal or business relationship to you can sign the request.

### Extension Granted

If your application for this extension is approved, you will be notified by the IRS. Attach the notice to your return when you file it.

If an extension is granted and the IRS later determines that the statements made on your request for this extension are false or misleading and an extension would not have been granted based on the true facts, the extension is null and void. You may have to pay the failure-to-file penalty if you file after the regular due date.

### Extension Not Granted

If your application for this extension is not approved, you must file your return by the extended due date of the automatic extension. You may be allowed to file within 10 days of the date of the notice you get from the IRS if the end of the 10-day period is later than the due date. The notice will tell you if the 10-day grace period is granted.

### Further Extensions

You generally cannot get an extension of more than 6 months. However, if you are outside the United States and meet certain tests, you may be able to get a longer extension. See "Bona Fide Residence or Physical Presence Test Not Yet Met."

### Bona Fide Residence or Physical Presence Test Not Yet Met

You can get an extension of time to file your tax return if you need the time to meet either the bona fide residence test or the physical presence test to qualify for either the foreign earned income exclusion or the foreign housing exclusion or deduction. The tests, the exclusions, and the deduction are explained in Chapter 9.

You should request an extension if all three of the following apply.

1. You are a U.S. citizen or resident.
2. You expect to meet either the bona fide residence test or the physical presence test, but not until after your tax return is due.
3. Your tax home is in a foreign country (or countries) throughout your period of bona fide residence or physical presence, whichever applies.

Generally, if you are granted an extension, it will be to 30 days beyond the date on which you can reasonably expect to qualify under either the bona fide residence test or the physical presence test. However, if you have moving expenses that are for services performed in 2 years, you may be granted an extension to 90 days beyond the close of the year following the year of first arrival in the foreign country.

### How to Get Extension

To obtain an extension, you should file Form 2350 with the Internal Revenue Service Center, Philadelphia, PA 19255-0002, the local IRS representative, or other IRS employee.

You must file Form 2350 by the due date for filing your return. Generally, if both your tax home and your abode are outside the United States and Puerto Rico on the regular due date of your return and you file on a calendar year basis, the due date for filing your return is June 15.

### What if Tests Not Met

If you obtain an extension of time and unforeseen events make it impossible for you to satisfy either the bona fide residence test or the physical presence test, you should file your income tax return as soon as possible because you must pay interest on any tax due after the regular due date of the return (even though an extension was granted).

You should make any request for an extension early, so that if it is denied you still can file your return on time. Otherwise, if you file late and additional tax is due, you may be subject to a penalty.

### Return Filed Before Test Met

If you file a return before you meet the bona fide residence test or the physical presence test, you must include all income from both U.S. and foreign sources and pay the tax on that income. If you later qualify for the foreign earned income exclusion, the foreign housing exclusion, or the foreign housing deduction under the bona fide residence or physical presence rules, you can file a claim for refund of tax on Form 1040X. The refund will be the difference between the amount of tax already paid and the tax liability as figured after the exclusion or deduction.

## FOREIGN CURRENCY

You must express the amounts you report on your U.S. tax return in U.S. dollars. If you receive all or part of your income or pay some or all of your expenses in foreign currency, you must translate the foreign currency into U.S. dollars. How you do this depends on your functional currency. Your functional currency generally is the U.S. dollar unless you are required to use the currency of a foreign country.

You must make all federal income tax determinations in your functional currency. The U.S. dollar is the functional currency for all taxpayers except some qualified business units. A qualified business unit is a separate and clearly identified unit of a trade or business that maintains separate books and records. Unless you are self-employed, your functional currency is the U.S. dollar.

Even if you are self-employed and have a qualified business unit, your functional currency is the dollar if any of the following apply.

- You conduct the business in dollars.
- The principal place of business is located in the United States.
- You choose to or are required to use the dollar as your functional currency.
- The business books and records are not kept in the currency of the economic environment in which a significant part of the business activities is conducted.

If your functional currency is the U.S. dollar, you must immediately translate into dollars all items of income, expense, etc. (including taxes), that you receive, pay, or accrue in a foreign currency and that will affect computation of your income tax. Use the exchange rate prevailing when you receive, pay, or accrue the item. If there is more than one exchange rate, use the one that most properly reflects your income. You can generally get exchange rates from banks and U.S. Embassies.

If your functional currency is not the U.S. dollar, make all income tax determinations in your functional currency. At the end of the year, translate the results, such as income or loss, into U.S. dollars to report on your income tax return.

### Blocked Income

You generally must report your foreign income in terms of U.S. dollars and, with one exception (see Fulbright grants later), you must pay taxes due on it in U.S. dollars.

If, because of restrictions in a foreign country, your income is not readily convertible into U.S. dollars or into other money or property that is readily convertible into U.S. dollars, your income is "blocked" or "deferrable" income. You can report this income in one of two ways:

1. Report the income and pay your federal income tax with U.S. dollars that you have in the United States or in some other country, or
2. Postpone the reporting of the income until it becomes unblocked.

If you choose to postpone the reporting of the income, you must file an information return with your tax return. For this information return, you should use another Form 1040 labeled "Report of Deferrable Foreign Income, pursuant to Rev. Rul. 74-351." You must declare on the information return that the deferrable income will be included in taxable income in the year that it becomes unblocked. You also must state that you waive any right to claim that the deferrable income was includible in income for any earlier year.

You must report your income on your information return using the foreign currency in which you received that income. If you have blocked income from more than one foreign country, include a separate information return for each country.

Income becomes unblocked and reportable for tax purposes when it becomes convertible, or when it is converted, into dollars or into other money or property that is convertible into U.S. currency. Also, if you use blocked income for your personal expenses or dispose of it by gift, bequest, or devise, you must treat it as unblocked and reportable.

If you have received blocked income on which you have not paid the tax, you should check to see whether that income is still blocked. If it is not, you should take immediate steps to pay the tax on it, file a declaration or amended declaration of estimated tax, and include the income on your tax return for the year in which the income became unblocked.

If you choose to postpone reporting blocked income and in a later tax year you wish to begin including it in gross income although it is still blocked, you must obtain the permission of the IRS to do so. To apply for permission, file Form 3115, "Application for Change in Accounting Method." You also must request permission from the IRS on Form 3115 if you have not chosen to defer the reporting of blocked income in the past, but now wish to begin reporting blocked income under the deferred method. See the instructions for Form 3115 for information.

### Fulbright Grants

All income must be reported in U.S. dollars. In most cases, the tax must also be paid in U.S. dollars. If, however, at least 70% of your Fulbright grant has been paid in nonconvertible foreign currency (blocked income), you can use the currency of the host country to pay part of the U.S. tax that is based on the blocked income. To determine the amount of the tax that you can pay in foreign currency get Publication 520. Details of these arrangements may also be obtained from the U.S. Educational Foundations or Commissions in foreign countries.

### WHERE TO FILE

If any of the following situations apply to you, you should file your return with the:

Internal Revenue Service Center
Philadelphia, PA 19255-0215.

1. You claim the foreign earned income exclusion.
2. You claim the foreign housing exclusion or deduction.
3. You claim the exclusion of income for bona fide residents of American Samoa.
4. You live in a foreign country or U.S. possession and have no legal residence or principal place of business in the United States.

The exclusions and the deductions are explained in Chapter 9.

If you do not know where your legal residence is and you do not have a principal place of business in the United States, you can file with the Philadelphia Service Center. The address for the Philadelphia Service Center is shown above.

However, you should not file with the Philadelphia Service Center if you are a bona fide resident of the Virgin Islands or a resident of Guam or the Commonwealth of the Northern Mariana Islands on the last day of your tax year.

### Resident of Virgin Islands

If you are a bona fide resident of the Virgin Islands on the last day of your tax year (even if your legal residence or principal place of business is in the United States), you must file your return with the Virgin Islands and pay your tax on income you have from all sources to the:

Virgin Islands Bureau of Internal Revenue
9601 Estate Thomas
Charlotte Amalie
St. Thomas, Virgin Islands 00802.

### *Non-Virgin Islands Resident with Virgin Islands Income*

If you are a U.S. citizen or resident and you have income from sources in the Virgin

Islands or income effectively connected with the conduct of a trade or business in the Virgin Islands, and you are not a bona fide resident of the Virgin Islands on the last day of your tax year, you must file identical tax returns with the United States and the Virgin Islands. File the original return with the United States and file a copy of the U.S. return (including all attachments, forms, and schedules) with the Virgin Islands Bureau of Internal Revenue.

The amount of tax you must pay to the Virgin Islands is figured by the following computation:

Form 8689, "Allocation of Individual Income Tax to the Virgin Islands," is used for this computation. You must complete this form and attach it to your return. You should pay any tax due to the Virgin Islands when you file your return with the Virgin Islands Bureau of Internal Revenue.

You should file your U.S. return with the Internal Revenue Service Center, Philadelphia, PA 19255-0215.

### Resident of Guam

If you are a resident of Guam on the last day of your tax year, you should file a return with Guam and pay your tax on income you have from all sources to the:

Department of Revenue and Taxation
Government of Guam
P.O. Box 23607
GMF, GU 96921.

However, if you are a resident of the United States on the last day of your tax year, you should file a return with the United States and pay your tax on income you have from all sources to the Internal Revenue Service Center, Philadelphia, PA 19255-0215.

See Publication 570, *Tax Guide for Individuals with Income from U.S. Possessions,* for information about the filing requirements for residents of Guam.

### Resident of the Commonwealth of the Northern Mariana Islands

If you are a resident of the Commonwealth of the Northern Mariana Islands on the last day of your tax year, you should file a return with the Northern Mariana Islands and pay your tax on income you have from all sources to the:

Division of Revenue and Taxation
Commonwealth of the Northern Mariana
  Islands
P.O. Box 5234, CHRB
Saipan, MP 96950.

However, if you are a resident of the United States on the last day of your tax year, you should file a return with the United States and pay your tax on income you have from all sources to the Internal Revenue Service Center, Philadelphia, PA 19255-0215.

See Publication 570 for information about the filing requirements for residents of the Commonwealth of the Northern Mariana Islands.

## TERRORIST OR MILITARY ACTION

U.S. income taxes are forgiven for U.S. Government military or civilian employees who die as a result of wounds or injuries sustained outside the United States in a terrorist or military action directed against the United States or its allies. The taxes are forgiven for the deceased employee's tax years beginning with the year immediately before the year in which the injury or wounds were incurred and ending with the year of death.

If the deceased government employee and the employee's spouse had a joint income tax liability for those years, the tax must be divided between the spouses to determine the amount forgiven.

For more information on how to have the tax forgiven or how to claim a refund of tax already paid, see Publication 559, *Survivors, Executors, and Administrators.*

# NONRESIDENT SPOUSE TREATED AS A RESIDENT

If, at the end of your tax year, you are married and one spouse is a U.S. citizen or a resident alien and the other is a nonresident alien, you can choose to treat the nonresident as a U.S. resident. This includes situations in which one of you is a nonresident alien at the beginning of the tax year, but a resident alien at the end of the year, and the other is a nonresident alien at the end of the year.

If you make this choice, the following two rules apply.

1. You and your spouse are treated, for income tax purposes, as residents for all tax years that the choice is in effect.
2. You must file a joint income tax return for the year you make the choice.

This means that neither of you can claim tax treaty benefits as a resident of a foreign country for a tax year for which the choice is in effect. You can file joint or separate returns in years after the year in which you make the choice.

*Example 1.* Pat Smith has been a U.S. citizen for many years. She is married to Norman, a nonresident alien. Pat and Norman make the choice to treat Norman as a resident alien by attaching a statement to their joint return. Pat and Norman must report their worldwide income for the year they make the choice and for all later years unless the choice is ended or suspended. Although Pat and Norman must file a joint return for the year they make the choice, they can file either joint or separate returns for later years.

*Example 2.* Bob and Sharon Williams are married, and both are nonresident aliens. In June of last year, Bob became a resident alien and remained a resident for the rest of the year. Bob and Sharon both choose to be treated as resident aliens by attaching a statement to their joint return for last year. Bob and Sharon must report their worldwide income for last year and all later years unless the choice is ended or suspended. Bob and Sharon must file a joint return for last year, but they can file either joint or separate returns for later years.

## Social Security Number (SSN)

If your spouse is a nonresident alien and you file a joint or separate return, your spouse must have either an SSN or an individual taxpayer identification number (ITIN).

To get an SSN for your spouse, apply at a social security office or U.S. consulate. You must complete Form SS-5. You must also provide original or certified copies of documents to verify your spouse's age, identity, and citizenship.

If your spouse is not eligible to get an SSN, he or she can file Form W-7 with the IRS to apply for an ITIN.

## How to Make the Choice

Attach a statement, signed by both spouses, to your joint return for the first tax year for which the choice applies. It should contain the following:

1. A declaration that one spouse was a nonresident alien and the other spouse a U.S. citizen or resident alien on the last day of your tax year, and that you choose to be treated as U.S. residents for the entire tax year, and
2. The name, address, and social security number (or individual taxpayer identification number) of each spouse. (If one spouse died, include the name and address of the person making the choice for the deceased spouse.)

You generally make this choice when you file your joint return. However, you can also make the choice by filing a joint amended return on Form 1040 or Form 1040A. Be sure to write the word "Amended" across the top of the amended return. If you make the choice with an amended return, you and your spouse must also amend any returns that you may have filed after the year for which you made the choice.

You generally must file the amended joint return within 3 years from the date you filed your original U.S. income tax return or 2 years from the date you paid your income tax for that year, whichever is later.

### Suspending the Choice

The choice to be treated as a resident alien does not apply to any later tax year if neither of you is a U.S. citizen or resident alien at any time during the later tax year.

*Example.* Dick Brown was a resident alien on December 31, 1995, and married to Judy, a nonresident alien. They chose to treat Judy as a resident alien and filed joint 1995 and 1996 income tax returns. On January 10, 1997, Dick became a nonresident alien. Judy had remained a nonresident alien throughout the period. Dick and Judy can file joint or separate returns for 1997. However, since neither Dick nor Judy is a resident alien at any time during 1998, their choice is suspended for that year. If either has U.S. source income or foreign source income effectively connected with a U.S. trade or business in 1998, they must file separate returns as nonresident aliens. If Dick becomes a resident alien again in 1999, their choice is no longer suspended. For years their choice is not suspended, they must include income received from both U.S. and foreign sources in their income for each tax year.

### Ending the Choice

Once made, the choice to be treated as a resident applies to all later years unless suspended (as explained above) or ended in one of the ways shown in Figure 1-A.

If the choice is ended for any of the reasons listed in Figure 1-A, neither spouse can make a choice in any later tax year.

If you do not choose to treat your nonresident spouse as a U.S. resident, you may be able to use head of household filing status. To use this status, you must pay more than half the cost of maintaining a household for certain dependents or relatives other than your nonresident alien spouse. For more information, see Publication 501.

### INFORMATION RETURNS AND REPORTS

If you acquire or dispose of stock in a foreign corporation, own a controlling interest in a foreign corporation, or acquire or dispose of any interest in a foreign partnership, you may have to file an information return. You also may have to file an information return if you transfer property to a foreign trust, or if you have transferred property to a foreign trust with at least one U.S. beneficiary. You may have to file reports if you ship currency to or from the United States or if you have an interest in a foreign bank or financial account.

### Form 5471

Form 5471 must generally be filed by certain U.S. shareholders of controlled foreign corporations and by certain shareholders, officers, and directors of foreign personal holding companies. Form 5471 must also be filed by officers, directors, and shareholders of U.S. entities that acquire, dispose of, or are involved in the reorganization of a foreign corporation.

If it is required, you must file Form 5471 at the time you file your income tax return. More information about the filing of Form 5471 can be found in the instructions for this information return.

### Form 3520

Form 3520, "Annual Return to Report Transactions with Foreign Trusts and Receipt of Certain Foreign Gifts," is used to report:

- Certain transactions with foreign trusts, and
- Receipt of certain large gifts or bequests from certain foreign persons.

It must be filed by:

- U.S. persons that are treated as owners of

**Figure 1A. Ending the Choice**

| Revocation | • Either spouse can revoke the choice for any tax year.<br>• The revocation must be made by the due date for filing the tax return for that tax year.<br>• The spouse who revokes must attach a signed statement declaring that the choice is being revoked.<br>• The statement revoking the choice must include the following:<br>   * The name, address, and Social Security number (or taxpayer identification number) of each spouse.<br>   * The name and address of any person who is revoking the choice for a deceased spouse.<br>   * A list of any states, foreign countries, and possessions that have community property laws in which either spouse is domiciled or where real property is located from which either spouse receives income.<br>• If the spouse revoking the choice must file a return, attach the statement to the return for the first year the revocation applies.<br>• If the spouse revoking the choice does not have to file a return but does file a return (for example, to obtain a refund), attach the statement to the return.<br>• If the spouse revoking the choice does not have to file a return and does not file a claim for refund, send the statement to the Internal Revenue Service Center where the last joint return was filed |
|---|---|
| Death | • The death of either spouse ends the choice, beginning with the first tax year following the year the spouse died.<br>• If the surviving spouse is a U.S. citizen or resident and is entitled to the joint tax rates as a surviving spouse, the choice will not end until the close of the last year for which these joint rates may be used.<br>• If both spouses die in the same tax year, the choice ends on the first day after the close of the tax year in which the spouses died. |
| Legal separation | • A legal separation under a decree of divorce or separate maintenance ends the choice as of the end of the tax year in which the legal separation occurs. |
| Inadequate records | • The Internal Revenue Service can end the choice for any tax year that either spouse has failed to keep adequate books, records, and other information necessary to determine the correct income tax liability, or to provide adequate access to these records. |

any portion of a foreign trust for U.S. income tax purposes under sections 671 through 679 (the "grantor trust rules") to report certain information,

• U.S. persons to provide information about distributions received from foreign trusts, and
• Other individuals as listed in the Form 3520 instructions.

You must file the form with your income tax return by the due date (including extensions) of your return. Also, send a copy of the form to the Internal Revenue Service Center, Philadelphia, PA 19255.

### Form 4790
Form 4790, "Report of International Transportation of Currency or Monetary Instruments," must be filed by each person who physically transports, mails, ships, or causes to be physically transported, mailed, or shipped, into or out of the United States, currency or other monetary instruments totaling more than $10,000 at one time. The filing requirement also applies to any person who attempts to transport, mail, or ship the currency or monetary instruments or attempts to cause them to be transported, mailed, or shipped. Form 4790 must also be filed by certain recipients of currency or monetary instruments.

The term "monetary instruments" includes coin and currency of the United States or of any other country, money orders, traveler's checks, investment securities in bearer form or otherwise in such form that title passes upon delivery, and negotiable instruments (except warehouse receipts or bills of lading) in bearer form or otherwise in such form that title passes upon delivery. The term includes bank checks, and money orders that are signed, but on which the name of the payee has been omitted. The term does not include bank checks, or money orders made payable to the order of a named person that have not been endorsed or that bear restrictive endorsements.

A transfer of funds through normal banking procedures (wire transfer) which does not involve the physical transportation of currency or bearer monetary instruments is not required to be reported on Form 4790.

### Recipients

Each person who receives currency or other monetary instruments from a place outside the United States for which a report has not been filed by the shipper must file Form 4790.

It must be filed within 15 days after receipt with the Customs officer in charge at any port of entry or departure, or by mail with the:

Commissioner of Customs
Attention: Currency Transportation
  Reports
Washington, DC 20229.

### Shippers or Mailers

If the currency or other monetary instrument does not accompany a person entering or departing the United States, Form 4790 can be filed by mail with the

Commissioner of Customs at the above address. It must be filed by the date of entry, departure, mailing, or shipping.

### Travelers

Travelers carrying currency or other monetary instruments with them must file Customs Form 4790 with the Customs officer in charge at any Customs port of entry or departure when entering or departing the United States.

### Penalties

Civil and criminal penalties are provided for failure to file a report, supply information, and for filing a false or fraudulent report. Also, the entire amount of the currency or monetary instrument may be subject to seizure and forfeiture.

More information about the filing of Form 4790 can be found in the instructions on the back of the form.

### Form TD F 90-22.1

Form TD F 90-22.1 must be filed if you had any financial interest in, or signature or other authority over, a bank, securities, or other financial account in a foreign country. You do not have to file the report if the assets are with a U.S. military banking facility operated by a U.S. financial institution or if the combined assets in the account(s) are $10,000 or less during the entire year.

You must file this form by June 30 each year with the Department of the Treasury at the address shown on the form. Form TD F 90-22.1 is not a tax return, so do not attach it to your Form 1040.

# CHAPTER 8
## *Internal Revenue Service, Publication 54:*
## *Tax Guide for U.S. Citizens and Resident Aliens Abroad,*
# Part Two

### WITHHOLDING

U.S. employers generally must withhold U.S. income tax from the pay of U.S. citizens performing services in a foreign country unless the employer is required by foreign law to withhold foreign income tax.

Your employer, however, is not required to withhold U.S. income tax from the portion of your wages earned abroad that are equal to the foreign earned income exclusion and foreign housing exclusion if your employer has good reason to believe that you will qualify for these exclusions.

### Statement

You can give a statement to your employer indicating that you will meet either the bona fide residence test or the physical presence test and indicating your estimated housing cost exclusion.

You can get copies of an acceptable statement (Form 673) by writing to:

Internal Revenue Service
Assistant Commissioner (International)
Attn: OP:IN:D:CS
950 L'Enfant Plaza South, SW
Washington, DC 20024.

You can use Form 673 only if you are a U.S. citizen. You do not have to use the form. You can prepare your own statement.

### Form 673

You must give the statement to your employer and not to the IRS.

Generally, the receipt of a signed statement from you that includes a declaration under penalties of perjury is considered authority for your employer to discontinue withholding. However, if your employer has reason to believe that you will not qualify for an exclusion of income, your employer must disregard the statement and withhold the tax.

If your employer has information about pay you received from any other source outside the United States, it must be considered in determining whether your foreign earned income is more than the limit on the exclusion.

Your employer should withhold taxes from any wages you earn for working in the United States.

### Foreign Tax Credit

If you plan to take a foreign tax credit, you may be eligible for additional withholding allowances on Form W-4. You can take these additional withholding allowances only for foreign tax credits attributable to taxable salary or wage income. See Publication 505 for further information.

### Withholding from Pension Payments

U.S. payers of benefits from employer deferred compensation plans, individual retirement plans, and commercial annuities generally must withhold income tax from the payments or distributions they make to you. Withholding will apply unless you choose exemption from withholding. You cannot choose either exemption unless you provide the payer of the benefits with a residence address in the United States or a U.S. possession or certify to the payer that you are not a U.S. citizen or resident alien or someone who left the United States to avoid tax.

### Checking your Withholding

Before you report U.S. income tax withholding on your tax return, you should carefully review all information documents, such as Form W-2 and Form 1099. Compare other records, such as final pay records or bank statements, with Form W-2 or Form 1099 to verify the withholding on these forms. Check your U.S. income tax withholding even if you pay someone else to prepare your tax return. You may be assessed penalties and interest if you claim more than your correct amount of withholding.

## SOCIAL SECURITY AND MEDICARE TAXES

Social security and Medicare taxes may apply to wages paid to an employee regardless of where the services are performed.

### General Information

In general, U.S. social security and Medicare taxes apply to payments of wages for services performed as an employee:

1. Within the United States, regardless of the citizenship or residence of either the employee or the employer,
2. Outside the United States on or in connection with an American vessel or aircraft, regardless of the citizenship or residence of either the employee or the employer, provided that either:

- The employment contract is entered into within the United States,
- The vessel or aircraft touches at a U.S. port while the employee is employed on it,
- Outside the United States, as provided by an applicable binational social security agreement (discussed later),
- Outside the United States by a U.S. citizen or a U.S. resident alien for an American employer (defined later), or
- Outside the United States by a U.S. citizen or U.S. resident alien for a foreign affiliate of an American employer under a voluntary agreement entered into between the American employer and the U.S. Treasury Department.

### American Vessel or Aircraft

An American vessel is any vessel documented or numbered under the laws of the United States, and any other vessel whose crew is employed solely by one or more U.S. citizens or residents or U.S. corporations. An American aircraft is an aircraft registered under the laws of the United States.

### American Employer

An American employer includes any of the following employers.

1. The U.S. Government or any of its instrumentalities.
2. An individual who is a resident of the United States.
3. A partnership of which at least two-thirds of the partners are U.S. residents.
4. A trust of which all the trustees are U.S. residents.

5. A corporation organized under the laws of the United States, any U.S. state, or the District of Columbia, Puerto Rico, the Virgin Islands, Guam, or American Samoa.

### Foreign Affiliate

A foreign affiliate of an American employer is any foreign entity in which the American employer has at least a 10% interest, directly or through one or more entities. For a corporation, the 10% interest must be in its voting stock, and for any other entity the 10% interest must be in its profits.

Form 2032, *Contract Coverage Under Title II of the Social Security Act*, is used by American employers to extend social security coverage to U.S. citizens and residents working abroad for foreign affiliates of the American employers. Coverage under an agreement in effect on or after June 15, 1989, cannot be terminated.

### Excludable Meals and Lodging

Social security tax does not apply to the value of meals and lodging provided to you for the convenience of your employer and excluded from your income.

### Binational Social Security (Totalization) Agreements

The United States has entered into agreements with several foreign countries to coordinate social security coverage and taxation of workers who are employed in those countries. These agreements are commonly referred to as totalization agreements and are in effect with the following countries.

Austria
Belgium
Canada
Finland
France
Germany
Greece
Ireland
Italy
Luxembourg

The Netherlands
Norway
Portugal
Spain
Sweden
Switzerland
The United Kingdom

Under these agreements, dual coverage and dual contributions (taxes) for the same work are eliminated. The agreements generally make sure that you pay social security taxes to only one country.

Generally, under these agreements, you will only be subject to social security taxes in the country where you are working. However, if you are temporarily sent to work in a foreign country, and your pay would otherwise be subject to social security taxes in both the United States and that country, you generally can remain covered only by U.S. social security. You can get more information on any specific agreement by contacting the United States Social Security Administration. If you have access to the internet, you can get more information at:

http://www.ssa.gov/international

To establish that your pay in a foreign country is subject only to U.S. social security tax and is exempt from foreign social security tax, your employer in the United States should write to the:

U.S. Social Security Administration
Office of International Programs
P.O. Box 17741
Baltimore, MD 21235.

Your employer should include the following information in the letter.

1. Your name.
2. Your U.S. social security number.
3. Your date and place of birth.
4. The country of which you are a citizen.

5. The country of your permanent residence.
6. The name and address of your employer in the United States and in the foreign country.
7. The date and place you were hired.
8. The beginning date and the expected ending date of your employment in the foreign country.

If you are permanently working in a foreign country with which the United States has a social security agreement and, under the agreement, your pay is exempt from U.S. social security tax, you or your employer should get a statement from the authorized official or agency of the foreign country verifying that your pay is subject to social security coverage in that country.

If the authorities of the foreign country will not issue such a statement, either you or your employer should get a statement from the U.S. Social Security Administration, Office of International Programs, at the above address, that your wages are not covered by the U.S. social security system.

This statement should be kept by your employer because it establishes that your pay is exempt from U.S. social security tax. Only wages paid on or after the effective date of the agreement can be exempt from U.S. social security tax.

### Exemption from Social Security and Medicare Taxes

The United States may reach agreements with foreign countries to eliminate dual coverage and dual contributions (taxes) to social security systems for the same work. See "Binational Social Security (Totalization) Agreements" on page 75 under Social Security and Medicare Taxes. As a general rule, self-employed persons who are subject to dual taxation will only be covered by the social security system of the country where they reside. For more information on how any specific agreement affects self-employed persons, contact the United States Social Security Administration.

If you are a U.S. citizen permanently working in a foreign country with which the United States has a social security agreement and you are exempt under the agreement from U.S. self-employment tax, you should get a statement from the authorized official or agency of the foreign country verifying that you are subject to social security coverage in that country.

If the authorities of the foreign country will not issue a statement, you should get a statement that your earnings are not covered by the U.S. social security system from the:

U.S. Social Security Administration
Office of International Programs
P.O. Box 17741
Baltimore, MD 21235.

Attach a photocopy of either statement to your federal income tax return each year you are exempt. Also enter "Exempt, see attached statement," on the line for self-employment tax on your return.

If you believe that your self-employment earnings should be exempt from foreign social security tax and subject only to U.S. self-employment tax, you should request a certificate of coverage from the United States Social Security Administration, Office of International Policy. The certificate will establish your exemption from the foreign social security tax.

### Who Must Pay Self-Employment Tax?

If you are abroad and you are a self-employed U.S. citizen or resident, other than a U.S. citizen employee of an international organization, foreign government, or wholly owned instrumentality of a foreign government, you generally are subject to the self-employment tax. This is a social security and Medicare tax on net earnings from self-employment of $400 or more a year. For 1999 the tax is on net earnings of $400 or more up to $72,600 for the social security portion. All net earnings are subject to the Medicare portion. Your net self-employment income is used to figure your net earnings from self-employment. Net self-employment income usually includes all business income less all business deductions allowed for income tax purposes. Net earnings from self-employment is a portion of net self-employment income. This amount is figured on Schedule SE (Short Schedule SE (Section A), line 4, or Long Schedule SE (Section B), line 6). The actual self-employment tax is figured on net earnings from self-employment.

### Employed by a U.S. Church

If you were employed by a U.S. church or a qualified church-controlled organization that chose exemption from social security and Medicare taxes and you received wages of $108.28 or more from the organization, the amounts paid to you are subject to self-employment tax. However, you can choose to be exempt from social security and Medicare taxes if you are a member of a recognized religious sect. (See Publication 517.)

### Effect of Exclusion

You must take all of your self-employment income into account in figuring your net earnings from self-employment, even income that is exempt from income tax because of the foreign earned income exclusion.

*Example.* You are in business abroad as a consultant and qualify for the foreign earned income exclusion. Your foreign earned income is $95,000, your business deductions total $27,000, and your net profit is $68,000. You must pay social security tax and Medicare tax on your net earnings even though you can exclude all of your earned income.

### Optional Method

You can use the nonfarm optional method if you are self-employed and your net nonfarm profits are less than $1,733 and less than 72.189% of your gross nonfarm income. You must have had $400 of net self-employment earnings in at least 2 of the 3 immediately preceding tax years. You cannot choose to report less than your actual net earnings from nonfarm self-employment. You cannot use the nonfarm optional method for more than 5 tax years. Use Long Schedule SE (Section B). For more details get Publication 533.

### Members of the Clergy

Although members of the clergy may be employees in performing their ministerial services, they are treated as self-employed for self-employment tax purposes. Their U.S. self-employment tax is based upon net earnings from self-employment figured without regard to the foreign earned income exclusion or the foreign housing exclusion.

Members of the clergy are covered automatically by social security and Medicare. You can receive exemption from coverage for your ministerial duties if you conscientiously oppose public insurance due to religious reasons or if you oppose it due to the religious principles of your denomination. You must file Form 4361 to apply for this exemption.

This subject is discussed in further detail in Publication 517.

### Puerto Rico, Guam, Commonwealth of the Northern Mariana Islands, American Samoa, or Virgin Islands

If you are a U.S. citizen or resident and you own and operate a business in Puerto Rico, Guam, the Commonwealth of the Northern Mariana Islands, American Samoa, or the Virgin Islands, you must pay tax on your net earnings from self-employment (if they are $400 or more) from those sources. You must pay the self-employment tax whether or not the income is exempt from U.S. income taxes (or whether or not you must otherwise file a U.S. income tax return). Unless your situation is described below, attach Schedule SE (Form 1040) to your U.S. income tax return.

If you do not have to file Form 1040 with the United States and you are a resident of:

Puerto Rico, Guam, The Commonwealth

of the Northern Mariana Islands, American Samoa, or The Virgin Islands,

figure your self-employment tax on either Form 1040-PR or Form 1040-SS, whichever applies.

You must file these forms with the Internal Revenue Service Center, Philadelphia, PA 19255-0215.

# CHAPTER 9
## *Internal Revenue Service, Publication 54:*
## *Tax Guide for U.S. Citizens and Resident Aliens Abroad,*
# Part Three

### REQUIREMENTS

To claim the foreign earned income exclusion, the foreign housing exclusion, or the foreign housing deduction, you must have foreign earned income, your tax home must be in a foreign country, and you must be one of the following:

- A U.S. citizen who is a bona fide resident of a foreign country or countries for an uninterrupted period that includes an entire tax year,
- A U.S. resident alien who is a citizen or national of a country with which the United States has an income tax treaty in effect and who is a bona fide resident of a foreign country or countries for an uninterrupted period that includes an entire tax year, or
- A U.S. citizen or a U.S. resident alien who is physically present in a foreign country or countries for at least 330 full days during any period of 12 consecutive months.

See Publication 519 to find out if you qualify as a U.S. resident alien for tax purposes and whether you keep that alien status when you temporarily work abroad.

If you are a nonresident alien married to a U.S. citizen or resident, and both you and your spouse choose to treat you as a resident, you are a resident alien for tax purposes. For information on making the choice, see the discussion in **Chapter 7** under "Nonresident Spouse Treated as a Resident" (page 69).

### Waiver of Minimum Time Requirements
The minimum time requirements for bona fide residence and physical presence can be waived if you must leave a foreign country because of war, civil unrest, or similar adverse conditions in that country. See "Waiver of Time Requirements," later.

### TAX HOME IN FOREIGN COUNTRY
To qualify for the foreign earned income exclusion, the foreign housing exclusion, or the foreign housing deduction, your tax home must be in a foreign country throughout your period of bona fide residence or physical presence abroad. Bona fide residence and physical presence are explained later.

#### *Tax Home*
Your tax home is the general area of your main place of business, employment, or post of duty, regardless of where you maintain your

**Figure 4-A. Can I Claim the Exclusion or Deduction?**

```
Start Here

┌──────────────────┐  Yes  ┌──────────────────┐  Yes  ┌──────────────────┐  No  ┌──────────────────┐  No
│ Do you have      │──────▶│ Is your tax home │──────▶│ Are you a U.S.   │─────▶│ Are you a U.S.   │─────▶
│ foreign earned   │       │ in a foreign     │       │ citizen?         │      │ resident alien?  │
│ income?          │       │ country?         │       │                  │      │                  │
└──────────────────┘       └──────────────────┘       └──────────────────┘      └──────────────────┘
        │ No                       │ No                        │ Yes                     │ Yes
                                                               ▼                         ▼
                              ┌──────────────────────┐  Yes   ┌──────────────────────┐
                              │ Were you a bona fide │◀───────│ Are you a citizen or │
                              │ resident of a foreign│        │ national of a country│
                              │ country or countries │        │ with which the United│
                              │ for an uninterrupted │        │ States has an income │
                              │ period that includes │        │ tax treaty in effect?│
                              │ an entire tax year?  │        └──────────────────────┘
                              └──────────────────────┘                 │ No
                                    │ No         │ Yes
                                                 ▼
                                    ┌──────────────────────┐
                                    │ You CAN claim the     │
                                    │ foreign earned income │
                                    │ exclusion and the     │
                                    │ foreign housing       │
                                    │ exclusion or the      │
                                    │ foreign housing       │
                                    │ deduction.            │
                                    └──────────────────────┘
                                    ┌──────────────────────┐  Yes
                                    │ Were you physically   │─────▶
                                    │ present in a foreign  │
                                    │ country for at least  │
                                    │ 330 full days during  │
                                    │ any period of 12      │
                                    │ consecutive months?   │
                                    └──────────────────────┘
                                                │ No
                                                ▼
                          ┌─────────────────────────────────────────────┐
                          │ You CANNOT claim the foreign earned income   │
                          │ exclusion, the foreign housing exclusion, or │
                          │ the foreign housing deduction.               │
                          └─────────────────────────────────────────────┘
```

family home. Your tax home is the place where you are permanently or indefinitely engaged to work as an employee or self-employed individual. Having a "tax home" in a given location does not necessarily mean that the given location is your residence or domicile for tax purposes.

If you do not have a regular or main place of business because of the nature of your work, your tax home may be the place where you regularly live. If you have neither a regular or main place of business nor a place where you regularly live, you are considered an itinerant and your tax home is wherever you work.

You are not considered to have a tax home in a foreign country for any period in which your abode is in the United States. However, your abode is not necessarily in the United States while you are temporarily in the United States. Your abode is also not necessarily in the United States merely because you maintain a dwelling in the United States, whether or not your spouse or dependents use the dwelling.

"Abode" has been variously defined as one's home, habitation, residence, domicile, or place of dwelling. It does not mean your principal place of business. "Abode" has a domestic rather than a vocational meaning and does not mean the same as "tax home." The location of your abode often will depend on where you maintain your economic, family, and personal ties.

*Example 1.* You are employed on an offshore oil rig in the territorial waters of a foreign country and work a 28-day on/28-day off schedule. You return to your family residence in the United States during your off periods. You are considered to have an abode in the United States and do not satisfy the tax home test in the foreign country. You cannot claim either of the exclusions or the housing deduction.

*Example 2.* For several years, you were a marketing executive with a producer of machine tools in Toledo, Ohio. In November of last year your employer transferred you to London, England, for a minimum of 18 months to set up a sales operation for Europe. Before you left, you distributed business cards showing your business and home addresses in London. You kept ownership of your home in Toledo but rented it to another family. You placed your car in storage. In November of last year, you moved your spouse, children, furniture, and family pets to a home your employer rented for you in London.

Shortly after moving, you leased a car, and you and your spouse got British driving licenses. Your entire family got library cards for the local public library. You and your spouse opened bank accounts with a London bank and secured consumer credit. You joined a local business league, and both you and your spouse became active in the neighborhood civic association and worked with a local charity. Your abode is in London for the time you live there, and you satisfy the tax home test in the foreign country.

## Temporary or Indefinite Assignment

The location of your tax home often depends on whether your assignment is temporary or indefinite. If you are temporarily absent from your tax home in the United States on business, you may be able to deduct your away-from-home expenses (for travel, meals, and lodging) but you would not qualify for the foreign earned income exclusion. If your new work assignment is for an indefinite period, your new place of employment becomes your tax home, and you would not be able to deduct any of the related expenses that you have in the general area of this new work assignment. If your new tax home is in a foreign country and you meet the other requirements, your earnings may qualify for the foreign earned income exclusion.

If you expect your employment away from home in a single location to last, and it does last, for 1 year or less, it is temporary unless facts and circumstances indicate otherwise. If you expect it to last for more than 1 year, it is indefinite. If you expect it to last for 1 year or less, but at some later date you expect it to last longer than 1 year, it is temporary (in the absence of facts and circumstances indicating otherwise) until your expectation changes.

## Foreign Country

To meet the bona fide residence test or the physical presence test, you must live in or be present in a foreign country. A foreign country usually is any territory (including the air space and territorial waters) under the sovereignty of a government other than that of the United States.

The term "foreign country" includes the seabed and subsoil of those submarine areas adjacent to the territorial waters of a foreign country and over which the foreign country has exclusive rights under international law to explore and exploit the natural resources.

The term "foreign country" does not include Puerto Rico, Guam, the Commonwealth of the Northern Mariana Islands, the Virgin Islands, or U.S. possessions such as American Samoa. For purposes of the foreign earned income exclusion, the foreign housing exclusion, and the foreign housing deduction, the terms "foreign," " abroad," and "overseas" refer to areas outside the United States, American Samoa, Guam, the Commonwealth of the Northern Mariana

Islands, Puerto Rico, the Virgin Islands, and the Antarctic region.

### American Samoa, Guam, and the Commonwealth of the Northern Mariana Islands

Residence or presence in a U.S. possession does not qualify you for the foreign earned income exclusion. You may, however, qualify for the possession exclusion.

### American Samoa

There is a possession exclusion available to individuals who are bona fide residents of American Samoa for the entire tax year. Gross income from sources within American Samoa, Guam, or the Commonwealth of the Northern Mariana Islands may be eligible for this exclusion. Income that is effectively connected with the conduct of a trade or business within those possessions also may be eligible for this exclusion. Use Form 4563, "Exclusion of Income for Bona Fide Residents of American Samoa," to figure the exclusion.

### Guam and the Commonwealth of the Northern Mariana Islands

New exclusion rules will apply to residents of Guam and the Commonwealth of the Northern Mariana Islands if, and when, new implementation agreements take effect between the United States and those possessions.

For more information, see Publication 570.

### Puerto Rico and Virgin Islands

Residents of Puerto Rico and the Virgin Islands are not entitled to the possession exclusion (discussed above) or to the exclusion of foreign earned income or the exclusion or deduction of foreign housing amounts under the bona fide residence or physical presence rules discussed later.

### Puerto Rico

Generally, if you are a U.S. citizen who is a bona fide resident of Puerto Rico for the entire tax year, you are not subject to U.S. tax on income from Puerto Rican sources. This does not include amounts paid for services performed as an employee of the United States. However, you are subject to U.S. tax on your income from sources outside Puerto Rico. You cannot deduct expenses allocable to the exempt income.

### Bona Fide Residence Test

The bona fide residence test applies to U.S. citizens and to any U.S. resident alien who is a citizen or national of a country with which the United States has an income tax treaty in effect.

### Bona Fide Residence

To see if you meet the test of bona fide residence in a foreign country, you must find out if you have established such a residence.

Your bona fide residence is not necessarily the same as your domicile. Your domicile is your permanent home, the place to which you always return or intend to return.

*Example.* You could have your domicile in Cleveland, Ohio, and a bona fide residence in London if you intend to return eventually to Cleveland.

The fact that you go to London does not automatically make London your bona fide residence. If you go there as a tourist, or on a short business trip, and return to the United States, you have not established bona fide residence in London. But if you go to London to work for an indefinite or extended period and you set up permanent quarters there for yourself and your family, you probably have established a bona fide residence in a foreign country, even though you intend to return eventually to the United States.

You are clearly a transient in the first instance. However, in the second, you are a resident because your stay in London appears to be permanent. If your residency is not as clearly defined as either of these illustrations, it may be more difficult to decide whether you have established a bona fide residence.

### Determination

Questions of bona fide residence are

determined according to each individual case, taking into account such factors as your intention or the purpose of your trip and the nature and length of your stay abroad.

You must show the Internal Revenue Service (IRS) that you have been a bona fide resident of a foreign country or countries for an uninterrupted period that includes an entire tax year. The IRS decides whether you qualify as a bona fide resident of a foreign country largely on the basis of facts you report on Form 2555. File this form with your income tax return on which you claim the exclusion of foreign earned income. IRS cannot make this determination until you file Form 2555.

### Statement to Foreign Authorities

You are not considered a bona fide resident of a foreign country if you make a statement to the authorities of that country that you are not a resident of that country and the authorities hold that you are not subject to their income tax laws as a resident.

If you have made such a statement and the authorities have not made a final decision on your status, you are not considered to be a bona fide resident of that foreign country.

### Special Agreements and Treaties

The income tax exemption provided in a treaty or other international agreement will not in itself prevent you from being a bona fide resident of a foreign country. Whether a treaty prevents you from becoming a bona fide resident of a foreign country is determined under all provisions of the treaty, including specific provisions relating to residence or privileges and immunities.

*Example 1.* You are a U.S. citizen employed in the United Kingdom by a U.S. employer under contract with the U.S. Armed Forces. You do not qualify for special status under the North Atlantic Treaty Status of Forces Agreement. You are subject to United Kingdom income taxes and may qualify as a bona fide resident.

*Example 2.* You are a U.S. citizen in the United Kingdom who qualifies as an "employee" of an armed service or as a member of a "civilian component" under the North Atlantic Treaty Status of Forces Agreement. You do not qualify as a bona fide resident.

*Example 3.* You are a U.S. citizen employed in Japan by a U.S. employer under contract with the U.S. Armed Forces. You are subject to the agreement of the Treaty of Mutual Cooperation and Security between the United States and Japan. You do not qualify as a bona fide resident.

*Example 4.* You are a U.S. citizen employed as an "official" by the United Nations in Switzerland. You are exempt from Swiss taxation on the salary or wages paid to you by the United Nations. This does not prevent you from qualifying as a bona fide resident if you meet all the requirements for that status.

### Effect of Voting by Absentee Ballot

If you are a U.S. citizen living abroad, you can vote by absentee ballot in any elections held in the United States without risking your status as a bona fide resident of a foreign country.

However, if you give information to the local election officials about the nature and length of your stay abroad that does not match the information you give for the bona fide residence test, the information given in connection with absentee voting will be considered in determining your status, but will not necessarily be conclusive.

### Uninterrupted Period Including Entire Tax Year

To qualify for bona fide residence, you must reside in a foreign country for an uninterrupted period that includes an entire tax year. An entire tax year is from January 1 through December 31 for taxpayers who file their income tax returns on a calendar year basis.

During the period of bona fide residence in a foreign country, you can leave the country for brief or temporary trips back to the United States or elsewhere for vacation or business. To keep your status as a bona fide resident of a foreign country, you must have a clear intention of returning from such trips, without unreasonable delay, to your foreign residence or to a new bona fide residence in another foreign country.

*Example 1.* You are the Lisbon representative of a U.S. employer. You arrived with your family in Lisbon on November 1, 1997. Your assignment is indefinite, and you intend to live there with your family until your company sends you to a new post. You immediately established residence there. On April 1, 1998, you arrived in the United States to meet with your employer, leaving your family in Lisbon. You returned to Lisbon on May 1, and continue living there. On January 1, 1999, you completed an uninterrupted period of residence for a full tax year (1998), and you may qualify as a bona fide resident of a foreign country.

*Example 2.* Assume that in Example 1, you transferred back to the United States on December 13, 1998. You would not qualify under the bona fide residence test because your bona fide residence in the foreign country, although it lasted more than a year, did not include a full tax year. You may, however, qualify for the foreign earned income exclusion or the housing exclusion or deduction under the physical presence test discussed later.

### Bona Fide Residence Status Not Automatic

You do not automatically acquire bona fide resident status merely by living in a foreign country or countries for 1 year.

*Example.* If you go to a foreign country to work on a particular construction job for a specified period of time, you ordinarily will not be regarded as a bona fide resident of that country even though you work there for one tax year or longer. The length of your stay and the nature of your job are only some of the factors to be considered in determining whether you meet the bona fide residence test.

### Bona Fide Resident for Part of a Year

Once you have established bona fide

residence in a foreign country for an uninterrupted period that includes an entire tax year, you will qualify as a bona fide resident for the period starting with the date you actually began the residence and ending with the date you abandon the foreign residence. You could qualify as a bona fide resident for an entire tax year plus parts of 1 or 2 other tax years.

*Example.* You were a bona fide resident of England from March 1, 1997, through September 14, 1999. On September 15, 1999, you returned to the United States. Since you were a bona fide resident of a foreign country for all of 1998, you also qualify as a bona fide resident from March 1, 1997, through the end of 1997 and from January 1, 1999, through September 14, 1999.

### Reassignment

If you are assigned from one foreign post to another, you may or may not have a break in foreign residence between your assignments, depending on the circumstances.

*Example 1.* You were a resident of France from October 1, 1998, through November 30, 1999. On December 1, 1999, you and your family returned to the United States to wait for an assignment to another foreign country. Your household goods also were returned to the United States.

Your foreign residence ended on November 30, 1999, and did not begin again until after you were assigned to another foreign country and physically entered that country. Since you were not a bona fide resident of a foreign country for the entire tax year of 1998 or 1999, you do not qualify under the bona fide residence test in either year. You may, however, qualify for the foreign earned income exclusion or the housing exclusion or deduction under the physical presence test, discussed later.

*Example 2.* Assume the same facts as in Example 1, except that upon completion of your assignment in France you were given a new assignment to England. On December 1,

1999, you and your family returned to the United States for a month's vacation. On January 2, 2000, you arrived in England for your new assignment. Because you did not interrupt your bona fide residence abroad, you qualify at the end of 1999 as a bona fide resident of a foreign country.

## Physical Presence Test

You meet the physical presence test if you are physically present in a foreign country or countries 330 full days during a period of 12 consecutive months. The 330 qualifying days do not have to be consecutive. The physical presence test applies to both U.S. citizens and resident aliens.

The physical presence test is concerned only with how long you stay in a foreign country or countries. This test does not depend on the kind of residence you establish, your intentions about returning, or the nature and purpose of your stay abroad. However, your intentions with regard to the nature and purpose of your stay abroad are relevant in determining whether you meet the tax home test explained earlier under "Tax Home in Foreign Country."

### 12-Month Period

Your 12-month period can begin with any day of any calendar month. It ends the day before the same calendar day, 12 months later.

*Example.* Your flight touches down in London on June 13, 1999. Your 12-month period ends on June 12, 2000.

### Purpose of Stay

You do not have to be in a foreign country only for employment purposes. You can be on vacation time.

### Less Than 330 Full Days

Generally, to meet the physical presence test, you must be physically present in a foreign country or countries for at least 330 full days during the 12-month period. This means that if illness, family problems, a vacation, or your employer's orders cause you to be present for less than the required amount of time, you cannot meet the physical presence test.

*Exception.* You can be physically present in a foreign country or countries for less than 330 full days and still meet the physical presence test if you are required to leave a country because of war or civil unrest. See "Waiver of Time Requirements," later.

### Full Day

A full day is a period of 24 consecutive hours, beginning at midnight. You must spend each of the 330 full days in a foreign country. When you leave the United States to go directly to a foreign country or when you return directly to the United States from a foreign country, the time you spend on or over international waters does not count toward the 330-day total.

*Example.* You leave the United States for France by air on June 10. You arrive in France at 9:00 A.M. on June 11. Your first full day in France is June 12.

### Passing Over Foreign Country

If, in traveling from the United States to a foreign country, you pass over a foreign country before midnight of the day you leave, the first day you can count toward the 330-day total is the day following the day you leave the United States.

*Example.* You leave the United States by air at 9:30 A.M. on June 10 to travel to Spain. You pass over a part of France at 11:00 P.M. on June 10 and arrive in Spain at 12:30 A.M. on June 11. Your first full day in a foreign country is June 11.

### Foreign Move

You can move about from one place to another in a foreign country or to another foreign country without losing full days. But if any part of your travel is not within a foreign country or countries and takes 24 hours or more, you will lose full days.

*Example 1.* You leave London by air at 11:00 P.M. on July 6 and arrive in Stockholm at 5:00 A.M. on July 7. Your trip takes less than 24 hours, and you lose no full days.

*Example 2.* You leave Norway by ship at 10:00 P.M. on July 6 and arrive in Portugal at 6:00 A.M. on July 8. Since your travel is not within a foreign country or countries and the trip takes more than 24 hours, you lose as full days July 6, 7, and 8. If you remain in Portugal, your next full day in a foreign country is July 9.

### In U.S. While in Transit

If you are in transit between two points outside the United States and are physically present in the United States for less than 24 hours, you are not treated as present in the United States during the transit. You are treated as traveling over areas not within any foreign country.

### How to Figure the 12-Month Period

There are four rules you should know when figuring the 12-month period.

1. Your 12-month period can begin with any day of the month. It ends the day before the same calendar day, 12 months later.
2. Your 12-month period must be made up of consecutive months. Any 12-month period can be used if the 330 days in a foreign country fall within that period.
3. You do not have to begin your 12-month period with your first full day in a foreign country or to end it with the day you leave. You can choose the 12-month period that gives you the greatest exclusion.
4. In determining if the 12-month period falls within a longer stay in the foreign country, any 12-month period can overlap another.

*Example 1.* You are a construction worker who works on and off in a foreign country over a 20-month period. You might pick up the 330 full days in a 12-month period only during the middle months of the time you work in the foreign country because the first few and last few months of the 20-month period are broken up by long visits to the United States.

*Example 2.* You work in Canada for a 20-month period from January 1, 1998, through August 31, 1999, except that you spend February 1998 and February 1999 on vacation in the United States. You are present in Canada 330 full days during each of the following two 12-month periods. One 12-month period can begin January 1, 1998, and end December 31, 1998; the second period can begin September 1, 1998, and end August 31, 1999. By overlapping the 12-month periods in this way, you meet the physical presence test for the whole 20-month period.

See Table 4-1.

### Exceptions to Tests

There are two exceptions to meeting the requirements under the bona fide residence and the physical presence tests.

**Table 4-1. How to Figure Overlapping 12-Month Periods**
(This table illustrates Example 2 under "How to Figure the 12-Month Period.")

| | | | | | | | | | | | | | | | | | | | |
|---|---|---|---|---|---|---|---|---|---|---|---|---|---|---|---|---|---|---|---|
| | | | | | First Full 12-Month Period | | | | | | | | | | | | | | |
| Jan. 98 | * Feb. 98 | Mar. 98 | Apr. 98 | May 98 | June 98 | July 98 | Aug. 98 | Sep. 98 | Oct. 98 | Nov. 98 | Dec. 98 | Jan. 99 | * Feb. 99 | Mar. 99 | Apr. 99 | May 99 | June 99 | July 99 | Aug. 99 |
| | | | | | | | | Second Full 12-Month Period | | | | | | | | | | | |

* 28-day vacation in the United States

## *Waiver of Time Requirements*

Both the bona fide residence test and the physical presence test contain minimum time requirements. The minimum time requirements can be waived, however, if you must leave a foreign country because of war, civil unrest, or similar adverse conditions in that country. You also must be able to show that you reasonably could have expected to meet the minimum time requirements if not for the adverse conditions. To qualify for the waiver, you must actually have your tax home in the foreign country and be a bona fide resident of, or be physically present in, the foreign country on or before the beginning date of the waiver.

Early in 2000, the IRS will publish in the *Internal Revenue Bulletin* a list of countries qualifying for the waiver for 1999 and the effective dates. If you left one of the countries on or after the date listed for each country, you can qualify for the bona fide residence test or physical presence test for 1999 without meeting the minimum time requirement. However, in figuring your exclusion, the number of your qualifying days of bona fide residence or physical presence includes only days of actual residence or presence within the country.

You can read the *Internal Revenue Bulletins* on the Internet at www.irs.gov. Select "Tax Info For You." Or, you can get a copy of the list of countries by writing to:

Internal Revenue Service
Assistant Commissioner (International)
Attention: OP:IN:D:CS
950 L'Enfant Plaza South, SW
Washington, D.C. 20024

### U.S. Travel Restrictions

If you are present in a foreign country in violation of U.S. law, you will not be treated as a bona fide resident of a foreign country or as physically present in a foreign country while you are in violation of the law. Income that you earn from sources within such a country for services performed during a period of violation does not qualify as foreign earned income. Your housing expenses within that country (or outside that country for housing your spouse or dependents) while you are in violation of the law cannot be included in figuring your foreign housing amount.

Currently, the countries to which travel restrictions apply and the beginning dates of the restrictions are as follows:

Cuba—January 1, 1987
Iraq—August 2, 1990
Libya—January 1, 1987

The restrictions are still in effect in all three countries.

### Foreign Earned Income

The foreign earned income exclusion, the foreign housing exclusion, and the foreign housing deduction are based on foreign earned income. For this purpose, foreign earned income is income you receive for services you perform in a foreign country during a period your tax home is in a foreign country and during which you meet either the bona fide residence test or the physical presence test, discussed earlier.

Foreign earned income does not include the following amounts.

1.  The previously excluded value of meals and lodging furnished for the convenience of your employer.
2.  Pension or annuity payments including social security benefits (see "Pensions and Annuities," later).
3.  U.S. Government payments to its employees (see "U.S. Government Employees," later).
4.  Amounts included in your income because of your employer's contributions to a nonexempt employee trust or to a nonqualified annuity contract.
5.  Recaptured unallowable moving expenses (see "Moving Expenses" on page 91).

6. Payments received after the end of the tax year following the tax year in which you performed the services that earned the income.

Earned income is pay for personal services performed, such as wages, salaries, or professional fees. The list that follows classifies many types of income into three categories. The column headed "Variable Income" lists income that may fall into either the earned income category, the unearned income category, or partly into both. For more information on earned and unearned income, see "Earned and Unearned Income," later.

Unearned income
Variable income
Earned income
Salaries and wages
Dividends
Business profits
Interest
Commissions
Capital gains
Royalties
Bonuses
Gambling winnings
Rents
Professional fees
Tips
Alimony
Social security benefits
Pensions
Annuities

In addition to the types of earned income listed, certain noncash income and allowances or reimbursements are considered earned income. They must be included in the listing of earned income on Form 2555.

### Noncash Income

The fair market value of property or facilities provided to you by your employer in the form of lodging, meals, or use of a car is earned income.

### Allowances or Reimbursements

Earned income includes amounts paid to you as allowances or reimbursements for the following items:

Cost of living.
Overseas differential.
Family.
Education.
Home leave.
Quarters.
Moving (unless excluded from income as discussed later).

### Source of Earned Income

The source of your earned income is the place where you perform the services for which you received the income. Foreign earned income is income you receive for performing personal services in a foreign country. Where or how you are paid has no effect on the source of the income. For example, income you receive for work done in France is income from a foreign source even if the income is paid directly to your bank account in the United States and your employer is located in New York City.

If you receive a specific amount for work done in the United States, you must report that amount as U.S. source income. If you cannot determine how much is for work done in the United States, or for work done partly in the United States and partly in a foreign country, determine the amount of U.S. source income using the method that most correctly shows the proper source of your income.

In most cases you can make this determination on a time basis. U.S. source income is the amount that results from multiplying your total pay including allowances, reimbursements other than for foreign moves, and noncash fringe benefits by a fraction. The numerator (top number) is the number of days you worked within the United States. The denominator (bottom number) is the total number of days of work for which you were paid.

*Example*. You are a U.S. citizen, a bona fide resident of Country A, and working as a mining engineer. Your salary is $76,800 per year. You also receive a $6,000 cost of living allowance and a $6,000 education allowance. Your employment contract did not indicate that you were entitled to these allowances only while outside the United States. Your total pay is $88,800. You work a 5-day week, Monday through Friday. After subtracting your vacation, you have a total of 240 workdays in the year. You worked in the United States during the year for 6 weeks (30 workdays). The following shows how to figure your wages paid for work done in the United States during the year.

Number of days worked in the United States during the year (30) ÷ Number of days of work during the year for which payment was made (240) X Total pay ($88,800) = $11,100.

Your U.S. source income is $11,100.

### Earned and Unearned Income

Earned income was defined earlier as pay for personal services performed. Some types of income are not easily identified as earned or unearned income. These types of income—specifically, income from sole proprietorships, partnerships, and corporations; stock options; pensions and annuities; royalties; rents; and fringe benefits—are further explained here. Income from sole proprietorships and partnerships generally is treated one way, and income from corporations is treated another way.

### Trade or Business— Sole Proprietorship or Partnership

Generally, income from a business in which capital investment is an important part of producing the income is unearned income. However, if you are a sole proprietor or partner and your personal services are also an important part of producing the income, part

of the income will be treated as your pay (earned income).

The amount treated as your pay cannot be more than the smaller of:

1. The value of your personal services to the business, or
2. If there are net profits, 30% of your share of the net profits of the business.

*Example 1*. You are a U.S. citizen and meet the bona fide residence test. You invest in a partnership based in Italy that is engaged solely in selling merchandise outside the United States. You perform no services for the partnership. At the end of the tax year, your share of the net profits is $80,000. The entire $80,000 is unearned income.

*Example 2*. Assume that in Example 1 you spend time operating the business. Your share of the net profits is $80,000; 30% of your share of the profits is $24,000. If the value of your services for the year is $15,000, your earned income is limited to the value of your services, $15,000.

### No Net Profits

If you have no net profits, the part of your gross profit that represents a reasonable allowance for personal services actually performed is considered earned income. Because you do not have a net profit, the 30% limit does not apply.

If capital is not an income-producing factor and personal services produce the business income, the 30% rule does not apply. The entire amount of business income is earned income.

*Example*. You and Lou Green are management consultants and operate as equal partners in performing services outside the United States. Because capital is not an income-producing factor, all the income from the partnership is considered earned income.

### Trade or Business—Corporation

Income from a corporation is not treated the same as income from a sole proprietorship or partnership. The salary you receive from a corporation is earned income only if it represents a reasonable allowance as compensation for work you do for the corporation. Any amount over what is considered a reasonable salary is unearned income.

*Example 1.* You are a U.S. citizen and an officer and stockholder of a corporation in Canada. You perform no work or service of any kind for the corporation. During the tax year you receive a $10,000 "salary" from the corporation. The $10,000 clearly is not for personal services and is unearned income.

*Example 2.* You are a U.S. citizen and devote full time as secretary-treasurer of your corporation. During the tax year you receive $100,000 as salary from the corporation. If $80,000 is a reasonable allowance as pay for the work you did, then $80,000 is earned income.

### Stock Options

You may have earned income if you disposed of stock that you got by exercising a stock option granted to you under an employee stock purchase plan.

If your gain on the disposition of option stock is treated as capital gain, your gain is unearned income.

However, if you disposed of the stock less than 2 years after you were granted the option or less than 1 year after you got the stock, part of the gain on the disposition may be earned income. It is considered received in the year you disposed of the stock and earned in the year you performed the services for which you were granted the option. Any part of the earned income that is due to work you did outside the United States is foreign earned income.

See Publication 525, *Taxable and Nontaxable Income,* for a discussion of treatment of stock options.

### Pensions and Annuities

For purposes of the foreign earned income exclusion, the foreign housing exclusion, and the foreign housing deduction, amounts received as pensions or annuities are unearned income.

### Royalties

Royalties from the leasing of oil and mineral lands and patents generally are a form of rent or dividends and are unearned income.

Royalties received by a writer are earned income if they are received:

1. For the transfer of property rights of the writer in the writer's product, or
2. Under a contract to write a book or series of articles.

### Rental Income

Generally, rental income is unearned income. If you perform personal services in connection with the production of rent, up to 30% of your net rental income can be considered earned income.

*Example.* Larry Smith, a U.S. citizen living in France, owns and operates a rooming house in Paris. If he is operating the rooming house as a business that requires capital and personal services, he can consider up to 30% of net rental income as earned income. On the other hand, if he just owns the rooming house and performs no personal services connected with its operation, except perhaps making minor repairs and collecting rents, none of his net income from the house is considered earned income. It is all unearned income.

### Income of an Artist

Income you receive from the sale of paintings is earned income if you painted the pictures yourself.

### Use of Employer's Property or Facilities

If you receive fringe benefits in the form of the right to use your employer's property or facilities, you must add the fair market value of that right to your pay. Fair market value is the price at which the property would change hands between a willing buyer and a willing seller, neither being required to buy or sell, and both having reasonable knowledge of all the necessary facts.

*Example.* You are privately employed and live in Japan all year. You are paid a salary of $6,000 a month. You live rent-free in a house provided by your employer that has a fair rental value of $3,000 a month. The house is not provided for your employer's convenience. You report on the calendar year, cash basis. You received $72,000 salary from foreign sources plus $36,000 fair rental value of the house, or a total of $108,000 of earned income.

### Reimbursement of Employee Expenses

If you are reimbursed under an accountable plan (defined below) for expenses you incur on your employer's behalf and you have adequately accounted to your employer for the expenses, do not include the reimbursement for those expenses in your earned income.

The expenses for which you are reimbursed are not considered allocable (related) to your earned income. If expenses and reimbursement are equal, there is nothing to allocate to excluded income. If expenses are more than the reimbursement, the unreimbursed expenses are considered to have been incurred in producing earned income and must be divided between your excluded and included income in determining the amount of unreimbursed expenses you can deduct. (See Chapter 10.) If the reimbursement is more than the expenses, no expenses remain to be divided between excluded and included income and the excess must be included in earned income.

These rules do not apply to straight-commission salespersons or other individuals who are employees and have arrangements with their employers under which, for withholding tax purposes, their employers consider a percentage of the commissions to be attributable to the expenses of the employees and do not withhold taxes on that percentage.

### Accountable Plan

An accountable plan is a reimbursement or allowance arrangement that includes all three of the following rules.

1. The expenses covered under the plan must have a business connection.
2. The employee must adequately account to the employer for these expenses within a reasonable period of time.
3. The employee must return any excess reimbursement or allowance within a reasonable period of time.

### Reimbursement of Moving Expenses

Earned income may include reimbursement of moving expenses. You must include as earned income:

1. Any reimbursements of, or payments for, nondeductible moving expenses;
2. Reimbursements that are more than your deductible expenses and that you do not return to your employer;
3. Any reimbursements made (or treated as made) under a nonaccountable plan (any plan that does not meet the rules listed above for an accountable plan), even if they are for deductible expenses; and
4. Any reimbursement of moving expenses you deducted in an earlier year.

This section discusses reimbursements that must be included in earned income. Publication 521, *Moving Expenses*, discusses additional rules that apply to moving expense deductions and reimbursements.

The rules for determining when the reimbursement is considered earned or where the reimbursement is considered earned may differ somewhat from the general rules previously discussed.

Although you receive the reimbursement in one tax year, it may be considered earned for services performed, or to be performed, in another tax year. You must report the reimbursement as income on your return in the year you receive it, even if it is considered earned during a different year.

### Move from U.S. to Foreign Country

If you move from the United States to a foreign country, your moving expense reimbursement is considered pay for future services to be performed at the new location. The reimbursement is considered earned solely in the year of the move if your tax home is in a foreign country and you qualify under the bona fide residence test or physical presence test for at least 120 days during that tax year.

If you do not qualify under either test for 120 days during the year of the move, the reimbursement is considered earned in the year of the move and the year following the year of the move. To figure the amount earned in the year of the move, multiply the reimbursement by a fraction. The numerator (top number) is the number of days in your qualifying period that fall within the year of the move, and the denominator (bottom number) is the total number of days in the year of the move.

The difference between the total reimbursement and the amount considered earned in the year of the move is the amount considered earned in the year following the year of the move. The part earned in each year is figured as shown in the following example.

*Example.* You are a U.S. citizen working in the United States. You were told in October of last year that you were being transferred to a foreign country. You arrived in the foreign country on December 15 of last year, and you qualify as a bona fide resident for the remainder of last year and all of this year. Your employer reimburses you $2,000 in January of this year for the part of the moving expense that you were not allowed to deduct. Because you did not qualify as a bona fide resident for at least 120 days last year (the year of the move), the reimbursement is considered pay for services performed in the foreign country for both last year and this year.

You figure the part of the moving expense reimbursement for services performed in the foreign country last year by multiplying the total reimbursement by a fraction. The fraction is the number of days during which you were a bona fide resident during the year of the move divided by 365 (366 if it was a leap year). The remaining part of the reimbursement is for services performed in the foreign country this year.

This computation is used only to determine when the reimbursement is considered earned. You would report the amount you include in income in this tax year, the year you received it.

### Move Between Foreign Countries

If you move between foreign countries and you qualify for at least 120 days during the tax year under the bona fide residence test or the physical presence test, the moving expense reimbursement that you must include in income is considered earned in the tax year of the move.

### Move to U.S.

If you move to the United States, the moving expense reimbursement that you must include in income is generally considered to be U.S. source income.

However, if under either an agreement between you and your employer or a statement of company policy that is reduced to writing before your move to the foreign country, your employer will reimburse you for your move back to the United States regardless of whether you continue to work for the employer, the includible reimbursement is considered compensation for past services performed in the foreign country. The includible reimbursement is considered earned in the tax year of the move if you qualify under the bona fide residence test or the physical presence test for at least 120 days during that tax year. Otherwise, you treat the includible reimbursement as received for services performed in the foreign country in the year of the move and the year immediately before the year of the move.

See the discussion under "Move from U.S." to foreign country (earlier) to figure the amount of the includible reimbursement considered earned in the year of the move. The amount earned in the year before the year of the move is the difference between the total includible reimbursement and the amount earned in the year of the move.

*Example.* You are a U.S. citizen employed in a foreign country. You retired from employment with your employer on March 31 of last year, and returned to the United States after having been a bona fide resident of the foreign country for several years. A written agreement with your employer entered into before you went abroad provided that you would be reimbursed for your move back to the United States.

In April of last year, your former employer reimbursed you $2,000 for the part of the cost of your move back to the United States that you were not allowed to deduct. Because you were not a bona fide resident for at least 120 days last year (the year of the move), the includible reimbursement is considered pay for services performed in the foreign country for both last year and the year before last.

You figure the part of the moving expense reimbursement for services performed in the foreign country last year by multiplying the total includible reimbursement by a fraction. The fraction is the number of days of foreign residence during the year (90) divided by the number of days in the year (365 or 366). The remaining part of the includible reimbursement is for services performed in the foreign country the year before last. You report the amount of the includible reimbursement on your Form 1040 for last year, the tax year you received it.

In this example, if you qualify to exclude income under the physical presence test instead of the bona fide residence test for last year, you may have had more than 120 qualifying days in the year of the move because you can choose the 12-month qualifying period that is most advantageous to you. (See "Physical Presence Test," later under "Part-Year Exclusion.") If so, the moving expense reimbursement would be considered earned entirely in the year of the move (last year).

### Storage Expense Reimbursements

If you are reimbursed for storage expenses, the reimbursement is for services you perform during the period you are in the foreign country.

## U.S. Government Employees

For purposes of the foreign earned income exclusion and the foreign housing exclusion or deduction, foreign earned income does not include any amounts paid by the United States or any of its agencies to its employees. Payments to employees of nonappropriated fund activities are not foreign earned income. Nonappropriated fund activities include the following employers.

1. Armed forces post exchanges.
2. Officers' and enlisted personnel clubs.
3. Post and station theaters.
4. Embassy commissaries.

Amounts paid by the United States or its agencies to persons who are not their employees may qualify for exclusion or deduction.

If you are a U.S. Government employee paid by a U.S. agency that assigned you to a foreign government to perform specific services for which the agency is reimbursed by the foreign government, your pay is from the U.S. Government and does not qualify for the exclusion or deduction.

If you have questions about whether you are an employee or an independent contractor, get Publication 15-A, *Employer's Supplemental Tax Guide.*

### Panama Canal Commission

U.S. employees of the Panama Canal Commission are employees of a U.S.

Government agency and are not eligible for the foreign earned income exclusion on their salaries from that source.

Furthermore, no provision of the Panama Canal Treaty or Agreement exempts their income from U.S. taxation.

Employees of the Panama Canal Commission and civilian employees of the Defense Department of the United States stationed in Panama can exclude certain foreign-area and cost-of-living allowances. See Publication 516, *U.S. Government Civilian Employees Stationed Abroad*, for more information.

These employees cannot exclude any overseas tropical differential they receive.

### American Institute in Taiwan

Amounts paid by the American Institute in Taiwan are not considered foreign earned income for purposes of the exclusion of foreign earned income or the exclusion or deduction of foreign housing amounts. If you are an employee of the American Institute in Taiwan, allowances you receive are exempt from U.S. tax up to the amount that equals tax-exempt allowances received by civilian employees of the U.S. Government.

### Allowances

Cost-of-living and foreign-area allowances paid under certain Acts of Congress to U.S. civilian officers and employees stationed in Alaska and Hawaii or elsewhere outside the 48 contiguous states and the District of Columbia can be excluded from gross income. See Publication 516 for more information. Post differentials are wages that must be included in gross income, regardless of the Act of Congress under which they are paid.

## Exclusion of Meals and Lodging

You do not include in your income the value of meals and lodging provided to you and your family by your employer at no charge if the following conditions are met:

1. The meals are:
   —Furnished on the business premises of your employer, and
   —Furnished for the convenience of your employer.
2. The lodging is:
   —Furnished on the business premises of your employer,
   —Furnished for the convenience of your employer, and
   —A condition of your employment. (You are required to accept it).

Amounts you do not include in income because of these rules are not foreign earned income.

### Family

Your family, for this purpose, includes only your spouse and your dependents.

### Lodging

The value of lodging includes the cost of heat, electricity, gas, water, sewer service, and similar items needed to make the lodging fit to live in.

### Business Premises of Employer

Generally, the business premises of your employer are wherever you work. For example, if you work as a housekeeper, meals and lodging provided in your employer's home are provided on the business premises of your employer. Similarly, meals provided to cowhands while herding cattle on land leased or owned by their employer are considered provided on the premises of their employer.

### Convenience of Employer

Whether meals or lodging are provided for your employer's convenience must be determined from all the facts. Meals or lodging provided to you and your family by your employer will be considered provided for your employer's convenience if there is a good business reason for providing the meals or lodging, other than to give you more pay.

If your employer has a good business reason for providing the meals or lodging, do not include their value in your income, even though your employer may also intend them as part of your pay. You can exclude the value of meals or lodging from your income even if a law or your employment contract says that they are provided as compensation.

On the other hand, if meals or lodging are provided to you or your family by your employer as a means of giving you more pay, and there is no other business reason for providing them, their value is extra income to you.

### Condition of Employment

Lodging is provided as a condition of employment if you must accept the lodging to properly carry out the duties of your job. You must accept lodging to properly carry out your duties if, for example, you must be available for duty at all times.

### Foreign Camps

If you are provided lodging by or for your employer in a camp located in a foreign country, the camp is considered to be part of your employer's business premises. For this purpose, a camp is lodging that is:

1. Provided for your employer's convenience because the place where you work is in a remote area where satisfactory housing is not available to you on the open market within a reasonable commuting distance,
2. Located as close as reasonably possible in the area where you render services, and
3. Provided in a common area or enclave that is not available to the general public for lodging or accommodations and that normally houses at least ten employees.

### Foreign Earned Income Exclusion

If your tax home is in a foreign country and you meet the bona fide residence test or the physical presence test, you can choose to exclude from your income a limited amount of your foreign earned income. Foreign earned income is defined earlier. You cannot deduct expenses directly connected with the earning of excluded income. (See Chapter 10.)

You can also choose to exclude from your income a foreign housing amount. This is explained later. If you choose to exclude a foreign housing amount, you must figure the foreign housing exclusion first. Your foreign earned income exclusion is limited to your foreign earned income minus your foreign housing exclusion.

### Limit on Excludable Amount

You may be able to exclude up to $74,000 of income earned. (See Table 4.2 for the maximum amount excludable for other years.)

---

### TABLE 4.2
The maximum amount you can exclude depends on the calendar year.

| YEAR | MAXIMUM EXCLUDABLE AMOUNT |
|------|---------------------------|
| 1997 and earlier | $70,000 |
| 1998 | $72,000 |
| 1999 | $74,000 |
| 2000 | $76,000 |
| 2001 | $78,000 |
| 2002 and later | $80,000 |

---

### Limits
Currently, you cannot exclude more than the smaller of:

1. $74,000, or
2. Your foreign earned income (discussed earlier) for the tax year minus your foreign housing exclusion (discussed later).

If both you and your spouse work abroad

and you each meet either the bona fide residence test or the physical presence test, you can each choose the foreign earned income exclusion. It is possible for a married couple together to exclude as much as $148,000.

If you perform services one year but do not get paid for those services until the following year, the income is generally considered earned in the year you performed the services. If you report your income on the cash basis, you report the income on your return for the year you receive it. You can exclude as much of the income in the year you receive it as you could have excluded in the year you performed the services had you received the income that year.

*Example.* You qualify as a bona fide resident of a foreign country for all of last year and this year. You report your income on the cash basis. You received $65,000 last year for services you performed last year in the foreign country. You can exclude all of the $65,000.

This year you will receive $85,000: $10,000 for services performed in the foreign country last year and $75,000 for services performed in the foreign country this year. You can exclude $7,000 of the $10,000 received for services performed last year. This is the $72,000 maximum exclusion allowable last year minus the $65,000 you excluded last year. You must include the remaining $3,000 in income (this year) because you could not have excluded that income last year had you received it then. You can also exclude $74,000 of the $75,000 received for services performed during this year.

Your total foreign earned income excluded on your return for this year would be $81,000 ($7,000 attributable to last year and $74,000 attributable to this year). You would have $4,000 of includible income.

### Year-End Payroll Period

There is an exception to the rule that you exclude income in the year you earn it. If you are a cash basis taxpayer, a salary or wage payment that you receive after the end of the tax year in which you perform the services is considered earned entirely in the year you receive it if all four of the following apply:

1. The period for which the payment is made is a normal payroll period of your employer that regularly applies to you.
2. The payroll period includes the last day of your tax year.
3. The payroll period is not longer than 16 days.
4. The payday comes at the same time in relation to the payroll period that it would normally come, and it comes before the end of the next payroll period.

### Income Earned Over More than 1 Year

Regardless of when you actually receive income, you must credit it to the tax year in which you earned it in figuring your excludable amount for that year. For example, a bonus that you receive in 1 year may be based on services you performed over several tax years. You determine the amount of the bonus that is considered earned in a particular tax year by dividing the bonus by the number of calendar months in the period when you performed the services that resulted in the bonus and then multiplying the result by the number of months you performed these services during the tax year. This is the amount that is subject to the exclusion limit for that tax year.

### Income Received More Than 1 Year After It Was Earned

You cannot exclude income you receive after the end of the tax year following the tax year in which you perform the services that earned it.

*Example.* You qualify as a bona fide resident of a foreign country for 1997, 1998, and 1999. You report your income on the cash basis. You received $65,000 for 1997 and $70,000 for 1998 for services performed in the foreign country. You excluded $65,000 on your

1997 federal income tax return and $70,000 for your 1998 return.

In 1999 you receive $85,000; $75,000 for services performed in the foreign country during 1999, and $5,000 for services performed in the foreign country in 1997. You cannot exclude any of the $5,000 received for services performed in 1997 because you received it after the year following the year in which you earned it. You must include the $5,000 in income. You can exclude $74,000 of the $75,000 received for services performed in 1999.

### Community Income

The maximum exclusion applies individually to the earnings of a husband and wife. Ignore any community property laws when you figure your limit on the foreign earned income exclusion.

### Part-Year Exclusion

If you qualify under either the bona fide residence test or the physical presence test for only part of the tax year, you must adjust the maximum limit based on the number of qualifying days in your tax year. The number of qualifying days in your tax year is the number of days within the period on which you both have your tax home in a foreign country and meet either test.

For this purpose, you can count as qualifying days all days within a period of 12 consecutive months once you are physically present and have your tax home in a foreign country for 330 full days. To figure your maximum exclusion, multiply the maximum excludable amount for the year by the number of your qualifying days in the year, and then divide the result by the number of days in your tax year.

*Example.* You report your income on the calendar-year basis, and you qualified under the bona fide residence test for 75 days in 1999. You can exclude a maximum of 75/365 of $74,000, or $15,205, of your foreign earned income for 1999. If you qualify under the

bona fide residence test for all of 2000, you can exclude your foreign earned income up to the full $76,000 limit.

### Physical Presence Test

Under the physical presence test, a 12-month period can be any period of 12 consecutive months that includes 330 full days. If you qualify under the physical presence test for part of a tax year, it is important to carefully choose the 12-month period that will allow the maximum exclusion for that year.

*Example.* You are physically present and have your tax home in a foreign country for a 16-month period from June 1, 1998, through September 30, 1999, except for 15 days in December 1998 that you spend on vacation in the United States. You figure the maximum exclusion for 1998 as follows:

1. Beginning with June 1, 1998, count forward 330 full days (disregarding the 15 days in the United States). The 330th day, May 11, 1999, is the last day of a 12-month period.
2. Count backward 12 months from May 11, 1999, to find the first day of this 12-month period, May 12, 1998. This 12-month period runs from May 12, 1998, through May 11, 1999.
3. Count the total days during 1998 that fall within this 12-month period. This is 234 days (May 12, 1998–December 31, 1998).
4. Multiply $72,000 by the fraction 234/365 to find your maximum exclusion for 1998 ($46,159).

You figure the maximum exclusion for 1999 in the opposite manner:

1. Beginning with your last full day, September 30, 1999, count backward 330 full days (disregarding the 15 days in the United States). That day, October 21, 1998, is the first day of a 12-month period.
2. Count forward 12 months from October

21, 1998, to find the last day of this 12-month period, October 20, 1999. This 12-month period runs from October 21, 1998, through October 20, 1999.

3. Count the total days during 1999 that fall within this 12-month period. This is 293 days (January 1, 1999—October 20, 1999).

4. Multiply $74,000, the maximum limit, by the fraction 293/365 to find your maximum exclusion for 1999 ($59,402).

These are limits on the amount you can exclude. You can never exclude more pay than you actually earned during your qualifying period.

### Choosing the Exclusion

The foreign earned income exclusion is voluntary. You can separately choose the foreign earned income exclusion and the foreign housing exclusion by completing the appropriate parts of Form 2555. Your initial choice of the exclusions on Form 2555 or Form 2555-EZ generally must be made with a timely filed return (including any extensions), a return amending a timely filed return, or a late-filed return filed within 1 year from the original due date of the return (determined without regard to any extensions).

### *Date a Return Is Considered to Be Filed*

If a return is delivered to Internal Revenue Service by:

- The U.S. mail with a U.S. postmark, or
- A designated delivery service,

the return is considered to have been filed on or before the due date if it is postmarked or dated by the specified delivery service on or before that date. If a return is not timely filed, the postmark or date mark of the designated delivery service date is not considered. A return postmarked or date marked after the due date is not considered to be filed until it is received by IRS.

You can use certain private delivery services designated by the IRS to meet the "timely mailing as timely filing/paying" rule for tax returns and payments. The IRS publishes a list of the designated private delivery services in September of each year.

You can choose the exclusion on a return filed after the periods described above provided you owe no federal income tax after taking into account the exclusion. If you owe federal income tax after taking into account the exclusion, you can choose the exclusion on a return filed after the periods described above provided you file before IRS discovers that you failed to choose the exclusion. You must type or legibly print at the top of the first page of the Form 1040 "FILED PURSUANT TO SECTION 1.911-7(a)(2)(i)(D)." If you owe federal income tax after taking into account the foreign earned income exclusion and the IRS discovered that you failed to choose the exclusion, you must request a private letter ruling under Revenue Procedure 92-85 (as modified by Revenue Procedure 93-28).

Revenue procedures are published in the *Internal Revenue Bulletin* (*I.R.B.*) and in the *Cumulative Bulletin* (*C.B.*), which are volumes containing official matters of the Internal Revenue Service. You can buy the *C.B.* containing a particular revenue procedure from the Superintendent of Documents, U.S. Government Printing Office, Washington, D.C. 20402.

You may also be able to choose the foreign earned income exclusion by completing Form 2555-EZ.

Once you choose to exclude your foreign earned income or housing amount, that choice remains in effect for that year and all later years unless you revoke it.

### *Revocation*

You can revoke your choice for any tax year. You do this by attaching a statement that you are revoking one or more previously made choices to the return or amended return for the first year that you do not wish to claim the exclusion(s). You must specify which choice(s) you are revoking. You must revoke separately a choice to exclude foreign earned income and a choice to exclude foreign housing amounts.

If you revoked a choice and within 5 tax years again wish to choose the same exclusion, you must apply for IRS approval. You do this by requesting a ruling from the Internal Revenue Service.

Mail your request for a ruling in duplicate to:

Associate Chief Counsel (International)
Internal Revenue Service
CC:DOM:CORP:TSS
P.O. Box 7604
Ben Franklin Station
Washington, D.C. 20044.

Because requesting a ruling can be complex, you may need professional help. Also, the IRS charges a fee for issuing these rulings. For more information, see Revenue Procedure 99-1, which is published in *Internal Revenue Bulletin* No. 1999-1.

In deciding whether to give approval, the IRS will consider any facts and circumstances that may be relevant. These may include a period of residence in the United States, a move from one foreign country to another foreign country with different tax rates, a substantial change in the tax laws of the foreign country of residence or physical presence, and a change of employer.

### Foreign Tax Credit

Once you choose to exclude either foreign earned income or foreign housing costs, you cannot take a foreign tax credit for taxes on income you can exclude. If you do take the credit, one or both of the choices may be considered revoked. See "Credit for Foreign Income Taxes" in Chapter 10 for more information.

### Earned Income Credit

You will not qualify for the earned income credit if you claim the foreign earned income exclusion, the foreign housing exclusion, or the foreign housing deduction for the year. For

more information on this credit, see Publication 596.

### Foreign Housing Exclusion or Deduction

In addition to the foreign earned income exclusion, you can also claim an exclusion or a deduction from gross income for your housing amount if your tax home is in a foreign country and you qualify under either the bona fide residence test or the physical presence test.

The housing exclusion applies only to amounts considered paid for with employer-provided amounts. The housing deduction applies only to amounts paid for with self-employment earnings.

If you are married and you and your spouse each qualifies under one of the tests, see "Married Couples Living Apart" (page 102).

### Housing Amount

Your housing amount is the total of your housing expenses for the year minus a base amount.

### Base Amount

The base amount is 16% of the annual salary of a GS-14, step 1, U.S. Government employee, figured on a daily basis, times the number of days during the year that you meet the bona fide residence test or the physical presence test. The annual salary is determined on January 1 of the year in which your tax year begins.

On January 1, 1999, the GS-14 salary was $61,656 per year; 16% of this amount comes to $9,865 or $27.03 per day. To figure your base amount if you are a calendar-year taxpayer, multiply $27.03 by the number of your qualifying days during 1999 (see "Limit on Excludable Amount," page 95). Subtract the result from your total housing expenses for 1999 to find your housing amount.

*Example.* You qualify under the physical presence test for all of 1999. During the year, you spend $12,500 for your housing. Your housing amount is $12,500 minus $9,865, or $2,635.

### U.S. Government Allowance

You must reduce your housing amount by any U.S. Government allowances or similar nontaxable allowances intended to compensate you or your spouse for the expenses of housing during the period for which you claim a foreign housing exclusion or deduction.

### Housing Expenses

Housing expenses include your reasonable expenses paid or incurred for housing in a foreign country for you and (if they live with you) for your spouse and dependents.

Consider only housing expenses for the part of the tax year that your tax home is in a foreign country and that you meet either the bona fide residence test or the physical presence test.

Housing expenses include:

- Rent,
- The fair rental value of housing provided in kind by your employer,
- Repairs,
- Utilities (other than telephone charges),
- Real and personal property insurance,
- Nondeductible occupancy taxes,
- Nonrefundable fees for securing a leasehold,
- Rental of furniture and accessories, and
- Residential parking.

Housing expenses do not include:

- Expenses that are lavish or extravagant under the circumstances,
- Deductible interest and taxes (including deductible interest and taxes of a tenant-stockholder in a cooperative housing corporation),
- The cost of buying property, including principal payments on a mortgage,
- The cost of domestic labor (maids, gardeners, etc.),
- Pay television subscriptions,
- Improvements and other expenses that increase the value or appreciably prolong the life of property,
- Purchased furniture or accessories, or
- Depreciation or amortization of property or improvements.

### No Double Benefit

You cannot include in housing expenses any amounts that you exclude from gross income as meals or lodging provided for your employer's convenience on the business premises (see "Exclusion of Meals and Lodging," page 94) or that you deduct as moving expenses.

### Second Foreign Household

Ordinarily, if you maintain two foreign households, your reasonable foreign housing expenses include only costs for the household that bears the closer relationship (not necessarily geographic) to your tax home. However, if you maintain a second, separate household outside the United States for your spouse or dependents because living conditions near your tax home are dangerous, unhealthful, or otherwise adverse, include the expenses for the second household in your reasonable foreign housing expenses. You cannot include expenses for more than one second foreign household at the same time.

If you maintain two households and you exclude the value of one because it is provided by your employer, you can still include the expenses for the second household in figuring a foreign housing exclusion or deduction.

Adverse living conditions include a state of warfare or civil insurrection in the general area of your tax home and conditions under which it is not feasible to provide family housing (for example, if you must live on a construction site or drilling rig).

## Foreign Housing Exclusion

If you have no self-employment income, your entire housing amount is considered paid for with employer-provided amounts. This means that you can exclude (up to the limits) the entire amount.

Employer-provided amounts include any

amounts paid to you or paid or incurred on your behalf by your employer that are taxable foreign earned income (without regard to the foreign earned income exclusion) to you for the tax year. This includes:

1. Your salary,
2. Any reimbursement for housing expenses,
3. Amounts your employer pays to a third party for your housing,
4. The fair rental value of company-owned housing furnished to you unless that value is excluded from your income because it is provided for your employer's convenience,
5. Amounts paid to you by your employer as part of a tax equalization plan, and
6. Amounts paid to you or a third party by your employer for the education of your dependents.

Your only earnings that are not employer-provided amounts are earnings from self-employment.

### Choosing the Exclusion

You can choose the housing exclusion by completing the appropriate parts of Form 2555. Follow the rules explained earlier in "Choosing the Exclusion," under "Foreign Earned Income Exclusion." You cannot use Form 2555-EZ to claim the housing exclusion.

Your housing exclusion is the lesser of:

- That part of your housing amount paid for with employer-provided amounts, or
- Your foreign earned income.

If you choose the housing exclusion, you must figure it before figuring your foreign earned income exclusion. You cannot claim less than the full amount of the housing exclusion to which you are entitled.

### Foreign Tax Credit

Once you choose to exclude either foreign earned income or foreign housing costs, you cannot take a foreign tax credit for taxes on

income you can exclude. If you do take the credit, one or both of the choices may be considered revoked.

### Foreign Housing Deduction

If you have no self-employment income, you cannot take a foreign housing deduction.

How you figure your housing deduction depends on whether you have only self-employment income or both self-employment income and employer-provided income. In either case, the amount you can deduct is subject to the limit explained below.

### Self-Employed—No Employer-Provided Amounts

If none of your housing amount is considered paid for with employer-provided amounts, such as when all of your income is from self-employment, you can deduct your housing amount, subject to the limit below, in figuring your adjusted gross income.

Take the deduction by including it in the total on line 32 of Form 1040. Write the amount and "Form 2555" on the dotted line next to line 32.

### Self-Employed and Employer-Provided Amounts

If you are both an employee and a self-employed individual during the year, you can deduct part of your housing amount and exclude part of it. To find the part that you can take as a housing exclusion, multiply your housing amount by the employer-provided amounts (discussed earlier) and then divide the result by your foreign earned income. The balance of the housing amount can be deducted, subject to the limit below.

*Example.* Your housing amount for the year is $12,000. During the year, your total foreign earned income is $80,000, of which half ($40,000) is from self-employment and half is from your services as an employee. Half ($40,000/$80,000) of your housing amount ($12,000/2) is considered provided by your employer. You can exclude $6,000 as a housing exclusion. You can deduct the remaining $6,000 as a housing deduction subject to the following limit.

### Limit

Your housing deduction cannot be more than your foreign earned income minus the total of:

1. Your foreign earned income exclusion, plus
2. Your housing exclusion.

You can carry over to the next year any part of your housing deduction that is not allowed because of this limit.

### Carryover

You are allowed to carry over your excess housing deduction to the next year only. If you cannot deduct it in the next year, you cannot carry it over to any other year. You deduct the carryover in figuring adjusted gross income. The amount of carryover you can deduct is limited to your foreign earned income for the year of the carryover minus the total of your foreign earned income exclusion, housing exclusion, and housing deduction for that year.

## Married Couples Living Apart

If you and your spouse live apart and maintain separate households, you both may be able to claim the foreign housing exclusion or the foreign housing deduction. You can do this if you have different tax homes that are not within reasonable commuting distance of each other and neither spouse's residence is within reasonable commuting distance of the other spouse's tax home. Otherwise, only you or your spouse can exclude or deduct a housing amount.

If you both claim the housing exclusion or the housing deduction, neither of you can claim the expenses for a qualified second foreign household maintained for the other. If one of you qualifies for but does not claim the exclusion or the deduction, the other spouse can claim the expenses for a qualified second household maintained for the first spouse. This would usually result in a larger total housing exclusion or deduction since you would apply only one base amount against the combined housing expenses.

If you and your spouse live together, both of you claim a foreign housing exclusion or a foreign housing deduction, and you file a joint return, you can figure your housing amounts either separately or jointly. If you file separate returns, you must figure your housing amounts separately. In figuring your housing amounts separately, you can allocate your housing expenses between yourselves in any proportion you wish, but each spouse must use his or her full base amount.

In figuring your housing amount jointly, you can combine your housing expenses and figure one base amount. If you figure your housing amount jointly, only one spouse can claim the housing exclusion or housing deduction. Either spouse can claim the exclusion or deduction. However, if you and your spouse have different periods of residence or presence and the one with the shorter period of residence or presence claims the exclusion or deduction, you can claim as housing expenses only the expenses for that shorter period.

*Example.* Tom and Jane live together and file a joint return. Tom was a bona fide resident of, and had his tax home in, a foreign country from August 17, 1999, through December 31, 2000. Jane was a bona fide resident of, and had her tax home in, the same foreign country from September 15, 1999, through December 31, 2000.

During 1999 Tom received $75,000 of foreign earned income, and Jane earned and received $50,000 of foreign earned income. Tom paid $10,000 for housing expenses in 1999, of which $7,500 was for expenses incurred from September 15 through the end of the year. Jane paid $3,000 for housing expenses in 1999, all of which were incurred during her period of foreign residence.

Tom and Jane can choose to figure their housing amount jointly. If they do so, and Tom claims the housing exclusion, their housing expenses would be $13,000, and their base amount, using Tom's period of residence (Aug. 11–Dec. 31,1999), would be

$3,703.11 ($27.03 – 137 days). Tom's housing amount would be $9,296.89 ($13,000 – $3,703.11). If, instead, Jane claims the housing exclusion, their housing expenses would be limited to $10,500 ($7,500 + $3,000), and their base amount, using Jane's period of residence (Sept. 15–Dec. 31,1999), would be $2,919.24 ($27.03 – 108 days). Jane's housing amount would be $7,580.76 ($10,500 – $2,919.24).

If Tom and Jane choose to figure their housing amounts separately, then Tom's separate base amount would be $3,619.54 and Jane's separate base amount would be $2,853.36. They could divide their total $13,000 housing expenses between them in any proportion they wished.

### Housing Exclusion

Each spouse claiming a housing exclusion must figure separately the part of the housing amount that is attributable to employer-provided amounts, based on his or her separate foreign earned income.

# CHAPTER 10
## *Internal Revenue Service, Publication 54:*
### *Tax Guide for U.S. Citizens and Resident Aliens Abroad,*
# Part Four

### EXCLUSION VS. DEDUCTION

U.S. citizens and resident aliens living outside the United States generally are allowed the same deductions as citizens and residents living in the United States.

If you choose to exclude foreign earned income or housing amounts, you cannot deduct, exclude, or claim a credit for any item that can be allocated to or charged against the excluded amounts. This includes any expenses, losses, and other normally deductible items that are allocable to the excluded income. You can deduct only those expenses connected with earning includible income.

These rules apply only to items definitely related to the excluded earned income, and they do not apply to other items that are not definitely related to any particular type of gross income. These rules do not apply to items such as personal exemptions, qualified retirement contributions, alimony payments, charitable contributions, medical expenses, mortgage interest, or real estate taxes on your personal residence. For purposes of these rules, your housing deduction is not treated as allocable to your excluded income, but the deduction for self-employment tax is.

If you receive foreign earned income in a tax year after the year in which you earned it, you may have to file an amended return for the earlier year to properly adjust the amounts of deductions, credits, or exclusions allocable to your foreign earned income and housing exclusions.

*Example.* If you excluded all of your $72,000 foreign earned income in 1998, you would not have been able to claim any deductions allocable to that excluded income. If you then receive a bonus of $10,000 in 1999 for work you did abroad in 1998, you cannot exclude it because it exceeds the $72,000 foreign earned income exclusion limit in effect for 1998. (You have no housing exclusion.) But, you can file an amended return for 1998 to claim the 10/80 of your allocable deductions that are now allowable ($10,000 included foreign earned income over $80,000 total foreign earned income).

### Exemptions

You can claim an exemption for your nonresident alien spouse on your separate return, provided your spouse has no gross income for U.S. tax purposes and is not the dependent of another U.S. taxpayer.

You can also claim exemptions for dependents who qualify under all the dependency tests. The dependent must be a U.S. citizen or national, or must be a resident of the United States, Canada, or Mexico for some part of the calendar year in which your tax year begins.

### Social Security Number

You must include on your return the social security number of each dependent for whom you claim an exemption. To get a social security number for a dependent, apply at a social security office or U.S. consulate outside the United States. You must provide original or certified copies of documents to verify the dependent's age, identity, and citizenship and complete Form SS-5.

If your dependent is a nonresident alien who is not eligible to get a social security number, you must apply for an IRS Individual Taxpayer Identification Number (ITIN). To apply for an ITIN, file Form W-7 with the IRS. It usually takes 30 days to get an ITIN. Enter your dependent's ITIN wherever an SSN is requested on your tax return.

### Children

Children usually are citizens or residents of the same country as their parents. If you were a U.S. citizen when your child was born, your child may be a U.S. citizen. He or she may be a U.S. citizen even if the child's other parent is a nonresident alien, the child was born in a foreign country, and the child lives abroad with the other parent.

If you are a U.S. citizen living abroad and have a legally adopted child who is not a U.S. citizen or resident, you can claim an exemption for the child as a dependent if your home is the child's main home and the child is a member of your household for your entire tax year. For more information, see Publication 501.

## Contributions

If you make contributions directly to a foreign church or other foreign charitable organization, you cannot deduct the contributions (unless you make them to certain Canadian, Israeli, or Mexican organizations). However, you can deduct contributions to a U.S. organization that transfers funds to a charitable foreign organization if the U.S. organization controls the use of the funds by the foreign organization, or if the foreign organization is just an administrative arm of the U.S. organization.

Under income tax treaties, you can deduct contributions to certain Canadian, Israeli, and Mexican charitable organizations. These organizations must meet the qualifications that a U.S. charitable organization must meet under U.S. tax law. The organization can tell you whether it qualifies. If you are unable to get this information from the organization itself, contact IRS at the address below.

You cannot deduct more than the percentage limit on charitable contributions applied to your Canadian, Israeli, or Mexican source income. If you or a member of your family is enrolled at a Canadian college or university, the limit does not apply to gifts to that school. For additional information on the deduction of contributions to Canadian charities, see Publication 597.

For more information these treaty provisions, write to:

Internal Revenue Service
Assistant Commissioner (International)
Attn: OP:IN:D:CS
950 L'Enfant Plaza South, SW
Washington, D.C. 20024.

## Moving Expenses

If you moved to a new home because of your job or business, you may be able to deduct the expenses of your move. To be deductible, the moving expenses must have been paid or incurred in connection with starting work at a new job location.

### Requirements

You may be able to deduct moving expenses if you meet the following requirements.

### Distance

The distance from your new job location to your former home must be at least 50 miles more than the distance from your old job location to your former home. If you did not have an old job location, your new job location must be at least 50 miles from your former home.

### Time

You must work full time for at least 39 weeks during the first 12 months after you move. If you are self-employed, you must work full time for at least 39 weeks during the first 12 months AND for at least 78 weeks during the first 24 months after you move.

*Retirees*—You can deduct your allowable moving expenses if you move to the United States when you permanently retire if your principal place of work and former home were outside the United States and its possessions. You do not have to meet the time test. The other requirements must be met.

*Survivors*—You can deduct moving expenses for a move to a home in the United States if you are the spouse or dependent of a person whose principal place of work at the time of death was outside the United States or its possessions. The move must begin within 6 months after the decedent's death and must be from the decedent's former home outside the United States in which you lived with the decedent at the time of death. You are not required to meet the time test. The other requirements must be met.

### Closely Related to the Start of Work

Your move must be closely related, both in time and in place, to the start of work at your new job location.

Closely related in time—In general, moving expenses incurred within one year from the date you first reported to work at the new location are considered closely related in time to the start of work.

If you do not move within one year, you ordinarily cannot deduct the expenses unless you can show that circumstances existed that prevented the move within that time.

*Example.* Your family moved more than a year after you started work at a new location. Their move was delayed because you allowed your child to complete high school. You can deduct your allowable moving expenses.

Closely related in place—A move is generally considered closely related in place to the start of work if the distance from your new home to the new job location is not more than the distance from your former home to the new job location. A move that does not meet this requirement may qualify if you can show that:

1. A condition of employment requires you to live at your new home, or
2. You will spend less time or money commuting from your new home to your new job.

## Deductible Expenses

You can only deduct certain expenses.

### Reasonable Expenses

You can only deduct expenses that are reasonable for the circumstances of your move. The cost of traveling from your former home to your new one should be by the shortest, most direct route available by conventional transportation.

### Reimbursements

If you are reimbursed by your employer for allowable moving expenses, these reimbursements may have been excluded from your income. You cannot deduct moving expenses for which you were reimbursed by your employer unless the reimbursement was included in your income.

### Deductible Moving Expenses

Some of the moving expenses that you

may be able to deduct include the reasonable costs of:

1. Moving household goods and personal effects (including packing, crating, in-transit storage, and insurance) of both you and members of your household. For foreign moves, costs of moving household goods and personal effects include reasonable expenses of moving the items to and from storage and storing them while your new place of work abroad is your principal place of work.
2. Transportation and lodging for yourself and members of your household for one trip from your former home to your new home (including costs of getting passports).

### Members of Your Household

A member of your household includes anyone who has both your former and new home as his or her home. It does not include a tenant or employee unless that person is your dependent.

### Foreign Moves

A foreign move is a move in connection with the start of work at a new job location outside the United States and its possessions. A foreign move does not include a move back to the United States or its possessions.

### Allocation of Moving Expenses

Your deductible moving expenses must be incurred in connection with the start of your work at a new job location.

When your new place of work is in a foreign country, your moving expenses are directly connected with the income earned in that foreign country. If all or part of the income that you earn at the new location is excluded under the foreign earned income exclusion or the housing exclusion, the part of your moving expense that is allocable to the excluded income is not deductible.

Also, if you move from a foreign country to the United States and:

- You are reimbursed for your move by your employer:
- You are able to treat the reimbursement as compensation for services performed in the foreign country, and
- You choose to exclude your foreign earned income,

you cannot deduct the part of the moving expense that is related to the excluded income.

The moving expense is connected with earning the income (including reimbursements, as discussed in Chapter 9 under "Reimbursement of Moving Expenses," page 91) either entirely in the year of the move or in 2 years. It is connected with earning the income entirely in the year of the move if you qualify under the bona fide residence test or physical presence test for at least 120 days during that tax year.

If you do not qualify under either the bona fide residence test or the physical presence test for at least 120 days during the year of the move, the expense is connected with earning the income in 2 years. The moving expense is connected with the year of the move and the following year if the move is from the United States to a foreign country, or the year of the move and the preceding year if the move is from a foreign country to the United States.

To figure the amount of your moving expense that is allocable to your excluded foreign earned income (and not deductible), you must multiply your total moving expense deduction by a fraction. The numerator (top number) of the fraction is your total excluded foreign earned income and housing amounts for both years and the denominator (bottom number) of the fraction is the total foreign earned income for both years.

*Example.* You are transferred by your employer as of November 1, 1998, to a foreign country. Your tax home is in the foreign country, and you qualify as a bona fide resident for the entire tax year 1999. In 1998 you paid $6,000 for allowable moving expenses for your move from the United States to the foreign country. You were fully reimbursed (under a nonaccountable plan) for these expenses in the same year. The reimbursement is included in your income. Your only other income consists of $14,000 wages earned in 1998 after the date of your move, and $80,000 wages earned in the foreign country for the entire year 1999. You exclude the maximum amount under the foreign earned income exclusion and have no housing exclusion.

Because you did not meet the bona fide residence test for at least 120 days during 1998, the year of the move, the moving expenses are for services you performed in both 1998 and the following year, 1999. Your total foreign earned income for both years is $100,000, consisting of $14,000 wages for 1998, $80,000 wages for 1999, and $6,000 moving expense reimbursement for both years.

Of this total, $86,033 is excluded, consisting of the $74,000 full-year exclusion for 1999 and a $12,033 part-year exclusion for 1998 ($72,000 times the fraction of 61 qualifying bona fide residence days over 365 total days in the year). To find the part of your moving expenses that is not deductible, multiply your $6,000 total expenses by the fraction $86,033 over $100,000. The result, $5,162, is your nondeductible amount.

You must report the full amount of the moving expense reimbursement in the year in which you received the reimbursement. In the preceding example, this year was 1999. You attribute the reimbursement to both 1998 and 1999 only to figure the amount of foreign earned income eligible for exclusion for each year.

### Move between Foreign Countries

If you move between foreign countries and you qualified under the bona fide residence test or the physical presence test for at least 120 days during the year of the move, your moving expense is allocable to the income earned in the year of the move.

### New Place of Work in U.S.

If your new place of work is in the United States, the deductible moving expenses are directly connected with the income earned in the United States. If you treat a reimbursement from your employer as foreign earned income (see the discussion in Chapter 9), you must allocate deductible moving expenses to foreign earned income.

### Storage Expenses

These expenses are attributable to services you perform during the year in which the storage expenses are incurred. The amount allocable to excluded income is not deductible.

### Recapture of Moving Expense Deduction

If your moving expense deduction is attributable to your foreign earnings in 2 years (the year of the move and the following year), you should request an extension of time to file your return for the year of the move until after the end of the following year. You should then have all the information needed to properly figure the moving expense deduction. See "Extensions" under "When to File and Pay," in Chapter 7.

If you do not request an extension, you should figure the part of the entire moving expense deduction that is disallowed. You do this by multiplying the moving expense by a fraction, the numerator (top number) of which is your excluded foreign earned income for the year of the move, and the denominator (bottom number) of which is your total foreign earned income for the year of the move. Once you know your foreign earnings and exclusion for the following year, you must either:

1. Adjust the moving expense deduction by filing an amended return for the year of the move, or
2. Recapture any additional unallowable amount as income on your return for the following year.

If, after you make the final computation,

you have an additional amount of allowable moving expense deduction, you can claim this only on an amended return for the year of the move. You cannot claim it on the return for the second year.

### Forms to File

Report your moving expenses on Form 3903. Report your moving expense deduction on line 26 of Form 1040. If you must reduce your moving expenses by the amount allocable to excluded income as explained later under "How to Report Deductions," attach a statement to your return showing how you figured this amount.

For more information about figuring moving expenses, see Publication 521.

### Individual Retirement Arrangements

Contributions to your individual retirement arrangements (IRAs) that are traditional IRAs or Roth IRAs are generally limited to the lesser of $2,000 or your compensation that is includible in your gross income for the tax year. For example, do not take into account compensation up to the amount of your foreign earned income exclusion and foreign housing exclusion, if any. Do not reduce your compensation by the foreign housing deduction.

If you are covered by an employer retirement plan at work, your deduction for your contributions to your traditional IRAs are generally limited based on your modified adjusted gross income. The adjusted gross income shown on your return is modified by figuring it without regard to the foreign earned income exclusion, the foreign housing exclusion, or the foreign housing deduction. Other modifications are also required. For more information on IRAs, see Publication 590.

### Taxes of Foreign Countries and U.S. Possessions

You can take either a credit or a deduction for income taxes imposed on you by a foreign country or a U.S. possession. Taken as a deduction, foreign income taxes reduce your

taxable income. Taken as a credit, foreign income taxes reduce your tax liability. You must treat all foreign income taxes in the same way. You generally cannot deduct some foreign income taxes and take a credit for others. See "Deduction for Other Foreign Taxes," later.

There is no specific rule that will let you choose the more advantageous method. If foreign income taxes were imposed at a high rate, and the proportion of foreign income to U.S. income is small, a lower final tax may result from taking the foreign income tax deduction. In any event, you should figure your tax liability both ways and then use the one that is better for you. In most cases, it is to your advantage to take foreign income taxes as a tax credit, which you subtract directly from your U.S. tax liability, rather than as a deduction in figuring taxable income.

You can make or change your choice within 10 years from the due date for filing your U.S. tax return for the tax year for which you make the claim.

The terms "foreign country" and "foreign taxes" also refer to possessions of the United States and the income taxes imposed by these possessions. See "Foreign Country," in Chapter 9 (page 81).

### Foreign Income Taxes

These are generally income taxes you pay to any foreign country.

The foreign income tax you can claim is the amount of foreign income tax that is the legal and actual tax liability you pay or accrue during the year. The amount you claim is not necessarily the amount of tax withheld by the foreign country. You cannot take a foreign tax credit or deduction for income tax you paid to a foreign country that would be refunded by the foreign country if you made a claim for refund.

### Subsidies

If a foreign country returns your foreign tax payments to you in the form of a subsidy, you cannot claim these payments as taxes qualified for the foreign tax credit. This rule applies to a subsidy provided by any means that is determined, directly or indirectly, by reference to the amount of tax, or to the base used to figure the tax.

Some ways of providing a subsidy are refunds, credits, deductions, payments, or discharges of obligations. The credit is also not allowed if the subsidy is given to a person related to you, or persons who participated in a transaction or a related transaction with you.

### Foreign Income Taxes on U.S. Return

Foreign income taxes can only be taken as a credit on Form 1116 or a deduction on Schedule A. These amounts cannot be included as withheld income taxes on Form 1040, line 57.

### Foreign Taxes Paid on Excluded Income

You cannot take a credit or deduction for foreign income taxes paid on income that is exempt from tax under the foreign earned income exclusion, the foreign housing exclusion, or the possession exclusion. If your wages are completely excluded, you cannot deduct or take a credit for any of the foreign taxes paid on these wages.

If only part of your wages is excluded, you cannot deduct or take a credit for the foreign income taxes allocable to the excluded part. You find the taxes allocable to your excluded wages by applying a fraction to the foreign taxes paid on foreign earned income received during the tax year. The numerator (top number) of the fraction is your excluded foreign earned income received during the tax year minus deductible expenses allocable to that income (not including the foreign housing deduction). The denominator (bottom number) of the fraction is your total foreign earned income received during the tax year minus all deductible expenses allocable to that income (including the foreign housing deduction).

If foreign law taxes both earned income and some other amount (for example, unearned income, earned income from U.S.

sources, or a type of income not subject to U.S. tax), and the taxes on the other amount cannot be segregated, the denominator of the fraction is the total amount of income subject to foreign tax minus deductible expenses allocable to that income.

If you take a foreign tax credit for tax on income you could have excluded under your choice to exclude foreign earned income or your choice to exclude foreign housing costs, one or both of the choices may be considered revoked.

### Credit for Foreign Income Taxes

If you take the foreign tax credit, you may have to file Form 1116 with Form 1040. Use Form 1116 to figure the amount of foreign tax paid or accrued that you can claim as a foreign tax credit. Do not include the amount of foreign tax paid or accrued as withheld federal income taxes on Form 1040, line 57.

### Limit

The foreign tax credit is limited to the part of your total U.S. tax that is in proportion to your taxable income from sources outside the United States compared to your total taxable income. The allowable foreign tax credit cannot be more than your actual foreign tax liability.

### Exemption from Limit

You will not be subject to this limit and will not have to file Form 1116 if you meet all three of the following requirements.

1. Your only foreign source income for the tax year is passive income (dividends, interest, royalties, etc.) that is reported to you on a payee statement (such as a Form 1099-Div or 1099-INT).
2. Your foreign taxes for the tax year that qualify for the credit are not more than $300 ($600 if filing a joint return) and are reported on a payee statement.
3. You elect this procedure for the tax year.

If you make this election, you cannot carry back or carry over any unused foreign tax to or from this tax year.

### Separate Limit

You must figure the limit on a separate basis with regard to each of the following categories of income (see the instructions for Form 1116).

- Passive income.
- High withholding tax interest.
- Financial services income.
- Shipping income.
- Certain dividends from a domestic international sales corporation (DISC) or former DISC.
- Certain distributions from a foreign sales corporation (FSC) or former FSC.
- Any lump-sum distributions from employer benefit plans for which the 5- or 10-year tax option is used to determine your tax.
- Section 901(j) income.
- Income re-sourced by treaty.
- All other income not included above (general limitation income).

### Figuring the Limit

In figuring taxable income in each income category, you take into account only the income that you must include in income on your federal income tax return. Do not take any excluded income into account.

To determine your taxable income in each category from sources outside the United States, deduct expenses and losses that are definitely related to that income.

Other expenses (such as itemized deductions or the standard deduction) not definitely related to specific items of income must be apportioned to the foreign income in each category by multiplying them by a fraction. The numerator (top number) of the fraction is your gross foreign income in the separate limit category. The denominator (bottom number) of the fraction is your gross income from all sources. For this purpose, gross income includes amounts that are otherwise exempt or excluded. You must use special rules for deducting interest expenses. For more information on allocating and apportioning your deductions, see Publication 514.

### Exemptions

Do not take the deduction for exemptions for yourself, your spouse, or your dependents in figuring taxable income for purposes of the limit.

### Recapture of Foreign Losses

If you have an overall foreign loss and the loss reduces your U.S. source income (resulting in a reduction of your U.S. tax liability), you must recapture the loss in later years when you have taxable income from foreign sources. This is done by treating a part of your taxable income from foreign sources in later years as U.S. source income. This reduces the numerator of the limiting fraction and the resulting foreign tax credit limit.

### Foreign Tax Credit Carryback and Carryover

The amount of foreign income tax not allowed as a credit because of the limit

More information on figuring the foreign tax credit can be found in Publication 514.

## Deduction for Foreign Income Taxes

Instead of taking the foreign tax credit, you can deduct foreign income taxes as an itemized deduction on Schedule A (Form 1040).

You can claim a deduction only for those foreign income taxes paid on income that is subject to U.S. tax. You cannot claim a deduction for foreign taxes paid on income you exclude under the foreign earned income or housing exclusions.

*Example.* You are a U.S. citizen and qualify to exclude your foreign earned income. Your excluded wages in Country X are $70,000 on which you paid income tax of $10,000. You received dividends from Country X of $2,000 on which you paid income tax of $600.

You can claim a deduction for the $600 tax payment because the dividends relating to it are subject to U.S. tax. Because the wages are exempt from U.S. tax, you cannot claim a deduction for the income tax of $10,000.

If only a part of your earnings are excluded, see the earlier discussion under Foreign taxes paid on excluded income.

### Deduction for Other Foreign Taxes

You can deduct real property taxes you pay that are imposed on you by a foreign country. You take this deduction on Schedule A (Form 1040). You cannot deduct other foreign taxes, such as personal property taxes, unless you incurred the expenses in a trade or business or in the production of income.

On the other hand, you generally can deduct personal property taxes when you pay them to U.S. possessions. But if you claim the possession exclusion, see Publication 570.

The deduction for foreign taxes other than foreign income taxes is not related to the foreign tax credit. You can take deductions for these miscellaneous foreign taxes and also claim the foreign tax credit for income taxes imposed by a foreign country.

# CHAPTER 11
## *Internal Revenue Service, Publication 54:*
## *Tax Guide for U.S. Citizens and Resident Aliens Abroad,*
# Part Five

## THE PURPOSE OF TAX TREATIES

The United States has tax treaties or conventions with many countries under which citizens and residents of the United States who are subject to taxes imposed by foreign countries are entitled to certain credits, deductions, exemptions, and reductions in the rate of taxes of those foreign countries. If a foreign country with which the United States has a treaty imposes a tax on you, you may be entitled to benefits under the treaty. (See Table 6-1 on page 118.)

Treaty benefits generally are available to residents of the United States. They generally are not available to U.S. citizens who do not reside in the United States. However, certain treaty benefits and safeguards, such as the nondiscrimination provisions, are available to U.S. citizens residing in the treaty countries. U.S. citizens residing in a foreign country may also be entitled to benefits under that country's tax treaties with third countries.

You should carefully examine the specific treaty articles that may apply to find if you are entitled to a tax credit, tax exemption, reduced rate of tax, or other treaty benefit or safeguard.

### Common Benefits

Some common tax treaty benefits are explained below. The credits, deductions, exemptions, reductions in rate, and other benefits provided by tax treaties are subject to conditions and restrictions that vary from one treaty to another. Also, benefits provided by certain treaties are not provided by others.

1. *Personal service income*. If you are a U.S. resident who is in a treaty country for a limited number of days in the tax year and you meet certain other requirements, any pay you receive for personal services performed in that country may be exempt from that country's income tax.
2. *Professors and teachers*. If you are a U.S. resident, pay you receive for the first 2 or 3 years that you are teaching or doing research in a treaty country may be exempt from that country's income tax.
3. *Students, trainees, and apprentices*. If you are a U.S. resident, amounts you receive from the United States for study, research, or business, professional and technical training may be exempt from a treaty country's income tax.

Some treaties exempt grants,

allowances, and awards received from governmental and certain nonprofit organizations. Also, under certain circumstances, a limited amount of pay received by students, trainees, and apprentices may be exempt from the income tax of many treaty countries.

4. *Pensions and annuities*. If you are a U.S. resident, any nongovernment pensions and annuities you receive may be exempt from the income tax of treaty countries.

    Most treaties contain separate provisions for exempting government pensions and annuities from treaty country income tax, and some treaties provide exemption from the treaty country's income tax for social security payments.

5. *Investment income*. If you are a U.S. resident, investment income, such as interest and dividends, that you receive from sources in a treaty country may be exempt from that country's income tax or taxed at a reduced rate.

    Several treaties provide exemption for capital gains (other than from sales of real property in most cases) if specified requirements are met.

6. *Tax credit provisions*. If you are a U.S. resident who receives income from or owns capital in a foreign country, you may be taxed on that income or capital by both the United States and the treaty country.

    Most treaties allow you to take a credit against or deduction from the treaty country's taxes based on the U.S. tax on the income.

7. *Nondiscrimination provisions*. Most U.S. tax treaties provide that the treaty country cannot discriminate by imposing more burdensome taxes on U.S. citizens who are residents of the treaty country than it imposes on its own citizens in the same circumstances.

8. *Saving clauses*. U.S. treaties contain saving clauses that provide that the treaties do not affect the U.S. taxation of its own citizens and residents. As a result, most of the treaty benefits and safeguards with reference to a treaty country's taxes are available only to U.S. citizens who are not residents of the treaty country and to U.S. residents who are not citizens of the treaty country.

    However, some treaties provide certain limited exceptions to saving clauses. It is important that you examine the applicable saving clause to determine if such an exception applies.

### Competent Authority Assistance

If you are a U.S. citizen or resident, you can request assistance from the U.S. competent authority if you think that the actions of the United States, a treaty country, or both cause or will cause a tax situation not intended by the treaty between the two countries. You should read any specific treaty articles, including the mutual agreement procedure article, that apply in your situation.

If your request provides a basis for competent authority assistance, the U.S. competent authority will consult with the treaty country competent authority on how to resolve the situation.

The U.S. competent authority cannot consider requests involving countries with which the United States does not have an applicable tax treaty.

It is important that you make your request for competent authority consideration as soon as you have been denied treaty benefits or the actions of both the United States and the foreign country have resulted in double taxation or will result in taxation not intended by the treaty.

In addition to a timely request for assistance, you should take the following measures to protect your right to the review of your case by the competent authorities.

1. File a timely protective claim for credit or refund of U.S. taxes on Form 1040X to preserve your right to a foreign tax credit if you do not qualify for the treaty benefit in question.

2. Take appropriate action under the procedures of the foreign country to avoid the lapse or termination of your right of appeal under the foreign country's income tax law.

Your request for competent authority consideration should be addressed to:

Internal Revenue Service
Assistant Commissioner (International)
Attn: OP:IN:I:T
950 L'Enfant Plaza South, SW
Washington, D.C. 20024

The request should contain all essential items of information including the following items:

- The facts from which the issue arises.
- The amounts of income and tax involved.
- A description of the issue and identification of the relevant treaty provisions.
- The respective positions taken by you and the foreign country.
- Copies of any protests, briefs, or other pertinent documents.

Additional details on the procedures for requesting competent authority assistance are included in Revenue Procedure 96-13, which is in Cumulative Bulletin 1996-1. You can obtain copies of this procedure by writing to:

Internal Revenue Service
Assistant Commissioner (International)
Attn: OP:IN:D:CS:HQ
950 L'Enfant Plaza South, SW
Washington, D.C. 20024.

### More Information on Treaties and Problems

You can get more information about the benefits and safeguards provided by U.S. tax treaties or information concerning double taxation problems by writing to the IRS Assistant Commissioner (International).

Publication 901 contains an explanation of treaty provisions that apply to amounts received by teachers, students, workers, and government employees and pensioners who are alien nonresidents or residents of the United States.

Since treaty provisions generally are reciprocal, you can usually substitute "United States" for the name of the treaty country whenever it appears, and vice versa when "U.S." appears in the treaty exemption discussions in Publication 901.

Publication 597 contains an explanation of a number of frequently used provisions of the United States–Canada income tax treaty.

### Obtaining Copies of Tax Treaties

Table 6-1, shown on the following page, lists those countries with which the United States has income tax treaties. This table is updated through December 31, 1999.

You can get complete information about treaty provisions from the taxing authority in the country from which you receive income or from the treaty itself. The text of some of the treaties can be obtained from:

Department of Treasury
Office of Public Liaison
1500 Pennsylvania Ave. NW—Rm. 4418
Washington, D.C. 20220.

If you have specific questions about a treaty, you can get this information from most Internal Revenue Service offices or from:

Internal Revenue Service
Attn: OP:IN:D:CS:HQ
950 L'Enfant Plaza South, SW
Washington, D.C. 20024.

### SERVICES AVAILABLE ONLY OUTSIDE THE UNITED STATES

During the filing period (January to mid-June), you can get the necessary federal tax forms and publications from U.S. Embassies and consulates.

Also during the filing season, the IRS conducts an overseas taxpayer assistance

Table 6-1. **Table of Tax Treaties** (Updated through December 31, 1999)

| Country | Official Text Symbol[1] | General Effective Date | Citation | Applicable Treasury Explanations or Treasury Decision (T.D.) |
|---|---|---|---|---|
| Australia | TIAS 10773 | Dec. 1, 1983 | 1986-2 C.B. 220 | 1986-2 C.B. 246 |
| Austria | TIAS | Jan. 1, 1999 | | |
| Barbados | TIAS 11090 | Jan. 1, 1984 | 1991-2 C.B. 436 | 1991-2 C.B. 466 |
| Protocol | TIAS | Jan. 1, 1994 | | |
| Belgium | TIAS 7463 | Jan. 1, 1971 | 1973-1 C.B. 619 | |
| Protocol | TIAS 11254 | Jan. 1, 1988 | | |
| Canada[2] | TIAS 11087 | Jan. 1, 1985 | 1986-2 C.B. 258 | 1987-2 C.B. 298 |
| Protocol | TIAS | Jan. 1, 1996 | | |
| China, People's Republic of | TIAS | Jan. 1, 1987 | 1988-1 C.B. 414 | 1988-1 C.B. 447 |
| Commonwealth of Independent States[3] | TIAS 8225 | Jan. 1, 1976 | 1976-2 C.B. 463 | 1976-2 C.B. 475 |
| Cyprus | TIAS 10965 | Jan. 1, 1986 | 1989-2 C.B. 280 | 1989-2 C.B. 314 |
| Czech Republic | TIAS | Jan. 1, 1993 | | |
| Denmark | TIAS 1854 | Jan. 1, 1948 | 1950-1 C.B. 77 | T.D. 5692, 1949-1 C.B. 104; T.D. 5777, 1950-1 C.B. 76 |
| Egypt | TIAS 10149 | Jan. 1, 1982 | 1982-1 C.B. 219 | 1982-1 C.B. 243 |
| Finland | TIAS | Jan. 1, 1991 | | |
| France | TIAS | Jan. 1, 1996 | | |
| Germany | TIAS | Jan. 1, 1990[4] | | |
| Greece | TIAS 2902 | Jan. 1, 1953 | 1958-2 C.B. 1054 | T.D. 6109, 1954-2 C.B. 638 |
| Hungary | TIAS 9560 | Jan. 1, 1980 | 1980-1 C.B. 333 | 1980-1 C.B. 354 |
| Iceland | TIAS 8151 | Jan. 1, 1976 | 1976-1 C.B. 442 | 1976-1 C.B. 456 |
| India | TIAS | Jan. 1, 1991 | | |
| Indonesia | TIAS 11593 | Jan. 1, 1990 | | |
| Ireland | TIAS | Jan. 1, 1998 | | |
| Israel | TIAS | Jan. 1, 1995 | | |
| Italy | TIAS 11064 | Jan. 1, 1985 | 1992-1 C.B. 442 | 1992-1 C.B. 473 |
| Jamaica | TIAS 10207 | Jan. 1, 1982 | 1982-1 C.B. 257 | 1982-1 C.B. 291 |
| Japan | TIAS 7365 | Jan. 1, 1973 | 1973-1 C.B. 630 | 1973-1 C.B. 653 |
| Kazakstan | TIAS | Jan. 1, 1996 | | |
| Korea, Republic of | TIAS 9506 | Jan. 1, 1980 | 1979-2 C.B. 435 | 1979-2 C.B. 458 |
| Luxembourg | TIAS 5726 | Jan. 1, 1964 | 1965-1 C.B. 615 | 1965-1 C.B. 642 |
| Mexico | TIAS | Jan. 1, 1994 | 1994-2 C.B. 424 | 1994-2 C.B. 489 |
| Protocol | TIAS | Oct. 26, 1995 | | |
| Morocco | TIAS 10195 | Jan. 1, 1981 | 1982-2 C.B. 405 | 1982-2 C.B. 427 |
| Netherlands | TIAS | Jan. 1, 1994 | | |
| New Zealand | TIAS 10772 | Nov. 2, 1983 | 1990-2 C.B. 274 | 1990-2 C.B. 303 |
| Norway | TIAS 7474 | Jan. 1, 1971 | 1973-1 C.B. 669 | 1973-1 C.B. 693 |
| Protocol | TIAS 10205 | Jan. 1, 1982 | 1982-2 C.B. 440 | 1982-2 C.B. 454 |
| Pakistan | TIAS 4232 | Jan. 1, 1959 | 1960-2 C.B. 646 | T.D. 6431, 1960-1 C.B. 755 |
| Philippines | TIAS 10417 | Jan. 1, 1983 | 1984-2 C.B. 384 | 1984-2 C.B. 412 |
| Poland | TIAS 8486 | Jan. 1, 1974 | 1977-1 C.B. 416 | 1977-1 C.B. 427 |
| Portugal | TIAS | Jan. 1, 1996 | | |
| Romania | TIAS 8228 | Jan. 1, 1974 | 1976-2 C.B. 492 | 1976-2 C.B. 504 |
| Russia | TIAS | Jan. 1, 1994 | | |
| Slovak Republic | TIAS | Jan. 1, 1993 | | |
| South Africa | TIAS | Jan. 1, 1998 | | |
| Spain | TIAS | Jan. 1, 1991 | | |
| Sweden | TIAS | Jan. 1, 1996 | | |
| Switzerland | TIAS | Jan. 1, 1998 | | |
| Thailand | TIAS | Jan. 1, 1998 | | |
| Trinidad and Tobago | TIAS 7047 | Jan. 1, 1970 | 1971-2 C.B. 479 | |
| Tunisia | TIAS | Jan. 1, 1990 | | |
| Turkey | TIAS | Jan. 1, 1998 | | |
| United Kingdom | TIAS 9682 | Jan. 1, 1975 | 1980-1 C.B. 394 | 1980-1 C.B. 455 |

[1] (TIAS) Treaties and Other International Act Series.

[2] Information on the treaty can be found in Publication 597, *Information on the United States Canada Income Tax Treaty*.

[3] The U.S. U.S.S.R. income tax treaty applies to the countries of Armenia, Azerbaijan, Belarus, Georgia, Kyrgyzstan, Moldova, Tajikistan, Turkmenistan, Ukraine, and Uzbekistan.

[4] The general effective date for the area that was the German Democratic Republic is January 1, 1991.

program. To find out if IRS personnel will be in your area, you should contact the consular office at the nearest U.S. Embassy.

### Phone

You can also call your nearest U.S. Embassy, consulate, or IRS office listed below to find out when and where assistance will be available. These IRS telephone numbers include the country and city codes required if you are outside the local dialing area.

Berlin, Germany (49) (30) 8305-1140
London, England (44) (207) 408-8077
Mexico City, Mexico (52) (5) 209-9100 (Ext. 3557)
Paris, France (33) (1) 4312-2555 (Ext. 1210)
Rome, Italy (39) (06) 4674-2560
Singapore (65) 476-9413
Tokyo, Japan (81) (3) 3224-5466

If you are in Guam, the Bahamas, U.S. Virgin Islands, or Puerto Rico, you can call the Puerto Rico call site at 1-800-829-1040 (toll free).

### Mail

For answers to technical or account questions, you can write to:

Internal Revenue Service
Assistant Commissioner (International)
Attn: OP:IN:D:CS:HQ
950 L'Enfant Plaza South, SW
Washington, D.C. 20024.

You can request Package 1040-7 for Overseas Filers, which contains special forms with instructions and Publication 54.

### TaxFax Service

Using the phone attached to your fax machine, you can receive forms and instructions by calling 202-874-5440. Follow the directions from the prompts. When you order forms, enter the catalog number for the form you need. The items you request will be faxed to you.

# CHAPTER 12
## *Protecting Your Nationality and Assets Abroad*

**PART I:**
*DUAL NATIONALITY*
(U.S. Department of State,
American Citizen Services)

The concept of dual nationality means that a person is a citizen of two countries at the same time. Each country has its own citizenship laws based on its own policy. Persons may have dual nationality by automatic operation of different laws rather than by choice. For example, a child born in a foreign country to U.S. citizen parents may be both a U.S. citizen and a citizen of the country of birth.

A U.S. citizen may acquire foreign citizenship by marriage, or a person naturalized as a U.S. citizen may not lose the citizenship of the country of birth. U.S. law does not mention dual nationality or require a person to choose one citizenship or another. Also, a person who is automatically granted another citizenship does not risk losing U.S. citizenship. However, a person who acquires a foreign citizenship by applying for it may lose U.S. citizenship. In order to lose U.S. citizenship, the law requires that the person must apply for the foreign citizenship voluntarily, by free choice, and with the intention to give up U.S. citizenship.

Intent can be shown by the persons statements or conduct. The U.S. Government recognizes that dual nationality exists but does not encourage it as a matter of policy because of the problems it may cause. Claims of other countries on dual national U.S. citizens may conflict with U.S. law, and dual nationality may limit U.S. Government efforts to assist citizens abroad. The country where a dual national is located generally has a stronger claim to that person's allegiance.

However, dual nationals owe allegiance to both the United States and the foreign country. They are required to obey the laws of both countries. Either country has the right to enforce its laws, particularly if the person later travels there. Most U.S. citizens, including dual nationals, must use a U.S. passport to enter and leave the United States. Dual nationals may also be required by the foreign country to use its passport to enter and leave that country. Use of the foreign passport does not endanger U.S. citizenship. Most countries permit a person to renounce or otherwise lose citizenship.

Information on losing foreign citizenship can be obtained from the foreign country's embassy and consulates in the United States. Americans can renounce U.S. citizenship in the proper form at U.S. embassies and consulates abroad.

## ADVICE ABOUT POSSIBLE LOSS OF U.S. CITIZENSHIP AND DUAL NATIONALITY

The Department of State is responsible for determining the citizenship status of a person located outside the United States or in connection with the application for a U.S. passport while in the United States.

### Potentially Expatriating Statutes

Section 349 of the Immigration and Nationality Act, as amended, states that U.S. citizens are subject to loss of citizenship if they perform certain acts voluntarily and with the intention to relinquish U.S. citizenship. Briefly stated, these acts include:

(1) obtaining naturalization in a foreign state (Sec. 349 (a) (1) INA);
(2) taking an oath, affirmation, or other formal declaration to a foreign state or its political subdivisions (Sec. 349 (a) (2) INA);
(3) entering or serving in the armed forces of a foreign state engaged in hostilities against the U.S. or serving as a commissioned or non-commissioned officer in the armed forces of a foreign state (Sec. 349 (a) (3) INA);
(4) accepting employment with a foreign government if (a) one has the nationality of that foreign state or (b) a declaration of allegiance is required in accepting the position (Sec. 349 (a) (4) INA);
(5) formally renouncing U.S. citizenship before a U.S. consular officer outside the United States (sec. 349 (a) (5) INA);
(6) formally renouncing U.S. citizenship within the U.S. (but only "in time of war") (Sec. 349 (a) (6) INA);
(7) conviction for an act of treason (Sec. 349 (a) (7) INA).

## ADMINISTRATIVE STANDARD OF EVIDENCE

As already noted, the actions listed above can cause loss of U.S. citizenship only if performed voluntarily and with the intention of relinquishing U.S. citizenship. The Department has a uniform administrative standard of evidence based on the premise that U.S. citizens intend to retain United States citizenship when they obtain naturalization in a foreign state, subscribe to routine declarations of allegiance to a foreign state, or accept non-policy level employment with a foreign government.

## DISPOSITION OF CASES WHEN ADMINISTRATIVE PREMISE IS APPLICABLE

In light of the administrative premise discussed above, a person who:

(1) is naturalized in a foreign country;
(2) takes a routine oath of allegiance or
(3) accepts non-policy level employment with a foreign government

and in so doing wishes to retain U.S. citizenship need not submit prior to the commission of a potentially expatriating act a statement or evidence of his or her intent to retain U.S. citizenship since such an intent will be presumed.

When, as the result of an individual's inquiry or an individual's application for registration or a passport it comes to the attention of a U.S. consular officer that a U.S. citizen has performed an act made potentially expatriating by Sections 349(a)(1), 349(a)(2), 349(a)(3), or 349(a)(4), the consular officer will simply ask the applicant if there was intent to relinquish U.S. citizenship when performing the act. If the answer is no, the consular officer will certify that it was not the person's intent to relinquish U.S. citizenship and, consequently, find that the person has retained U.S. citizenship.

## PERSONS WHO WISH TO RELINQUISH U.S. CITIZENSHIP

If the answer to the question regarding intent to relinquish citizenship is yes, the person concerned will be asked to complete a questionnaire to ascertain his or her intent toward U.S. citizenship. When the questionnaire is completed and the voluntary relinquishment statement is signed by the expatriate, the consular officer will proceed to prepare a certificate of loss of nationality. The certificate will be forwarded to the Department of State for consideration and, if appropriate, approval.

An individual who has performed any of the acts made potentially expatriating by statute who wishes to lose U.S. citizenship may do so by affirming in writing to a U.S. consular officer that the act was performed with an intent to relinquish U.S. citizenship. Of course, a person always has the option of seeking to formally renounce U.S. citizenship in accordance with Section 349 (a) (5) INA.

## DISPOSITION OF CASES WHEN ADMINISTRATIVE PREMISE IS INAPPLICABLE

The premise that a person intends to retain U.S. citizenship is not applicable when the individual:

(1) formally renounces U.S. citizenship before a consular officer;
(2) takes a policy level position in a foreign state;
(3) is convicted of treason; or
(4) performs an act made potentially expatriating by statute accompanied by conduct which is so inconsistent with retention of U.S. citizenship that it compels a conclusion that the individual intended to relinquish U.S. citizenship. (Such cases are very rare.)

Cases in categories 2, 3, and 4 will be developed carefully by U.S. consular officers to ascertain the individual's intent toward U.S. citizenship.

## APPLICABILITY OF ADMINISTRATIVE PREMISE TO PAST CASES

The premise established by the administrative standard of evidence is applicable to cases adjudicated previously.

Persons who previously lost U.S. citizenship may wish to have their cases reconsidered in light of this policy.

A person may initiate such a reconsideration by submitting a request to the nearest U.S. consular office or by writing directly to:

Director
Office of American Citizens Services
(CA/OCS/ACS)
Room 4817 NS
Department of State
2201 C Street N.W.
Washington, D.C. 20520

Each case will be reviewed on its own merits taking into consideration, for example, statements made by the person at the time of the potentially expatriating act.

## LOSS OF NATIONALITY AND TAXATION

P.L. 104-191 contains changes in the taxation of U.S. citizens who renounce or otherwise lose U.S. citizenship. In general, any person who lost U.S. citizenship within 10 years immediately preceding the close of the taxable year, whose principle purpose in losing citizenship was to avoid taxation, will be subject to continued taxation. For the purposes of this statute, persons are presumed to have a principle purpose of avoiding taxation if 1) their average annual net income tax for a five year period before the date of loss of citizenship is greater than $100,000, or 2) their net worth on the date of the loss of U.S. nationality is $500,000 or more (subject to cost of living adjustments). The effective date of the law is retroactive to February 6, 1995. Copies of approved Certificates of Loss of Nationality are provided by the Department of State to the Internal Revenue Service pursuant to P.L. 104-191. Questions regarding United States taxation consequences upon loss of U.S. nationality, should be addressed to the U.S. Internal Revenue Service.

## DUAL NATIONALITY

Dual nationality can occur as the result of a variety of circumstances. The automatic acquisition or retention of a foreign nationality, acquired, for example, by birth in a foreign country or through an alien parent, does not affect U.S. citizenship. It is prudent, however, to check with authorities of the other country to see if dual nationality is permissible under local law. Dual nationality can also occur when a person is naturalized in a foreign state without intending to relinquish U.S. nationality and is thereafter found not to have lost U.S. citizenship the individual consequently may possess dual nationality. While recognizing the existence of dual nationality and permitting Americans to have other nationalities, the U.S. Government does not endorse dual nationality as a matter of policy because of the problems which it may cause. Claims of other countries upon dual-national U.S. citizens often place them in situations where their obligation to one country are in conflict with the laws of the other. In addition, their dual nationality may hamper efforts to provide U.S. diplomatic and consular protection to them when they are abroad.

## ADDITIONAL INFORMATION

See also information flyers on related subject available via the Department of State, Bureau of Consular Affairs home page on the internet at http://travel.state.gov or via our automated fax service at 202-647-3000. These flyers include:

- *Dual Nationality*
- *Advice About Possible Loss of U.S. Citizenship and Seeking Public Office in a Foreign State*
- *Advice About Possible Loss of U.S. Citizenship and Foreign Military Service*
- *Renunciation of United States Citizenship*
- *Renunciation of U.S. Citizenship by Persons Claiming a Right of Residence in the United States*

## QUESTIONS

For further information, please contact the appropriate geographic division of the Office of American Citizens Services:

- Africa Division at (202) 647-6060;
- East Asia and Pacific Division at (202) 647-6769;
- Europe Division at (202) 647-6178;
- Latin America and the Caribbean Division at (202) 647-5118;
- Near East and South Asia Division at (202) 647-7899.

Counsel representing persons in matters related to loss of U.S. nationality may also address inquiries to Director, Office of Policy Review and Inter-Agency Liaison, Overseas Citizens Services, Room 4817 N.S., Department of State, 2201 C Street N.W., Washington, D.C. 20520, 202-647-3666.

## PART II:
### *ADVICE ABOUT POSSIBLE LOSS OF U.S. CITIZENSHIP AND FOREIGN MILITARY SERVICE*

A U.S. citizen who is a resident or citizen of a foreign country may be subject to compulsory military service in that country. Although the United States opposes service by U.S. citizens in foreign armed forces, there is little that we can do to prevent it since each sovereign country has the right to make its own laws on military service and apply them as it sees fit to its citizens and residents.

Such participation by citizens of our country in the internal affairs of foreign countries can cause problems in the conduct of our foreign relations and may involve U.S. citizens in hostilities against countries with which we are at peace. For this reason, U.S. citizens facing the possibility of foreign military service should do what is legally possible to avoid such service.

Federal statutes long in force prohibit certain aspects of foreign military service originating within the United States. The current laws are set forth in Section 958-960 of Title 18 of the United States Code. In Wiborg v. U.S., 163 U.S. 632 (1985), the Supreme Court endorsed a lower court ruling that it was not a crime under U.S. law for an individual to go abroad for the purpose of enlisting in a foreign army; however, when someone has been recruited or hired in the United States, a violation may have occurred. The prosecution of persons who have violated 18 U.S.C. 958-960 is the responsibility of the Department of Justice.

Although a person's enlistment in the armed forces of a foreign country may not constitute a violation of U.S. law, it could subject him or her to Section 349(a)(3) of the Immigration and Nationality Act [8 U.S.C. 1481(a)(3)] which provides for loss of U.S. nationality if an American voluntarily and with the intention of relinquishing U.S. citizenship enters or serves in foreign armed forces engaged in hostilities against the United States or serves in the armed forces of any foreign country as a commissioned or non-commissioned officer.

Loss of U.S. nationality was almost immediate consequences of foreign military service and the other acts listed in Section 349(a) until 1967 when the Supreme Court handed down its decision in Afroyim v. Rusk, 387 U.S. 253. In that decision, the court declared unconstitutional the provisions of Section 349(a) which provided for loss of nationality by voting in a foreign election. In so doing, the Supreme Court indicated foreign election. In so doing, the Supreme Court indicated that a U.S. citizen "has a constitutional right to remain a citizen . . . unless he voluntarily relinquishes that citizenship."

Further confirmation of the necessity to establish the citizen's intent to relinquish nationality before expatriation will result came in the opinion in Vance v. Terrazas, 444 U.S. 252 (1980). The Court stated that "expatriation depends on the will of the citizen rather than on the will of Congress and its assessment of his conduct." The Court

also indicated that a person's intention to relinquish U.S. citizenship may be shown by statements or actions.

Military service in foreign countries usually does not cause loss of citizenship since an intention to relinquish citizenship normally is lacking. Service as a high-ranking officer, particularly in a policy-making position, could be viewed as indicative of an intention to relinquish U.S. citizenship.

Pursuant to Section 351(b) of the Immigration and Nationality Act, a person who served in foreign armed forces while under the age of eighteen is not considered subject to the provisions of Section 349(a)(3) if, within six months of attaining the age of eighteen, he or she asserts a claim to United States citizenship in the manner prescribed by the Secretary of State.

## LOSS OF NATIONALITY AND TAXATION

P.L. 104-191 contains changes in the taxation of U.S. citizens who renounce or otherwise lose U.S. citizenship. In general, any person who lost U.S. citizenship within 10 years immediately preceding the close of the taxable year, whose principle purpose in losing citizenship was to avoid taxation, will be subject to continued taxation. For the purposes of this statute, persons are presumed to have a principal purpose of avoiding taxation if 1) their average annual net income tax for a five year period before the date of loss of citizenship is greater than $100,000, or 2) their net worth on the date of the loss of U.S. nationality is $500,000 or more (subject to cost of living adjustments). The effective date of the law is retroactive to February 6, 1995. Copies of approved Certificates of Loss of Nationality are provided by the Department of State to the Internal Revenue Service pursuant to P.L. 104-191. Questions regarding United States taxation consequences upon loss of U.S. nationality, should be addressed to the U.S. Internal Revenue Service.

## ADDITIONAL INFORMATION

See also information flyers on related subject available via the Department of State, Bureau of Consular Affairs home page on the internet at http://travel.state.gov or via our automated fax service at 202-647-3000. These flyers include:

- *Dual Nationality*
- *Advice About Possible Loss of U.S. Citizenship and Seeking Public Office in a Foreign State*
- *Advice About Possible Loss of U.S. Citizenship and Foreign Military Service*
- *Renunciation of United States Citizenship*
- *Renunciation of U.S. Citizenship by Persons Claiming a Right of Residence in the United States*

## QUESTIONS

For further information, please contact the appropriate geographic division of the Office of American Citizens Services:

- Africa Division at (202) 647-6060;
- East Asia and Pacific Division at (202) 647-6769;
- Europe Division at (202) 647-6178;
- Latin America and the Caribbean Division at (202) 647-5118;
- Near East and South Asia Division at (202) 647-7899.

Counsel representing persons in matters related to loss of U.S. nationality may also address inquiries to Director, Office of Policy Review and Inter-Agency Liaison, Overseas Citizens Services, Room 4817 N.S., Department of State, 2201 C Street N.W., Washington, D.C. 20520, 202-647-3666.

## PART III:
### ADVICE ABOUT POSSIBLE LOSS OF U.S. CITIZENSHIP AND SEEKING PUBLIC OFFICE IN A FOREIGN STATE

DISCLAIMER: THE INFORMATION IN

THIS CIRCULAR IS PROVIDED FOR GENERAL INFORMATION ONLY. QUESTIONS INVOLVING INTERPRETATION OF SECTION 349(A)(4) INA WITH RESPECT TO A PARTICULAR CASE SHOULD BE ADDRESSED TO THE BUREAU OF CONSULAR AFFAIRS' OFFICE OF POLICY REVIEW AND INTERAGENCY LIAISON.

The Department of State is the U.S. government agency responsible for determining whether a person located outside the United States is a U.S. citizen or national. A U.S. citizen who assumes foreign public office may come within the loss of nationality statute, which is Section 349 of the Immigration and Nationality Act of 1952 (INA), as amended, or other legal provisions as discussed below.

Currently, there is no general prohibition on U.S. citizens' running for an elected office in a foreign government. Under Article 1, section 9, clause 8 of the U.S. Constitution, however, U.S. federal government officers may not accept foreign government employment without the consent of Congress. In addition, certain retired and reserve U.S. uniformed personnel may not accept foreign government positions without the express permission of the Secretary of State and the Secretary of their department. These restrictions are reflected in the Department's regulations at 22 CFR Part 3a., and are based on 37 U.S.C. 801 Note; 22 U.S.C.2658.

With respect to loss of nationality, 349(a)(4) of the Immigration and Nationality Act (INA), as amended, is the applicable section of law. Pursuant to 349(a)(4), accepting, serving in, or performing duties of in a foreign government is a potentially expatriating act. In order to come within the Act, the person must either be a national of that country or take an oath of allegiance in connection with the position. Thus, the threshold question is whether the person's actions fall within the scope of this provision. Information used to make this determination may include official confirmation from the foreign government about the person's nationality, and whether an oath of allegiance is required.

In addition, the prefatory language of section 349 requires that expatriating act be performed voluntarily and "with the intention of relinquishing U.S. nationality." Thus, if it is determined that the person's action falls within the purview of 349(a)(4) INA, an adjudication of the person's intent must be made.

The Department has a uniform administrative standard of evidence based on the premise that U.S. citizens intend to retain U.S. citizenship when they obtain naturalization in a foreign state, subscribe to routine declarations of allegiance to a foreign state, or accept non-policy level employment with a foreign government. This administrative premise is not applicable when an individual seeks public office in a foreign state, instead, the Department of State will carefully ascertain the individual's intent toward U.S. citizenship.

Because the Department's administrative practice presumes that U.S. citizens employed in non-policy level positions in a foreign government do not have the requisite intent to relinquish U.S. citizenship, there are no efforts to seek out or adjudicate the citizenship of citizens who fall into this category of employment. On the other hand, because there is no administrative presumption that U.S. citizens who hold policy-level positions in foreign governments necessarily intend to retain their U.S. citizenship, efforts are made to fully adjudicate such cases to determine the individual's intent. (Service in a country's legislative body is considered by the Department to be a policy level position.)

An Attorney General's opinion of 1969 states that service in an important foreign political position constitutes highly persuasive evidence of intent to relinquish U.S. citizenship. In some cases, it would appear that holding a foreign office may be incompatible with maintaining U.S.

citizenship (e.g. if the position necessarily entails immunity from U.S. law). The Department does not normally consider such service alone as sufficient to sustain the burden of showing loss of U.S. citizenship by a preponderance of the evidence when the individual has explicitly expressed a contrary intent. This is particularly true when the individual continues to file U.S. tax returns, enters and leaves the U.S. on a U.S. passport, maintains close ties in the U.S. (such as maintaining a residence in the U.S.), and takes other actions consistent with an intent to retain U.S. citizenship notwithstanding the assumption of a foreign government position. Conversely, a person who publicly denied an intent to retain citizenship or who stopped paying his/her taxes, traveled to the United States on a foreign passport, and abandoned any residence in the United States might be found to have intended to relinquish U.S. citizenship notwithstanding self-serving statements to the contrary. Therefore, the Department will consider statements, as well as inferences drawn from the person's conduct, in determining one's intent to remain a U.S. citizen. Intent is determined on a case-by-case basis in light of the facts and circumstances of each individual's case. If expressed intent and conduct are consistent with a lack of intent to relinquish U.S. citizenship, the Department would generally conclude that no loss has occurred.

For further information about possible loss of U.S. citizenship and seeking public office in a foreign state, please contact:

Director
Office of Policy Review and Interagency
    Liaison
CA/OCS/PRI Room 4817 MS
U.S. Department of State
2201 C Street, NW
Washington, D.C. 20520-4818
(202) 647-3666

# CHAPTER 13
## *Security Guidelines for American Families Living Abroad*

(A series of publications by the Bureau of Diplomatic Security, Overseas Security Advisory Council [OSAC0, produced November 1995, providing guidance, suggestions, and planning for the American traveler on a variety of security related issues. Released on the Web June 5, 1996.)

## INTRODUCTION

Effective security precautions require a continuous and conscious awareness of the environment, especially when living in a foreign country. Security precautions lessen vulnerability to criminal and terrorist acts and greatly facilitate the assistance the U.S. Government can provide. Levels of risk in a foreign country can change very rapidly, sometimes overnight, and can be triggered by internal or external incidents or circumstances. Continually monitor the political climate and other factors that may impact the level of risk. Security precautions must be constantly reviewed so they may be adapted for effective response to changes in the level of risk.

## PRELIMINARY RESIDENTIAL SECURITY PLANNING

Begin to develop a tentative residential security plan for yourself and all members of your family before leaving the United States. This is essential in providing you with guidelines for selecting a home and determining where your children will go to school, the type of car you will buy, the kind of clothing you will and will not wear, and the information required to live securely in your overseas location. This plan should progress from tentative to active.

### Obtaining Information
Become informed about your new location. Much professional help is available for the family moving overseas. Major multinational corporations have large international travel and security departments that may serve as valuable resources. Contact the U.S. Government Printing Office at telephone number (202) 512-1800, or fax (202) 512-2158, to acquire current issues of the U.S. Department of State publications entitled *Key Officers of Foreign Service Posts, Guide for*

*Business Representatives,* and *Background Notes* for your country of assignment.

Obtain a current political profile of the country to which you will be moving to aid you in assessing the level of risk.

Study the culture and customs of the country. Use library sources and reference works. If you have school-aged children, obtain information and advice about schooling abroad from the Office of Overseas Schools at the U.S. Department of State, telephone number (703) 875-7800.

### Assessing the Level of Risk

Two factors must be taken into consideration when evaluating the seriousness of the personal risk to you and your family when living abroad: a risk assessment of the location to which you will be moving and the profile of the company for which you work. The threat assessment designators below were formulated by the Department of State, Diplomatic Security Service, Intelligence and Threat Analysis Division. This assessment is available to the business community through the regional security officer (RSO) at the U.S. Embassy. Risk levels are defined as:

CRITICAL: Constant criminal activity is reported and the threat of criminal violence is serious and abiding, with a history of recurrent incidents against expatriate personnel and interests.

HIGH: Frequent criminal activity is reported and the threat of criminal violence is serious, but more sporadic, with incidents against expatriate personnel and interest occasionally reported.

MEDIUM: Some criminal activity is reported and there is a potential for serious criminal violence; incidents against expatriate personnel of interest occur, but are infrequent.

LOW: There is little indication of serious criminal activity; incidents against expatriate personnel and interests seldom occur and involve stealth rather than confrontation.

### Location of a Residence

Choose a safe neighborhood. The local police, the RSO, or Post Security Officer (PSO) at the nearest U.S. diplomatic post will facilitate this process. Pay particular attention to the condition of the streets. If possible, choose streets that are paved, wide, two-way, and maintained. Dense vehicular or pedestrian traffic facilitates retention of anonymity of criminals and surveillants.

Note the overall security precautions that are taken in the neighborhood such as barred windows, security fences, extensive lighting, or large dogs. Such visible precautions may indicate a high level of security awareness or a high-crime area. Examine the quality of lighting at night to determine whether it is sufficient to illuminate the entrances to homes in the area. Ensure that trees or shrubbery do not provide cover for an intruder.

The vast majority of kidnappings and other serious crimes occur close to the residence, when the victim is leaving or returning home. Therefore, it is essential that access routes to and from the residence provide sufficient alternatives that do not lock you into predictable patterns. Dead-end or one-way streets should be avoided.

Underground parking, unless tightly controlled, should be avoided. Ideally, a garage that can be locked is the most suitable means of securing vehicles at single-family residences. Parking the car on the street should be avoided.

Residing near friends or coworkers facilitates car pooling and observation of suspicious activities.

### Selection of Residence

An apartment offers greater protection against intrusion than a single-dwelling home. A private or single dwelling affords greater opportunity to establish more rigid access control to the property. In certain high- and critical-crime threat areas, it may be prudent to consider the need for a safehaven in any residence. A safehaven should be furnished with a substantial door equipped with a deadbolt lock and a door viewer or a grill gate. Such a safe area should also possess reliable communications, such as a telephone, cellular telephone, or radio to contact help. Accessible windows and openings should be secured against forced entry.

### After Moving In

Visit the U.S. Embassy or Consulate with your passport and register as soon as possible. Registration greatly facilitates emergency evacuation from the country of residence.

After moving in, immediately familiarize yourself with your new surroundings. Get acquainted with at least one neighbor without delay; you may need a neighbor in an emergency. Locate the nearest hospital and police station.

### Assistance to Terrorist Victims

In the case of terrorist action against an American citizen or company, the embassy or consulate can facilitate communication with the home office and family of the victim, help establish useful liaison with local authorities, provide information, and suggest possible alternatives open to the family or company of the victim.

### Emergency Preparations

Before an emergency, obtain emergency fire and safety equipment. Train family members and domestic employees in the use of emergency equipment. Know beforehand where you will turn for help. Participate in an alert-calling list. If such a list does not exist, create one. Be aware of host country fire regulations and telephone numbers.

Determine if an emergency telephone call will be answered by someone who can understand English if you or family members do not speak the local language. Fill out and update yearly an Employee and Family Profile form and include current photos.

### Perimeter Security

Generally, there are two lines of defense for a residence: the outer and inner perimeters. The outer perimeter of a single residence is ordinarily a property line; in an apartment or high-rise condominium, the outer lobby door functions as the external perimeter. Any perimeter barrier, even if it is only a symbolic hedge, serves as a deterrent by causing a intruder to commit an overt act to cross the barrier. Inner perimeters include grills and locks. Building exterior openings over 96 square inches in size on the ground floor or accessible from trees, vehicle tops, or porches may need to be covered by grills. At least one window grill in each section of the sleeping quarters should be hinged and equipped with an emergency release.

All primary residential entry doors should be equipped with both a primary (main locks with handles) and an auxiliary lock (deadbolt). All exterior locks, including the garage door and mailbox lock, should be changed before moving into a new residence abroad. Maintain strict key control on all exterior locks. Never hide an exterior door key outside the house. Install an intercom between the primary entrance and the inside foyer or unprotected area. You should consider removing all name identification from your gate and doors.

### Alarms, Lighting, and Absences

In areas abroad where forced entry of a residence is commonplace, the use of a good residential alarm system is highly recommended. Security lighting should be an integral part of the intrusion system. The important elements of protective outdoor lighting are coverage and evenness of light. Lighting should illuminate the walls of the residence and the ground area adjacent to the perimeter walls. It also should illuminate shrubbery and eliminate building blind spots. It is a good idea to connect lighting to a photoelectric cell that automatically turns lights on at dusk and off at dawn. Ensure that all lighting systems are installed in compliance with local codes. Consider the installation of a diesel-powered auxiliary generator that turns on automatically when electric power fails; test the generator periodically to ensure it is in good working condition.

Extended absences present an intruder with the easiest opportunity to target a residence. While residents are away, automatic timers or photoelectric switches should turn on inside lights. Close friends or neighbors should be asked to look after the home. In many locations, it is advisable to have trusted domestic employees remain in the residence during extended absences.

### Domestic Employees

Domestic employees can either be a valuable asset to residential security or a decided liability. The chances of obtaining the services of a reliable servant can be improved by hiring one employed and recommended by a friend, acquaintance, or neighbor. Prospective applicants should be required to produce references and should be interviewed thoroughly. It is wise to check references. Do not accept the candidate's word as to his or her name and date of birth without an authentic government document to back up his or her claim. Do not permit domestics of untested integrity and reliability in your home. Domestic help should be briefed on security practices. It is critical that household help be rehearsed and briefed from time to time to refresh their memories and to update previous instructions. Domestic employees, rather than members of the household, should be trained to answer the door. They should not be allowed to admit visitors without specific approval and should not unlock or open a door until visitors have been properly identified. Family plans and official business should not be discussed within the hearing of domestic employees.

## AUTO TRAVEL

Potential victims of kidnapping and assault are probably most vulnerable when entering or leaving their homes or offices. Always carefully observe surroundings for possible

surveillance upon leaving and returning. Never enter a car without checking the rear seat to ensure that it is empty.

Do not develop predictable patterns. If possible, exchange company cars or swap with coworkers occasionally.

Know the location of police, hospital, military, and government buildings. Avoid trips to remote areas, particularly after dark. Select well-traveled streets as much as possible. Keep vehicles well-maintained at all times. When driving, keep automobile doors and windows locked. Be constantly alert to road conditions and surroundings. Never pick up hitchhikers. Carry 3 x 5 cards printed with important assistance phrases to aid with language problems.

Always carry appropriate coins for public phones. Practice using public telephones. Report all suspicious activity to the company security contact. Always lock the doors when parking a car, no matter where it is located.

## TELEPHONES AND MAIL

Do not answer the telephone by stating the name of the family or giving the residence telephone number in response to wrong-number calls. Be suspicious of any caller alleging to represent the telephone company. Be skeptical of telephone calls from strangers advising that a family member has been injured, followed by a request for another family member to leave the home immediately. Children should be advised not to converse on the telephone with strangers for any reason. When practical, home telephone numbers should be unlisted and unpublished. Emergency telephone numbers should be available for quick reference at each telephone in the home. A programmable telephone can be very useful during any emergency.

Businessmen should discourage the delivery of mail to their private residences. Family members and domestic help should not accept unexpected mail deliveries unless sure of the source. The door should not be opened to accept strange deliveries. Packages should be left by the door. Continuously remind yourself and others in the household to be suspicious of all incoming mail and parcels and to remain alert for the following danger signs:

- Unusual Appearance
- Peculiar Odor
- Suspicious Weight

If a parcel is at all suspicious, STOP further handling and call appropriate authorities.

## MISCELLANEOUS ITEMS

It may be prudent to use major U.S. credit cards, as opposed to writing checks on local banks, to reduce the audit trail your financial transactions can leave. DO NOT imprint your home address or phone number on personalized checks.

You should be aware of the attitude of the government, police, and the populace toward other nationals, particularly Americans. A strong anti-American attitude may be cause for diminished police responsiveness. Where police capability is in doubt, the use of a private guard service should be considered. All guards should be subjected to a security check. At a minimum, guards should be physically capable of performing their shift duties during the normal workday. When children are to be picked up at school by anyone other than immediate family members, an established procedure should be coordinated with school officials to assure that children are picked up only by authorized persons. Children should be instructed in observing good security procedures.

In the event of a coup d'etat, establish contact, if not already done, and maintain contact with the nearest U.S. diplomatic post.

DO NOT automatically pack and leave the country on your own initiative. Monitor local news media for any evidence of anti-American activity. In certain locations, it is recommended that adequate supplies of nonperishable foods and drinking water be stockpiled in the home to sustain family members for a reasonable period of time. Have a bag packed for each family member in the event you have to leave on short notice. An appropriate amount of currency and traveler's checks should be kept on hand. Maintain current passports and, where applicable, visas for a safehaven country.

Employees in high-threat areas should avoid social activities that are conducted at a set time and place, such as the same church service every Sunday morning. Each family member should be familiar with basic security procedures and techniques. Persons in high-threat areas should consider whether or not to participate in recreational or exercise activities that are conducted at a set time and place.

Despite repeated warnings, drug arrests and convictions of American citizens are still on the increase. If you are caught overseas with either soft or hard drugs, you are subject to local, not U.S., laws. All U.S. citizens living abroad should familiarize themselves with the selected laws of the host country, especially those relating to illegal drugs. All medicines containing habit-forming drugs or narcotics should be left in their original labeled containers; a copy of the doctor's prescription should be maintained.

Many people have been victimized by crime, and most individuals are acquainted with victims of crime. Yet, it is perhaps the most difficult job in the world to convince people to practice security and safety in their lives. Individuals must assume responsibility for their personal security and ensure that their loved ones do the same.

# CHAPTER 14
## *Guidelines for Protecting Business Information Overseas*

(A series of publications by the Bureau of Diplomatic Security, Overseas Security Advisory Council [OSAC], produced November 1995, providing guidance, suggestions, and planning for the American traveler on a variety of security related issues. Released on the Web June 5, 1996.)

### INTRODUCTION

Each day America becomes driven more and more by information. Proprietary information is our chief competitive asset, vital to both our industry and our society. Our livelihood and, indeed, our national strength depend on our ability to protect industrial and economic data.

This pamphlet outlines some steps that may be taken to protect information and to raise the general level of awareness to the threat by Americans living, working, or traveling abroad.

### WHAT INFORMATION SHOULD BE PROTECTED?

Any information that provides a U.S.

company with a competitive edge over its competitors, creative or innovative, whose loss would negatively impact an investment in time, product, finances, plants, or personnel should be protected.

It could be a trade secret, patent information, or intellectual property; a simple improvement in the way a certain American industry produces a product or does business; a technical modification, new technique, personnel policy, or management concept; or employee human resources information.

### COMPANY EMPLOYEES

Current government and industrial security studies and surveys reveal that the majority of competitive information theft cases that occur in the United States and overseas involve a company's employees, contractors, vendors, and suppliers.

An employee's rank in the company is not necessarily commensurate with the interest of a foreign intelligence agency, who besides targeting researchers, key managers, and corporate executives, will target:

- Secretaries
- Computer operators
- Technicians
- Maintenance personnel

The latter frequently have good, if not the best, access to competitive information.

Application of need-to-know procedures will help. Carefully compartmentalizing competitive information on that basis provides two advantages: it slows or stops an information thief, and it may provide an indicator of an employee seeking to obtain competitive information beyond his or her need to know.

When local laws allow, it is prudent to conduct background investigations on prospective employees. A comprehensive background investigation can provide, prior to offering an applicant employment with a company, the best information concerning the person's social, education, military, credit, civil and criminal litigation, and employment histories.

## VENDORS, CONTRACTORS, AND SUPPLIERS

Recent U.S. Government and security industry surveys regarding safeguarding of proprietary information revealed that vendors, contractors, and suppliers accounted for almost 15 percent of all disclosures, misappropriation, and thefts of U.S. business competitive information. Generally these groups should be:

- Controlled, documented, and required to wear a photo identification
- Escorted throughout the general premises by the person they are visiting
- Restricted from unnecessary admittance to high-security areas, or escorted at all times
- Required to sign nondisclosure and confidentiality agreements

## VISITOR TOURS

Public tours of buildings containing competitive information should be discouraged. Similarly visitor tours of high-security areas should be prohibited.

All requests for tours by academic, industrial, fraternal, social, or media groups should be passed to security departments for background checks.

## WORKPLACE VULNERABILITIES

U.S. businesses or research locations overseas are principal targets of those seeking to compromise competitive information. If possible, locate corporate offices in facilities totally controlled by the corporation.

### Location, Location, Location

Site location and construction should be the best that will allow for normal and prudent security measures.

Normal security steps dictate that building perimeters and internal sensitive areas be secure, and that the general public, unescorted visitors, and unauthorized personnel be restricted from research, production, and business areas where competitive information is used. Prudent security steps dictate that existing security controls should always be reviewed for improvement or modification and that an awareness program, as well as policy and guidelines be established to protect competitive information.

### Facilities Perimeter

All windows, external and internal doors, and high-security areas should be provided with intrusion alarm monitoring. Alarm systems should be supplemented by lighting, as discussed below. The alarm signal must be communicated to a location where a speedy and appropriate response can be provided.

The entire perimeter of any office building that serves as a perimeter barrier should be adequately illuminated during hours of darkness. Other perimeters, such as walls, fences, and natural barriers, should be illuminated to both detect and deter persons attempting to gain unauthorized access to the building. Adequate interior night lights should be left on whenever the building is not occupied. Security personnel should control:

- Perimeter and internal sensitive area access
- Keys and locks supervision
- Access card supervision
- Employee, visitor, contractor, and vendor identification badges

### High-Security Areas

High-security areas include, but are not limited to, design studios, strategic planning areas, engineering and research facilities, mailrooms, telephone switching rooms, computer facilities, and other similar areas. In general, office safeguards and possible restriction to a high-security level should be provided for:

- Designated photo copiers
- Encrypted telecommunication equipment
- Facsimile machines and other reproduction equipment. If this cannot be done, the equipment should be provided with access control devices to prevent unauthorized usage.
- Executive offices, research labs, and work areas
- Lockable file cabinets and desks and vaults to secure competitive information
- Keys, combination locks, and access cards to maintain the effectiveness of these devices Certain offices or portions thereof may require designation as high-security areas if:
  —Highly sensitive competitive information is present.
  —Access is limited and entry is restricted to only those persons who possess special identification and who are specifically permitted entry.
  —A higher level access control device is used above that operating at the perimeter of the building.

—A procedure, such as a receipt and copy accountability system, is established for the authorized removal of all competitive information, blueprints, drawings, and other documents contained in these areas.

### Storage Facilities

Provide secure facilities for the storage of competitive information such as desks, offices, safes, vaults, filing cabinets, etc.

### Clean-Desk Policy

Encourage a clean-desk policy for all offices during non-business hours.
Require a clean-desk policy in high-security areas.

### Cleaning and Maintenance

Cleaning and maintenance should be done during times when responsible company supervisors are present to monitor such activity.

### Disposal of Competitive Information

Competitive information must be destroyed when no longer needed.
Each work area must have adequate shredding capabilities or controlled disposal functions. Make each functional area responsible for verifying that competitive information is properly disposed.

## COMMUNICATIONS

Easily accessed and intercepted telecommunications present a highly vulnerable and lucrative target for anyone interested in obtaining competitive information. Increased usage by businesses of these links for bulk computer data transmission and electronic mail makes telecommunications intercept efforts cost effective for intelligence collectors worldwide.
U.S. companies should:

- Assume that all overseas

telecommunications are intercepted, recorded, and organized into reports and reviewed for economic intelligence.

- "Button-up" all competitive information communications to maintain their competitive edge.

### Threats

U.S. companies should be aware of, and sensitize their employees overseas to, the fact that:

- All foreign telephone systems are either owned or controlled by the host government. This allows the government to easily monitor transmissions of selected U.S. corporations.
- Intelligence agencies of third-party nations, terrorists, and criminals monitor electronic transmissions.
- Business and technical data obtained from U.S. corporations may be, and often are, provided to foreign competitors and potential customers.
- Personal information obtained may be used to kidnap executives for financial gain or political purposes.
- Electronic equipment, such as facsimile machines, telephones, and desktop computers, may be altered to make electronic monitoring easier.

### Vulnerabilities

Telecommunications monitoring may be done at a phone company's switching facilities; phone lines may be tapped or bugged; or microwave transmissions may be intercepted anywhere between the two microwave towers.

Telephones do not necessarily cease transmitting once they are hung-up. Conversations taking place near a phone may be transmitted to the foreign state's telephone system switching facility and can be monitored anywhere between the phone and that facility.

Many telecommunications transmissions will contain "key words" used to identify information of interest to a third party. A key word can be the name of a technology, product, project, or anything else that may identify the subject of the transmission.

Encryption should be the first line of defense since it is easier for foreign intelligence services to monitor lines than to place "bugs"; however, encryption will provide little, if any, security if a careful examination for audio "bugs" elsewhere in the room is not conducted.

Most international U.S. corporate telecommunications are not encrypted. Some countries do not allow encryption of telecommunications traffic within their borders, but it should be considered, where feasible, for any transmission of competitive information.

About half of all overseas telecommunications are facsimile transmissions which, because they are emanations, may be intercepted by foreign intelligence services since many of the foreign telephone companies are foreign owned.

In addition, many American companies have begun using what is called electronic data interchange, a system of transferring corporate bidding, invoice, and pricing data electronically overseas. This type of information is invaluable to many foreign intelligence services that support their national businesses.

### Video Conferences

The threat is essentially the same as that to other types of telecommunications. Adversaries can purchase or replicate specific equipment used by an American company and then either tap into the line or use other means to monitor both audio and video.

Although encryption is available for some video conferencing installations, many countries do not allow any type of encryption and others allow only that type which they can break.

### Electronic Transmissions

Most foreign common carriers are

government controlled or owned. Trade secrets, data, marketing strategies, and personnel information that are discussed or sent over host country telephone lines are easily obtained by foreign interests.

### Electronic Media Path

Electronic data is recovered easiest when a signal is not multiplexed or mixed with other data signals, i.e., data transmitted from a telephone instrument to a telephone switch. Only a minimal investment is required to retrieve data not masked with other voice or data. For this reason, it is better to use standard dial-up versus dedicated lines.

Data and voice that is routed on major transmission paths—such as microwave or satellite transmission—have less likelihood of being monitored by hackers or low-cost monitoring operations, because the cost of sifting through such a volume of information to access one target is often cost prohibitive. However, a well-financed intelligence gathering operation may find satellite or microwave transmissions the best intercept opportunity, since they can be monitored at great distances with little or no threat of detection.

### Suggested Telecommunication Countermeasures

Below is a list of suggested actions that may be taken in order to improve the security of your telecommunications transmissions.

- Whenever possible, use your corporate transmission facilities instead of those of the host government.
- Encrypt electronic transmissions whenever possible. Computer links, facsimile transmissions, E-mail, and voice transmissions can all be encrypted.
- The National Institute of Standards and Technology (NIST) conducts validations of products for conformance to cryptographic standards for encryption and publishes the results quarterly in the "Validated Products List."

Subscriptions are available from:

National Technical Information Service
U.S. Department of Commerce
5285 Port Royal Road
Springfield, VA 22161

Neutralize the vulnerability of telephones. A small, company-controlled switch installed within the facility can help ensure that conversations are not transmitted through handsets that are "hung-up," and also can serve to decrease the threat of covert line access.

Avoid "key words" or phrases that may be used by intelligence agencies and others to search recorded conversations for subjects of interest. Examples would be project names, product names, the names of persons of interest (e.g., heads of state, CEOs, etc.), and classification labels such as "sensitive" and "company confidential."

Positively identify all parties participating in phone conversations or receiving the facsimile transmissions.

Always keep at least one phone and facsimile machine secured in a container equipped with a combination lock, and restrict access to the combination. This will help maintain the integrity of that equipment.

Check connecting lines to telecommunication devices (telephones, computers, fax machines, etc.) monthly to ensure that the line has not been replaced or modified by unauthorized personnel.

Placing stickers on phones warning of hostile monitoring will be helpful to maintain awareness.

### COMPUTER TECHNOLOGY

Computers can pose enormous security problems. While they contain great volumes of information, they also concentrate it, and if not protected, they can make the task of the information thief much easier. When the facility is located overseas, the following additional security issues should be considered.

### Access

Because one cannot assume that employment practices are the same from country to country, it is not always possible to dictate what employees can do or where they can go.

For example, in some countries you are not permitted to log the fact that a specific person accessed a specific data set at a certain time on a certain date, because such a log could be misused to inappropriately monitor work habits, speed, and productivity.

Similarly, in some countries, there are resident fire marshals in the facility who do not work for the enterprise, but are authorized access to each and every part of the physical facility.

### Magnetic Media Control

Managers must be sensitive to mailing or physically carrying magnetic media between countries.

The information on magnetic media may be vulnerable during interaction with the local customs authorities, which could be far more damaging to a business.

In either mailing or carrying, accountability is lost once the material is turned over to local customs personnel to be "cleared." Often, the time involved, as well as the other details of what "cleared" means, [is] not always spelled out to private industry.

### Distributed Printer Control

Physical access to printers used within a computing center is usually well controlled. However, small, powerful, printing facilities, which can be readily hooked-up with printed output routed directly to such devices by any employee, are coming increasingly into use. It is strongly recommended that attention be given to ensuring that:

- Printed output may be picked up only by the information owner or his or her representatives.
- Printers are placed in a room having a controlled-access system.

### Cellular PCs

The cellular portable computer is relatively new technology, having unique security considerations that one might easily overlook. The system is essentially a personal computer with an integrated modem, which is a device used to change signals understood by telephone technology into signals understood by computers, and vice versa.

There is also a built-in cellular telephone that allows a person with a single action to place a call to a computer system, connect the personal computer to it, and interact with a host computer. Sometimes overlooked with this technology is the fact that cellular telephones:

- Use radio frequencies to communicate
- Are vulnerable to unauthorized interception, recording, and subsequent analysis. Monitoring equipment is readily available to foreign intelligence services and to the more sophisticated business espionage agent.

### Virus Contamination and Detection

Although it is a standard precaution to take special care when receiving a PC program from someone because of the possibility of virus contamination, it is exponentially greater during foreign travel.

Answering the questions in the checklist below can identify opportunities to improve the security of your computer software and hardware.

### Computer Security Checklist

#### International Travel

- Does the local power supply match your system's requirements?
- Are electrical power transformers, filters, surge protectors, or uninterruptible power supply (UPS) units available to protect your equipment?
- Does the government impose restrictions on the import of computer hardware and software into the country?

### Environment

- Will the computer be used in a low humidity area where damage from static electricity may be sustained?
- Are carpets treated?
- Are humidifiers available?
- Will the computer be used in a hot, dusty climate?
- Are office temperature controls sufficient?
- Are dust covers available?

### Physical Security

- Is the work area kept clear of soft drinks, coffee, and other liquids, that, when accidentally spilled, may damage equipment?
- Are diskettes physically labeled and handled as directed by the manufacturer? Are sensitive diskettes sufficiently write-protected to avoid accidental or malicious damage or destruction?
- Are backup copies stored off-site?
- Is the computer sufficiently protected from acts of sabotage, tampering, and theft?
- Are modems (particularly those with an automatic answer feature) disconnected or powered off when not in use?
- Are printer ribbons, sensitive printouts, and diskettes burned, shredded, or degaussed as appropriate to prevent inadvertent information disclosure?

### System Security

- Are spare, user-serviceable parts available in the event of failure?
- Are backup copies of software and data produced periodically?
- Has a backup system (contingency) been identified to continue critical operations in the event of a failure or disaster? Has it been tested?
- Are sufficient controls in place to prevent violation of manufacturers' copyrights and license agreements?
- Are software controls present to authenticate individual system users?
- Are passwords changed frequently and are they easily guessed?

- Is a security erase or file scrub program present on the system that will overwrite sensitive data on the hard disk when a file is deleted? Is it used?
- Are system hardware and software controls present to authenticate individual system users?

### Virus Protection

- Are software and data diskettes received from reliable, trustworthy sources?
- Is software received from outside sources scanned for computer viruses with current virus detection software?

### Computer Security Guidance

Under the Computer Security Act of 1987, the National Institute of Standards and Technology (NIST) develops standards and guidelines for the protection of sensitive information.

For a listing of available documents, including ordering information, request a free copy of Publications List 91 from the following:

CSL Publications Technology Building
Room B64
National Institute of Standards and
    Technology
U.S. Department of Commerce
Gaithersburg, MD 20899

## EFFECTS OF TELECOMMUNICATIONS ON COMPUTER SECURITY

Telecommunications technology provides for electronic "highways" that now enable a person to directly access a computer system on another continent. Many U.S. corporations are dependent for their very survival on data being stored and processed on these computer systems. It is therefore mandatory that access control security software and procedures are implemented for any computer interfacing with a network or telephone system.

Hacking into computers is now a standard

tool for those involved in espionage and computer crime. Once an intruder has gained entry, he or she may be able to view, change, or destroy valuable company data and information. Electronic terrorism, placing a corporation's information assets at risk, also is possible.

Consider the following tips to reduce the possibility of unauthorized access through networks:

- Apply access control software and procedures to the corporation's networks; keep the intruder off the "highway."
- Ensure that the corporation's computer systems are protected.
- Mandate that all users change passwords at least once every 60 days, allow no more than three consecutive invalid passwords before suspending a user ID, and ensure that all passwords are at least six characters in length. Also, encourage employees to use passwords that do not relate to their lives (names of family, pets, sports teams, etc.). Hackers often gain entry by simply guessing passwords.
- Control the phone numbers to the corporation's networks and computer systems as competitive information.
- Minimize their distribution and notify corporate employees that the numbers should be guarded.
- Test corporate networks for the existence of unauthorized modems that could provide access to eavesdroppers.
- Encrypt computer-to-computer sensitive transmissions, including electronic mail.
- Require all personnel to agree in writing before they are granted access to corporate networks and computer systems, that they will keep competitive information confidential, and that they will abide by the corporation's information protection standards.

### AT HOME

Many of the same principles that apply to maintaining a safe and secure office apply equally to a residence. These elements will vary depending on the foreign environment and the associated risk factors. As a general rule, competitive information should not be taken home. However, should it become necessary, the level of protection afforded competitive information in the home must be equal to or greater than the standard of protection it is afforded in the office.

A favorite technique of information thieves is the examination of trash containers. Consequently, the disposal of competitive information should not be done at home. Such materials should be transported to the workplace where they may be properly destroyed.

### HOME SECURITY CHECKLIST

Access to residential buildings where competitive information is located must be limited to only authorized persons. This will require appropriate locking devices and an alarm system that will detect an attempted intrusion and alert authorities and other responsible parties. A specific area or areas within the residence should be designated for working on competitive information.

Access should be limited to authorized family and service personnel. Such information, when left unattended, should be secured in an appropriate container. Control of the keys for these containers should be limited.

Cleaning activities should be done only when competitive information items are cleared from the area, secured, or when the area is monitored by the owner, custodian, or user of the information.

Residences and residential buildings should have appropriate:

- Access controls to restrict unauthorized persons and vehicles
- Locking devices on exterior windows and doors
- Intrusion-control alarm systems where possible

- Procedures for the positive identification of visitors and utility personnel prior to entry

Within the residence, the work area should include the following life and safety equipment:

- Flashlight
- First-aid kit
- Emergency radio and/or cellular phone
- Fire and smoke alarms
- Safehaven

Specific areas for competitive information work should include:

- Limited access to only authorized persons
- Lockable desk and computer equipment and files
- Procedures imposed for access safeguards on computer equipment
- Storage of authorized company software on designated computer
- An appropriate shredder
- Limited cleaning conducted only in the presence of the employee or other responsible person

## BUSINESS TRAVEL

### Travel with a Laptop Computer

Business personnel who travel should adopt normal and prudent computer safeguards while traveling.

Never:

- Leave a laptop unattended while in an airport terminal, checking in and out of hotels, or at a business location
- Operate a computer while in public areas such as airport waiting rooms, cafeterias, or snack bars
- Check a laptop with luggage. Laptops should always be stowed in carry-on baggage that will stay with the traveler at all times

- Check a laptop in a temporary airport or train station storage locker even for a short time

### Working in Hotels with a PC

Hotel rooms are not secure. Leaving important company information in your room, even in a locked briefcase or PC, is an invitation for material to be copied or photographed while you are out. Hotel vaults are not much better. Foreign intelligence officers can gain access without you becoming aware of the compromise.

Reduce hard copy material as much as possible and carry what you must take on your person, possibly on disk, or secure it in a company vault.

U.S. business travelers should not assume that the U.S. standards in telecommunication security will be the case when traveling overseas. The quality of service, as well as the technical standards and conventions used, vary dramatically from country to country.

## SCIENTIFIC CONFERENCES

Historically, scientific conferences and trade association meetings have been targeted by some foreign intelligence agencies. Today these meetings are still targeted, but the goal is to learn economic information that will improve the position of our foreign competitors. Individuals collecting this type of information may be managers, corporate officers, salespeople, and other business people, scientists, engineers, and other technical personnel. There is a growing trend for foreign corporations to employ former intelligence officers for industrial work. Protect yourself by practicing discretion and remembering that not only time, but information, is money.

### *Eavesdropping*

INFORMATION OF COMPETITIVE VALUE SHOULD NOT BE DISCUSSED IN PUBLIC PLACES.

Discussions on airplanes are overheard by

those around you. Eavesdropping can result in gathering meaningful information in a radius of 6–8 seats. Recent revelations in the media specifically mention valuable information gathered by eavesdropping on conversations held on aircraft and in bars and restaurants.

### Destruction of Information Waste
- Keep unwanted material until you can dispose of it securely.
- Paper should be burned or shredded. If shredded, the type of shredder should cut horizontally and vertically.
- Floppy disks should be cut in small pieces and discarded.

### Necessary Communications
- Avoid sending facsimiles or conducting sensitive conversations on local or international telephone lines.
- Fax, telex, and data systems are all vulnerable to interception, particularly in overseas hotels.

- On important issues, go to the extra trouble of identifying company travelers for the purpose of carrying information rather than entrusting it to less secure electronic means.

### Be Alert!!!
Be aware of new acquaintances who probe for information or attempt to place you in a compromising situation. In an unusual situation, have an American colleague present. The watchword in travel while in foreign countries is discretion.

## ADDITIONAL INFORMATION

We hope this pamphlet provided you with some basic information you should consider in dealing with important issues. For a more detailed discussion, please review our expanded version, *Guidelines for Protecting U.S. Business Information Overseas*, available through the Overseas Security Advisory Council.

# CHAPTER 15
## *Crisis Abroad*
(Bureau of Consular Affairs, U.S. Department of State, Travel Publications)

## PART I:
## HOW THE U.S. GOVERNMENT CAN HELP IN A CRISIS

What can the State Department's Bureau of Consular Affairs do for Americans caught in a disaster or a crisis abroad?

Earthquakes, hurricanes, political upheavals, acts of terrorism, and hijackings are only some of the events threatening the safety of Americans abroad. Each event is unique and poses its own special difficulties. However, for the State Department there are certain responsibilities and actions that apply in every disaster or crisis.

When a crisis occurs, the State Department sets up a task force or working group to bring together in one set of rooms all the people necessary to work on that event. Usually this Washington task force will be in touch by telephone 24 hours a day with our Ambassador and Foreign Service Officers at the embassy in the country affected.

In a task force, the immediate job of the State Department's Bureau of Consular Affairs is to respond to the thousands of concerned relatives and friends who begin to telephone the State Department immediately after the news of a disaster is broadcast.

Relatives want information on the welfare of their family members and on the disaster. The State Department relies for hard information on its embassies and consulates abroad. Often these installations are also affected by the disaster and lack electricity, phone lines, gasoline, etc. Nevertheless, foreign service officers work hard to get information back to Washington as quickly as possible. This is rarely as quickly as the press is able to relay information. Foreign Service Officers cannot speculate; their information must be accurate. Often this means getting important information from the local government, which may or may not be immediately responsive.

### WELFARE & WHEREABOUTS

As concerned relatives call in, officers of the Bureau of Consular Affairs collect the names of the Americans possibly involved in the disaster and pass them to the embassy and consulates. Officers at post attempt to locate these Americans in order to report on their welfare. The officers work with local authorities and, depending on the circumstances, may personally search hotels, airports, hospitals, or even prisons. As they try to get the information, their first priority is Americans dead or injured.

### Death

When an American dies abroad, the Bureau of Consular Affairs must locate and inform the next-of-kin. Sometimes discovering the next-of-kin is difficult. If the American's name is known, the Bureau's Office of Passport Services will search for his or her passport application. However, the information there may not be current.

The Bureau of Consular Affairs provides guidance to grieving family members on how to make arrangements for local burial or return of the remains to the U.S. The disposition of remains is affected by local laws, customs, and facilities which are often vastly different from those in the U.S. The Bureau of Consular Affairs relays the family's instructions and necessary private funds to cover the costs involved to the embassy or consulate. The Department of State has no funds to assist in the return of remains or ashes of American citizens who die abroad.

Upon completion of all formalities, the consular officer abroad prepares an official Foreign Service Report of Death, based upon the local death certificate, and sends it to the next-of-kin or legal representative for use in U.S. courts to settle estate matters.

A U.S. consular officer overseas has statutory responsibility for the personal estate of an American who dies abroad if the deceased has no legal representative in the country where the death occurred. The consular officer takes possession of personal effects, such as convertible assets, apparel, jewelry, personal documents, and papers. The officer prepares an inventory and then carries out instructions from members of the deceased's family concerning the effects. A final statement of the account is then sent to the next-of-kin. The Diplomatic Pouch cannot be used to ship personal items, including valuables, but legal documents and correspondence relating to the estate can be transmitted by pouch. In Washington, the Bureau of Consular Affairs gives next-of-kin guidance on procedures to follow in preparing Letters Testamentary, Letters of Administration, and Affidavits of Next-of-Kin as acceptable evidence of legal claim of an estate.

### Injury

In the case of an injured American, the embassy or consulate abroad notifies the task force which notifies family members in the U.S. The Bureau of Consular Affairs can assist in sending private funds to the injured American; frequently it collects information on the individual's prior medical history and forwards it to the embassy or consulate. When necessary, the State Department assists in arranging the return of the injured American to the U.S. commercially, with appropriate medical escort, via commercial air ambulance or, occasionally, by U.S. Air Force medical evacuation aircraft. The use of Air Force facilities for a medical evacuation is authorized only under certain stringent conditions, and when commercial evacuation is not possible. The full expense must be borne by the injured American or his family.

### Evacuation

Sometimes commercial transportation entering and leaving a country is disrupted during a political upheaval or natural disaster. If this happens, and if it appears unsafe for Americans to remain, the embassy and consulates will work with the task force in Washington to charter special airflights and ground transportation to help Americans to depart. The U.S. Government cannot order Americans to leave a foreign country. It can only advise and try to assist those who wish to leave.

### Privacy Act

The provisions of the Privacy Act are designed to protect the privacy and rights of Americans, but occasionally they complicate our efforts to assist citizens abroad. As a rule, consular officers may not reveal information regarding an individual American's location, welfare, intentions, or problems to anyone, including family members and Congressional representatives, without the expressed consent of that individual. Although sympathetic to the distress this can cause concerned families, consular officers must comply with the provisions of the Privacy Act.

—Department of State, Family Liaison Office Direct Communication Project, Paper No. 10

## PART II:
## EVACUATION PLAN:
## DON'T LEAVE HOME WITHOUT IT!

This material is written for employees and family members assigned to an American Embassy or Consulate abroad, but most of it is practical advice that would be useful to anyone living outside of their own country.

If you are assigned to an American Embassy or Consulate aboard, please contact your Community Liaison Office Coordinator at post or the Family Liaison Office for a copy of the complete pamphlet, including information about safehavens.

Evacuations are stressful experiences: Where to go? What to take? What personal papers are necessary? Stresses and frustrations can be reduced by advanced contingency planning on your part.

### ESSENTIALS FOR OVERSEAS LIVING

#### Before Going Overseas on Assignment

- Make a list of the following for all family members. Leave a copy of this list with a trusted contact at home. Update periodically and carry with
    —Passport numbers and dates of issue
    —Bank account numbers
    —Credit card numbers
    —Insurance policy numbers
    —Car registration, serial, and license numbers
    —U.S. driver's license numbers
    —Social Security numbers (including children's)
    —Current prescriptions, including eyeglasses
    —Contents and location of safe deposit box(es)
    —Assets and debts
    —Names and addresses of business and professional contacts

- Locate a safe depository in the United States and put the following into it (making copies of the items if you will need them at post):
    —Copy of will(s). Do not put original of will in safe depository. Originals should be left with lawyer or executor.
    —Power of attorney (one of the originals)
    —Birth and marriage certificates
    —Naturalization papers
    —Deeds
    —Mortgages
    —Stocks (or leave with broker in case you want to sell)
    —Bonds (or leave with broker in case you want to sell)
    —Insurance papers—life, car, house, medical, and household effects (HHE)
    —Current household and personal effects inventory

- Execute a current power of attorney for each adult family member and have several originals made. Make several copies as well. These are needed to transact business on behalf of spouse or other adult.
- Learn the current laws of your legal residence and place of domicile with regard to taxes and property.
- Establish credit that will be adequate for emergencies. Obtain individual credit

cards for employee and spouse.

- Establish a joint checking account, or two joint checking accounts, enabling each spouse to work from either account in the event they are separated for a period of time.
- Consider getting an ATM (automatic teller machine) card for your bank account that can be used all over the country. Make sure both spouses know the PIN (personal identification number).
- Have the employee's paycheck sent to a U.S. bank account rather than to post. Checks lost in the mail can cause extraordinary difficulties.
- Put checkbooks, bankbooks, credit cards, some travelers checks, and a small amount of cash in a safe (but easily accessible) place.
- Keep a list of regular billing dates for all recurring expenses—insurance, mortgages, and taxes.
- Make and continually update an inventory of all your possessions, including jewelry and clothing.
- Decide what to take to post and what to put into storage based on where you are assigned.
- Consider personal property insurance.
- Pack both winter and summer clothing, regardless of post.
- Update scrapbook and photo albums. Consider leaving sentimental photos or negatives in safe deposit box.
- Gather all employment documents for adult family members, including resumes and letters of reference. Keep duplicates in the United States.
- Keep an up-to-date locator card in the Foreign Service Lounge or with your agency. Be certain your emergency contact person is capable of dealing with an emergency.
- Make duplicates of all personal address lists.
- Discuss with your immediate and extended family what to do in case of an emergency (evacuation, hostage-taking, illness, or death). Give them the emergency

telephone numbers for your agency.
- Take the Security Overseas Seminar. Foreign Affairs agency employees are required to take it every 5 years; spouses and teens are encouraged to take it. During the summer months, there are special sessions for teens and younger children.

## WHEN YOU ARRIVE AT POST

- Attend the post security briefing.
- Keep up with the current security situation at post. Hold periodic family security meetings.
- Be aware of the warden system at post. Know who your warden is and ensure that your family information is current and accurate.
- Make an inventory of what you have brought to post and keep it updated.
- Learn some of the local language to help you in an emergency. In the local language, post a list of instructions and essential telephone numbers for household employees.
- Make the acquaintance of your neighbors early in your tour.
- Learn the location of the closest hospital, police station, and friendly embassy.
- Keep immunizations up to date and recorded in your yellow shot card.
- If you have children in local schools, check the school's emergency evacuation plan. Become an involved parent.
- If you have children, choose a surrogate parent at post and supply that person with a current power of attorney for medical or other emergencies in the event you need them to care for your children unexpectedly.
- Maintain a separate emergency supply/first-aid kit to be used only for emergency situations.
- Decide which necessary items should be taken with you in the event of evacuation or authorized departure and which items should be airfreighted later.

## EMERGENCY SITUATIONS:
## WHEN AN EVACUATION IS A POSSIBILITY

- Discuss possible contingency plans with family members. The United States is the designated safehaven. Families may go to any destination in the continental United States; employees are normally required to safehaven in Washington, D.C.
- Make a list of items to pack in each suitcase (normally each evacuee is allowed one suitcase).
- Make a list of items for carry-on baggage.
- Update current household effects inventory of items at post.
- Consolidate all personal records, financial documents, school records, etc.
- Prepare your house for departure—secure valuables, if possible.
- Plan for pets. In almost all evacuations, your pets will not be allowed to go out on evacuation with you. Make advance arrangements for their care, food, etc. Keep the pets' records updated.
- Decide how money will be handled. Who will pay bills? Will you continue to use the joint checking account?

### WHEN THERE IS AN AUTHORIZED
### OR ORDERED DEPARTURE

- Pack luggage with suitable clothing and essential items. Remember seasonal changes/weather conditions.
- Engage the children in packing their own backpacks or carry-on bags with toys, snacks, games, books, and other comforting items.
- Make sure carry-on baggage includes the following items:
  - —Medications (prescription and over the counter)
  - —Medical/dental records, immunization cards
  - —Extra glasses and prescriptions
  - —School records, report cards, test scores, and current samples of work
  - —Current power of attorney
  - —Birth certificates, naturalization certificates, marriage certificates (if at post)
  - —Passports
  - —Driver's license, auto insurance policies, auto registration, and title, if applicable
  - —Personal checks, check registers, latest bank statement
  - —Credit cards
  - —Bills/financial records
  - —Safe deposit box keys
  - —Address book
  - —Lists with names and addresses of doctors, dentists, lawyers, etc.
  - —Travelers checks; U.S. currency, if possible
  - —Household effects (HHE) inventory
  - —Household goods insurance policy
  - —Evacuation travel orders
  - —Personal items and a change of clothing for each traveler
  - —Snacks, juice, books
- Choose practical traveling clothes suitable to the climate of destination.

### WHEN YOU ARE AT SAFEHAVEN

Important Note: Ordinarily, safehavens are in the contintental United States. Permission must be obtained for a foreign safehaven. You will be moved to a safehaven only once; subsequent moves will be at your own expense.

- Assume that the evacuation/authorized departure will last longer than original estimates. Make plans accordingly.
- Keep busy. Think about the possibility of temporary, full- or part-time employment, or volunteer work.
- Keep in touch with fellow evacuees.

### WHEN YOU RETURN TO POST OR
### RECEIVE A NEW ASSIGNMENT

If you return to the evacuated post, it is

often helpful to meet with fellow evacuees to evaluate your experiences. As an evacuee, you can provide valuable input to post orientation programs at future posts.

## CONCLUSION

No matter how calm things are at your post, you should not be lulled into thinking that "it can't happen here." In 1 year alone, 11 posts (from every region of the world) were under ordered or authorized departure orders at some point. More than 600 people were suddenly faced with making the kinds of decisions described in this booklet. Early personal preparation can alleviate some of the difficulties of an evacuation.

# CHAPTER 16
## *Number of Resident Americans Living Abroad*

(This list was compiled in July 1999 by the Bureau of Consular Affairs. This list does NOT include U.S. Government [military and nonmilitary] employees and their dependents.)

| COUNTRY | POST | # AMERICANS |
|---|---|---|
| Albania | Tirana | 646 |
| Algeria | Algiers | 793 |
| Angola | Luanda | 845 |
| Argentina | Buenos Aires | 27,600 |
| Armenia | Yerevan | 229 |
| Australia | Canberra | 2,500 |
|  | Melbourne | 38,000 |
|  | Sydney | 55,500 |
|  | Perth | 6,800 |
| Austria | Vienna | 14,000 |
| Azerbaijan | Baku | 600 |
| Bahamas | Nassau | 7,050 |
| Bahrain | Manama | 1,800 |
| Bangladesh | Dhaka | 1,320 |
| Barbados | Bridgetown | 12,000 |
| Belarus | Minsk | 190 |
| Belgium | Brussels | 35,328 |
| Belize | Belize City | 2,700 |
| Benin | Cotonou | 250 |
| Bermuda | Hamilton | 4,300 |
| Bolivia | La Paz | 3,000 |
| Bosnia-Herzegovina | Sarajevo | 1600 |
| Botswana | Gaborone | 800 |

| | | |
|---|---|---|
| Brazil | Brasilia | 7,200 |
| | Rio De Janeiro | 14,460 |
| | Sao Paolo | 16,480 |
| | Recife | 2,500 |
| Brunei | Bandar Seri Begawan | 248 |
| Bulgaria | Sofia | 400 |
| Burkina Faso | Ouagadougou | 329 |
| Burma | Rangoon | 332 |
| Burundi | Bujumbura | 46 |
| Cambodia | Phnom Penh | 1,200 |
| Cameroon | Yaounde | 1,161 |
| Canada | Ottawa | 24,300 |
| | Calgary | 105,000 |
| | Halifax | 40,000 |
| | Montreal | 65,000 |
| | Quebec | 3,400 |
| | Toronto | 250,000 |
| | Vancouver | 200,000 |
| Cape Verde | Praia | 1,000 |
| Central African Republic | Bangui | 91 |
| Chad | N'djamena | 162 |
| Chile | Santiago | 11,790 |
| China | Beijing | 10,000 |
| | Guangzhou | 3,200 |
| | Hong Kong | 48,220 |
| | Shanghai | 2,382 |
| | Shenyang | 555 |
| | Chengdu | 800 |
| Colombia | Bogota | 30,680 |
| Democratic Republic of the Congo | Kinshasa | 440 |
| | Brazzaville | 233 |
| Costa Rica | San Jose | 19,800 |
| Cote D'ivoire | Abidjan | 2,100 |
| Croatia | Zagreb | 1,921 |
| Cuba | Havana | 2,000 |
| Cyprus | Nicosia | 4,175 |
| Czech Republic | Prague | 10,000 |
| Denmark | Copenhagen | 9,380 |
| Djibouti | Djibouti | 50 |
| Dominican Republic | Santo Domingo | 82,000 |
| Ecuador | Quito | 7,950 |
| | Guayquil | 5,874 |
| Egypt | Cairo | 10,892 |
| El Salvador | San Salvador | 10,000 |
| Equatorial Guinea | Malabo | 30 |
| Eritrea | Asmara | 356 |
| Estonia | Tallinn | 1,000 |

| | | |
|---|---|---:|
| Ethiopia | Addis Ababa | 2,190 |
| Fiji | Suva | 5,288 |
| Finland | Helsinki | 4,700 |
| France | Paris | 75,000 |
| | Marseille | 23,700 |
| | Strasbourg | 3,050 |
| Gabon | Libreville | 298 |
| Gambia | Banjul | 546 |
| Georgia | Tbilisi | 303 |
| Germany | Bonn | 692 |
| | Berlin | 14,619 |
| | Frankfurt am Main | 138,815 |
| | Hamburg | 11,754 |
| | Munich | 45,000 |
| Ghana | Accra | 3,780 |
| Greece | Athens | 65,000 |
| | Thessaloniki | 7,500 |
| Grenada | St. George's | 2,000 |
| Guatemala | Guatemala City | 10,000 |
| Guinea | Conakry | 660 |
| Guinea–Bissau | Bissau | 25 |
| Guyana | Georgetown | 1,500 |
| Haiti | Port-Au-Prince | 11,000 |
| Honduras | Tegucigalpa | 10,500 |
| Hungary | Budapest | 15,000 |
| Iceland | Reykjavik | 1,730 |
| India | New Delhi | 1,397 |
| | Mumbai | 9,400 |
| | Calcutta | 672 |
| | Madras | 3,900 |
| Indonesia | Jakarta | 6,818 |
| | Surabaya | 2,240 |
| Ireland | Dublin | 46,984 |
| | Jerusalem | 76,195 |
| Italy | Rome | 40,000 |
| | Milan | 20,000 |
| | Naples | 72,000 |
| | Florence | 36,967 |
| Jamaica | Kingston | 7,500 |
| Japan | Naha, Okinawa | 3,415 |
| | Osaka–Kobe | 13,484 |
| | Sapporo | 2,756 |
| | Fukuoka | 5,695 |
| Jordan | Amman | 8,000 |
| Kazakhstan | Almaty | 3,600 |
| Kenya | Nairobi | 4,237 |
| Korea | Seoul | 30,000 |

| | | |
|---|---|---|
| Kuwait | Kuwait | 7,710 |
| Kyrgyzstan | Bishkek | 150 |
| Laos | Vientiane | 293 |
| Latvia | Riga | 2,084 |
| Lebanon | Beirut | 10,000 |
| Lesotho | Maseru | 190 |
| Liberia | Monrovia | 220 |
| Lithuania | Vilnius | 1,500 |
| Luxembourg | Luxembourg | 1,527 |
| Macedonia | Skopje | 800 |
| Madagascar | Antananarivo | 372 |
| Malawi | Lilongwe | 863 |
| Malaysia | Kuala Lumpur | 6,639 |
| Mali | Bamako | 460 |
| Malta | Valletta | 700 |
| Marshall Islands | Majuro | 580 |
| Mauritania | Nouakchott | 100 |
| Mauritius | Port Louis | 320 |
| Mexico | Mexico City | 441,680 |
| | Ciudad Juarez | 63,480 |
| | Guadalajara | 111,100 |
| | Monterrey | 29,900 |
| | Tijuana | 196,000 |
| | Hermosillo | 80,600 |
| | Matamoros | 60,960 |
| | Merida | 49,000 |
| | Nuevo Laredo | 3,580 |
| Micronesia | Kolonia | 760 |
| Moldova | Chisinau | 125 |
| Mongolia | Ulaanbaatar | 450 |
| Morocco | Rabat | 1,401 |
| Mozambique | Maputo | 641 |
| Namibia | Windhoek | 350 |
| Nepal | Kathmandu | 1,600 |
| Netherlands | Amsterdam | 23,707 |
| Netherlands Antilles | Curacao | 6,075 |
| New Zealand | Auckland | 14,540 |
| Nicaragua | Managua | 5,000 |
| Niger | Niamey | 335 |
| Nigeria | Lagos | 10,000 |
| Norway | Oslo | 15,000 |
| Oman | Muscat | 1,444 |
| Pakistan | Islamabad | 506 |
| | Karachi | 2,100 |
| | Lahore | 1,250 |
| | Peshawar | 375 |
| Palau | Koror | 300 |

| | | |
|---|---|---|
| Panama | Panama City | 19,700 |
| Papua New Guinea | Port Moresby | 2,468 |
| Paraguay | Asuncion | 2,368 |
| Peru | Lima | 14,143 |
| Philippines | Manila | 105,000 |
| Poland | Warsaw | 21,300 |
| | Krakow | 18,000 |
| Portugal | Lisbon | 1,072 |
| | Ponta Delgada | 1,100 |
| Qatar | Doha | 3,775 |
| Romania | Bucharest | 13,152 |
| Russia | Moscow | 8,000 |
| | St. Petersburg | 900 |
| | Vladivostok | 348 |
| | Yekaterinburg | 200 |
| Rwanda | Kigali | 165 |
| Saudi Arabia | Riyadh | 11,506 |
| | Dhahran | 13,600 |
| | Jeddah | 10,883 |
| Senegal | Dakar | 791 |
| Serbia-Montenegro | Belgrade | 4,514 |
| Sierra Leone | Freetown | 130 |
| Singapore | Singapore | 15,000 |
| Slovak Republic | Bratislava | 850 |
| Slovenia | Ljubljana | 650 |
| Somalia | Mogadishu | 12 |
| South Africa | Pretoria | 8,100 |
| | Cape Town | 2,647 |
| | Durban | 720 |
| Spain | Barcelona | 18,917 |
| Sri Lanka | Colombo | 658 |
| Sudan | Khartoum | 425 |
| Swaziland | Mbabane | 352 |
| Sweden | Stockholm | 18,000 |
| Switzerland | Bern | 12,113 |
| Syria | Damascus | 3,856 |
| Taiwan | Taipei | 38,000 |
| Tajikistan | Dushanbe | 117 |
| Tanzania | Dar Es Salaam | 1,186 |
| Thailand | Bangkok | 16,500 |
| | Chiang Mai | 1,600 |
| Togo | Lome | 329 |
| Trinidad & Tobago | Port-Of-Spain | 3,200 |
| Tunisia | Tunis | 700 |
| Turkey | Ankara | 2,010 |
| | Istanbul | 4,800 |
| | Adana | 266 |

| | | |
|---|---|---:|
| Turkmenistan | Ashgabat | 107 |
| Uganda | Kampala | 1,350 |
| Ukraine | Kiev | 3,000 |
| United Arab Emirates | | |
| | Dubai | 9,000 |
| United Kingdom | London, England | 200,000 |
| | Belfast, Ireland | 4,000 |
| | Edinburgh, Scotland | 20,000 |
| Uruguay | Montevideo | 3,500 |
| Uzbekistan | Tashkent | 590 |
| Venezuela | Caracas | 25,000 |
| Vietnam | Hanoi | 3,000 |
| Western Samoa | Apia | 495 |
| Yemen | Sanaa | 15,300 |
| Zambia | Lusaka | 980 |
| Zimbabwe | Harare | 2,125 |

**TOTAL**                                           **3,784,693**

# CHAPTER 17
## Top 100 Web Sites for Americans Living or Working Abroad

Readers of this book are invited to visit an exclusive Web site especially for them: www.overseaslife.com. On this site you will be able to do the following:

- Link to all the documents included in this book
- Use the constantly updated "Top 100 Web Sites for Americans Living and Working Abroad"
- Read and subscribe to the free monthy newsletter *Overseas Digest*
- Browse through the back issues of *Overseas Digest* from 1997–2001
- Enjoy many other surprises

Author's note: All sites and addresses listed were current at time of publication. Please note, however, that links often change without notice. The inclusion of these sites does not imply that they are endorsed or advocated. They are simply provided here as a source for finding information.

### U.S. STATE DEPARTMENT INFORMATION

**Authentication of Documents for Use Abroad**
http://www.state.gov/www/authenticate/index.html
**Current Warnings and Announcements**
http://travel.state.gov/warnings_list.html
**Dual Nationality**
http://travel.state.gov/dualnationality.html
**Information for Americans Abroad**
http://travel.state.gov/acs.html
**International Adoption**
http://travel.state.gov/adopt.html
**International Parental Child Abduction**
http://travel.state.gov/abduct.html

**Links to Foreign Embassies in Washington, D.C.**
http://www.embassy.org/embassies/index.html
**Lists of Lawyers Abroad**
http://travel.state.gov/judicial_assistance.html#attorneys
**Marriage Abroad**
http://travel.state.gov/marriage.html
**More Links to Foreign Embassies (Worldwide)**
http://www.embpage.org/
**Overseas Security Advisory Council**
http://www.ds-osac.org/
**Passport Information**
http://travel.state.gov/passport_services.html
**Print Passport Applications**
http://travel.state.gov/download_applications.html
**Records of Birth, Death, and Marriage Abroad**
http://travel.state.gov/vital_records_services.html
**Travel Publications**
http://travel.state.gov/travel_pubs.html
**Travel Warnings/Consular Info Sheets**
http://travel.state.gov/travel_warnings.html

## EMPLOYMENT

**Monster — International Work Abroad Links**
http://international.monster.com/workabroad/resources/intllinks.stm
Just what the name implies—a huge site for finding overseas employment.
**A-Z Overseas Jobs Links**
http://www.advocacy-net.com/overseasmks.htm
This is the site to visit when you have a lot of time to look through comprehensive collection of links relevant to working abroad.
**Overseas Jobs Express**
http://www.overseasjobs.com/
A U.K.-based bimonthly newspaper listing international employment vacancies, with at least 1,500 new jobs printed per issue.
**Jobs Overseas Index Page—EscapeArtist.com**
http://www.escapeartist.com/jobs/overseas1.htm
Another extensive collection of links leading to international jobs, classified by country and other headings.

## MOVING OVERSEAS

**Craighead**
http://www.craighead.com
Craighead Countries Online provides information about living, working, and doing business in 84 countries.
**Resources for Living Abroad—Index Page**
http://www.escapeartist.com/expatriate/resources.htm
This excellent site has a comprehensive collection of links relevant to moving abroad.

**The Insider's Guide to Relocation**

http://www.insiders.com/relocation/

Everything you need to know about moving, including international relocation.

**BR Anchor Publishing**

http://www.branchor.com/

A recognized expert on relocation, Beverly Roman has been featured on CNN's *Parenting Today*, ABC's *Home Show*, and the Discovery Channel's *Home Matters* with relocation advice. Site offers advice, checklist, and resources for domestic and international moves.

**Appliances Overseas**

http://www.appliancesoverseas.com/

A source for 220 Volt, Dual Voltage, PAL, Secam, NTSC and Multi-System televisions, VCRs, stereos, telephones, fax machines, home appliances, refrigerators, power tools, and a complete selection of transformers, adapters, and converters for international relocation.

**Expat Exchange's General Store**

http://www.expatexchange.com/generalstore/generalstore.htm

An excellent selection of products, services, and links critical to those considering international relocation. Listings include such things as language courses, buying a car, and many others.

## MONEY AND FINANCES

**IRS Publication 54**

*Tax Guide for U.S. Citizens and Resident Aliens Abroad.*

http://overseasdigest.com/tax54.htm

It all starts here.

**Expat Financial**

http://www.expatfinancial.com

Offers solutions for life, health, and disability insurance needs, along with various offshore savings plans.

**Relocation Tax Services, LLC (RTS)**

http://www.taxmove.com/

Specializes in meeting the U.S. tax preparation and consulting needs of relocated individuals (domestic or international relocations).

**Social Security Payments While Outside the United States**

http://overseasdigest.com/your_ss.html

Social Security Administration report.

**GlobalTaxHelp.Com**

http://www.globaltaxhelp.com/

This site provides tax solutions for U.S. expatriates overseas and foreign nationals.

**Expatriate Taxation**

http://expattax.com

They can do your taxes regardless of where in the world you are.

**Introduction to Expatriate Taxes**

http://www.filetax.com/expat.html

This page and the related links discuss in general terms some provisions of the U.S. federal income tax law that apply to U.S. citizens and resident aliens who live or work abroad and expect to receive income from foreign sources.

**Taxhelper.Com**

http://taxhelper.com

Klarin & Associates is a group of CPAs who handle clients from all over the world.

## TEACHING ABROAD

**Teaching Jobs Overseas**

http://joyjobs.com/?digest

An excellent Web site which covers international teaching jobs, American and international schools abroad, overseas jobs, international employment, and more.

**Teaching in American/International Schools Abroad**

http://overseasdigest.com/odsamples/ambrose.html

An informative article by Jim Abrose of Search Associates.

**Choosing a Placement Agency and Placement Agency Reviews**

http://www.coe.uh.edu/projects/teaching_overseas/agency.html

**The International Educator**

http://www.tieonline.com/overseas.html

The International Educator newspaper is probably one of the most important news and job information resources available for teachers already abroad and those who want to go.

**International Schools Services**

http://www.iss.edu/

ISS employs teachers and administrators in the schools it operates worldwide. It publishes the famous Directory of Overseas Schools.

**O-Hayo Sensei: The Newsletter of (Teaching) Jobs in Japan**

http://www.ohayosensei.com/

A biweekly newsletter of teaching jobs available in Japan.

**Department of State Office of Overseas Schools**

http://www.state.gov/www/about_state/schools/

This site from the State Department provides good information about American and International schools overseas.

**Ed-U-Link Services, Inc.**

http://www.edulink.com/index.html

Provides those looking for international teaching jobs a place to place the curriculum vitae so that potential employers can read them.

**International Supply Teachers**

http://teachersonthemove.com/

An organization recruiting specialist teachers for short-term vacancies in international schools.

**Teach in China Job Board and Discussion Forum**

http://teach-in-China.com/wwwboard.html

**Iteachnet**

http://www.iteachnet.com/

A site by a team of international school teachers who have volunteered to make a useful resource for international school teachers and administrators.

**ESL Worldwide**

http://www.eslworldwide.com

ESLworldwide.com specializes in providing the latest language training jobs on its extensive posting service and helps to recruit instructors for language training schools all over the world.

**Tefl Professional Network**

http://tefl.com

A daily updated database of more than 100 English language teaching posts worldwide.

### Dave's ESL Café
http://www.eslcafe.com/
Dave runs an excellent service with lots of features: email lists, chat rooms, discussion forums, and much more.

### Teach and Travel
http://www.teachandtravel.com/
The International TESOL Program is a comprehensive training program for those wishing international accreditation as a teacher of english to speakers of other languages

### Teaching Abroad without a Certificate
http://www.ippu.purdue.edu/sa/work/teach1.htm
This page focuses on the great number of possibilities for those without teaching credentials.

### TeachAbroad.com
http://www.teachabroad.com/
A comprehensive on-line source for international teaching positions, English Language Certificate Programs, Jobs Abroad, volunteer positions abroad, study abroad, and a whole lot more.

### Transitions Abroad
http://www.transitionsabroad.com/
Resources on studying and teaching abroad, including *Transitions Abroad* magazine.

## EXPAT SUPPORT SITES

### ActiveAbroad.com
http://www.ActiveAbroad.com/
For people relocating to London and the U.K.

### Americans Abroad Greece:
http://www.geocities.com/Athens/7243/
Expatriate resources for those going to Greece.

### American Society of Sydney
http://www.americansociety.com.au/
For American expats in Sydney.

### Americans in Toulouse
http://www.geocities.com/AITonline/
For those moving to the Toulouse area of France.

### American Citizens Abroad
http://www.aca.ch/

### American Expatriates
http://www.expataccess.com/General/Americans.shtml

### The American Hour: 100 Percent Dedicated to American Expatriates in the U.K.
http://www.theamericanhour.com/

### American Women Overseas
http://www.awoscentral.com/
AWOS, a national nonprofit organization with an international outreach for the support of American women who are victims of domestic violence in foreign countries.

### Art of International Living
http://www.artintliving.com/
Bimonthly newsletter for expatriate families.

**Bratz.Net**
Online community for American children: military brats, missionary kids, and others.
**CountryNet**
http://www.countrynet.com
Country profiles from *The Economist* Intelligent Unit.
**Democrats Abroad: The Overseas Democrat**
http://www.democratsabroad.org/newsltr.html
**Educating the International Child**
http://www.culturebank.com/expated.html#Managingx
**Escape from America International Forum**
http://www.escapeartist.net/
**ESL Cafe's Job Discussion Forum Message Index**
http://www.eslcafe.com/jd2/index.cgi
**Expat Exchange**
http://www.expatexchange.com
**ExpatSingapore**
http://www.expatsingapore.com/index.htm
The information resource for expats in Singapore.
**Expatriates Moving to or Living in Europe**
http://www.expataccess.com/
**Expatriate Offshore Mexico**
http://www.offshorelife.com/
**Expat Chat**
http://www.expatforum.com/Msgboard/webx.cgi
**Expatica.com**
http://www.expatica.com/
News and community for expatriates in the Netherlands.
**Expat Village**
http://www.expatvillage.com/
For expats in Buenos Aires, Argentina.
**Federation of American Women's Clubs Overseas**
http://www.fawco.org
**Guatemala Lifestyles**
http://www.escapeartist.com/Guatemala_Lifestyles/Guatemala_Lifestyles.html
For anyone considering Guatemala.
**Global Assignment**
http://www.globalassignment.com/home.html
**Global Nomads**
http://globalnomads.association.com
Children who have lived outside of their native countries because of their parent's job.
**GoAbroad.com**
http://www.GoAbroad.com/
Directory for foreign language programs, volunteer abroad, and overseas internship.
**iAgora**
http://www.iagora.com/
For and by international people.

**In Your Pocket: The Ultimate City Guides**
http://www.inyourpocket.com/
**Inside a U.S. Embassy: Profiles**
http://www.afsa.org/inside/ch1.html
**International Executive Transfer Update**
http://www.bakernet.com/Publications/Display%20Pages/All%20Publications.asp
**International Living**
http://www.escapeartist.com/international/living.htm
The original newsletter about living an international expatriate lifestyle.
**Living Abroad Publishing**
http://www.livingabroad.com/
How-to-live and relocation information about 88 different countries.
**Living in Indonesia**
http://www.expat.or.id
For expatriates in Indonesia.
**Living in Russia**
http://www.amcham.ru/living.htm
**MOBILITY Magazine**
http://www.erc.org/fr_mobil.htm
**Network for Living Abroad**
http://www.liveabroad.com/
**Outpost Expatriate Information Centre**
http://www.OUTPOSTexpat.nl/
**PlanetExpat.com : Finding Your Way in the World**
http://www.planetexpat.com/
**Relocation Journal—Newsbreak**
http://www.relojournal.com/newsbrk.htm
**Republicans Abroad**
http://www.republicansabroad.org/
**Runzheimer News Releases**
http://www.runzheimer.com/
**Settling in Scotland—Frequently Asked Questions**
http://www.settlescot.com/faq.html
**SHRM Global Forum: Publications**
http://www.shrmglobal.org/publications/index.htm
**TIPS' International Teacher and Administrator's WWW Bulletin Board**
http://www.iteachnet.com/wwwboard/wwwboard.html#post
**TransAtlantic American Magazine**
http://www.escapeartist.com/transatlantic/american.htm
For American expatriates living in Europe.
**Transitions Abroad**
http://www.transabroad.com/
**U.S. Expatriate Handbook**
http://www.us-expatriate-handbook.com/contents.htm
**Windham International**
http://www.windhamint.com/